THE
GROOVE PROJECT

Two Unlikely Friends, an Unlucky Car, and a Lifetime They Never Imagined

PAUL HEAGEN

iUniverse, Inc.
New York   Bloomington

The Groove Project
Two Unlikely Friends, an Unlucky Car, and a Lifetime They Never Imagined

iUniverse books may be ordered through booksellers or by contacting:

iUniverse
1663 Liberty Drive
Bloomington, IN 47403
www.iuniverse.com
1-800-Authors (1-800-288-4677)

ISBN: 978-1-4502-4373-5 (pbk)
ISBN: 978-1-4502-4375-9 (cloth)
ISBN: 978-1-4502-4374-2 (ebk)

Printed in the United States of America

iUniverse rev. date: 8/10/10

We shall not cease from exploration
And the end of all our exploring
Will be to arrive where we started
And know the place for the first time.

T. S. Eliot—"Little Gidding"

Contents

Preface

It's both fascinating and baffling to me why some memories have such clarity while others fade into a haze we never notice until it has set in over the years. Some memories earn a place in our mental storage closet because they were so consequential, dramatic, or profound that they cannot be stripped from the effect we feel from them today. Yet that same closet is cluttered with nonsense and flotsam (as proof, I still remember our phone number from when I was in junior high school in 1967). It makes me worry sometimes that the reason I may not remember something really important—like my Social Security number or my wedding anniversary—is because that shelf in the closet is occupied by that worthless squatter of a forty-year-old phone number.

Sometimes we plead with our brains to resurface a memory that we want desperately to salvage: the first words of your child, the final words you spoke with your grandfather, or—as you pry a rusty nail out of your bare foot—the date of your last tetanus shot.

In my case, in writing this book, memories that I had long assumed were forever buried in the clutter emerged from the darkness and the haze with a sharpness and depth that startled me. It was as if I stood before a pile of rubble with a giant magnet in my hands and pieces of steel and iron began to worm through the morass and line up in front of me.

My hope for this book is that it might prompt you to rummage around a bit more in your own closet to discover events and people tucked back in the corners and upper shelves that might serve a purpose and take on a meaning in your life today.

Those memories matter, more than you might realize.

Find them.

Chapter One

Whump whump

I can't believe I'm working this late. Midnight flew past a while ago. At this rate I'll start wondering why I'm working this *early*.

Whump whump

Still, when you have your own home office, it's nice that if you have to work, at least you can do it in solitude; no phones ringing, no office gossiper trolling around your door shoveling the latest scoop, no noise to speak of except that lopsided *whump whump* of the ceiling fan overhead. One of these days I have to get out the stepladder and tape a quarter to one of the blades. I know I never will.

Whump whump
(blip)

The electronic tone startles me at first, until I glance down at the bottom of the computer monitor to see the bobbing icon.

(blip)

It's the alert telling me I just received an e-mail; an e-mail at 1:30 in the morning. Like it matters.

(blip)
(blip)

I stare at it as if somehow my stare alone will make it go away. The icon is that overanxious kid in grade school jumping up and down in the gymnasium class when captains are picking sides in dodge ball—"Hey, pick me! Pick me!" They never shut up or go away until you go ahead and pick them.

So I click on it.

To: paul
From: mark
Subject: '57 chevy

---

hey buddy ... remember stoned valley ... yeah ... you drank the muscle car juice my man ...

Mark. Now that's interesting. I've never received an e-mail from him. Funny; what's he up to at this hour? I flip a quick reply, like a ping of friendly sonar, but no sooner do I respond than the icon bobs its head and there is a volley of even more e-mails.

To: paul
From: mark
Subject: '57 chevy

---

it was awesome paul. no wonder people were so anxious to hear and see your 57. it was a huge story.

To: paul
From: mark
Subject: '57 chevy

---

paul, i don't think you ever understood what you meant to the school. that car had everyone anxiously wanting to see, and it took on mythical status. sometimes two weeks went by with no news and anxiety would grow over the whole school.

Every time I click on one of the notes, another one pops up, as if this is some kind of Internet Whack-A-Mole. I push my work out of my mind and concentrate on trying to slip in responses amid the repeated *blips* of his notes, but I am outrun.

To: paul
From: mark
Subject: '57 chevy

We had a good time, my friend ... the best time

Thirty-five years is a long time ago, but I am startled with how quickly the notes come to life, how text morphs into images and sounds. I close my eyes and, almost on reflex, inhale deeply. It's all still there, soaked into my senses as much as my memory—the aroma of fresh oil, the heat of the exhaust, the musty garage, the AM radio blasting. As I drift into the images in my mind, the *whump* of the ceiling fan falls away and is replaced by a throbbing bass guitar and drum kick, mingled with the jangle of box-end wrenches dropped on a cold, concrete garage floor (*"You're the only girl I know—CLANG—really love you so—CLANG—in the midnight hour, oh yeah ... "*).

It has been a long time. A very long time. But as I lean back in my chair in the quiet and the darkness, the sights, the sounds, and the smells surround me again and I am lost in them.

(blip-blip ... click)

For every reply I try to squeeze in, I am peppered with more notes—but he is not answering; he is just spilling it all out. The notes are hurried, frenetic, even desperate. Some I can barely read for all the misspellings and typos. In my office at this hour, time no longer matters to me, yet the e-mails coming at me seem to be racing against a clock I cannot see. After a while, I stop trying to make it a conversation and just let the notes come. For the next half hour, the monologue rattles on. Now, though sitting in the same solitude of my office, I am no longer alone. It is me and the icon as it taps out its rhythm.

Then, as suddenly as the barrage began, it stops. I probe the silence with a "Hey, buddy, you still there?" note, but there is no reply; the icon resting compliantly. I wait a few minutes more—it is not like I am going to shut down on the first e-mails I ever got from him without some pause—but the hours are weighing in on me now. It's time to call it a night.

"What time was it when you finally came to bed?" My wife Carol slips up behind me as I brace my elbows on the kitchen counter, watching the coffee drip into the carafe. She cuffs my neck, partly in affection, partly in annoyance. "You know you're always tired the next day when you stay up so late working."

"I wasn't working," I reply, handing her the first cup of coffee. "I was reading e-mails—a bunch of them. From Mark."

"You mean as in 'Mark' Mark?" Carol is puzzled. Mark is one to call at all hours with something on his mind—Carol fields as many of the calls as I do. But this was different. He never sends e-mails. Never.

Then he sends thirty in one night.

"Can I read them?" Carol's question is more than curiosity. She knows enough about Mark to spot his antics and his impulses, especially now that he is a virtual fixture in our lives, but now she senses something odd. You can hear it in her voice.

"Thirty is a lot. I need to read them."

We take our coffee back to my office and Carol sits in my chair as I stand behind her and point out the string of e-mails on the computer screen. I narrate the first few—*see, it's all about the Chevy, the Ducks, here he talks about the cheerleaders, the funk band*—but then my chatter is muted by Carol's waving hand as she scrolls through the notes. She reads each one, clicking through the list that trails out of sight at the bottom of the screen.

"After all these years, he dumps all this in one night." I rest back against the office wall and slurp some coffee. "What a character, huh?"

Carol leans in more, studying the notes.

"So what do you think?" I ask. "Pretty cool, huh?"

Carol is silent, scrolling back up through the notes, her eyes retracing the lines of text. I see her shoulders tighten as she speaks for the first time.

"No," she says quietly, never looking away from the screen. "Something's wrong. Something's really wrong."

To: paul
From: mark
Subject: '57 chevy

The Beast was awesome ... man ... the best ... nothing like it

"*Far-out* car, man!"

I glanced nervously to my left and am confronted by wiry knuckles rapping on the steel-blue sheet metal of the doorframe and a grinning face peering through the open driver's side window. It was a thin, long face with a sharp nose and darting eyes, blonde hair combed straight back on the sides but crowned with a rooster-style flip on top, all policed into place with cream. The head bobbed around like a bobble-head doll to a beat only he could hear.

I had first seen him amid a horde of students just minutes before as I made my way to the parking lot near the gym after my last class. The swarm had gathered near the blue/gray Chevy, cupping their hands over their eyes and peering inside. He was leading the pack, conducting an unauthorized but thoroughly authoritative inspection tour of the car, pointing out features and flaws like a Kelley Blue Book assessor. When he saw me approach, he called out, as much as anything to announce to his followers, "Hey, Mr. St. Louis! You bought Rocky's crate! *Far-out car, man!*"

I sheepishly wormed my way through the students, barely suppressing a smile of pride, and climbed into the front seat. That's when he strutted around from the front of the car to frame himself in the open driver's side window.

"My name's Mark. Most people just call me 'Mark.'" He cackled at his own joke but still thrust his hand into the open window to shake my hand. "Let me know if you need help." It never occurred to me I would need help, at least not this early. It wasn't supposed to be this way. I had dreamed of having my own car for nearly three years, and now here in just a few hours it was all seeming a little overwhelming.

My dad had a '66 Mustang.

I was fourteen years old when he got it. It had those classic spinner hubcaps, a three-speed manual transmission, and a 289-cubic-inch engine with four-barrel carburetor. When you are only a year or so away from getting your driver's permit, you pay attention to those details. It was yellow; Phoenician Yellow is what Ford called it. No doubt a name that some marketing guy pulled out of his dumb hat when you realize that the ancient Phoenicians were known for the deep purple colors of their fabrics, not *yellow*.

My father was not a car guy by any measure, so it was a bold stroke for him to buy that Mustang. It was a stroke that afflicted a lot of people in 1965 and '66; the car just seemed to speak to every guy's inner devil that there was still a place in their middle-class, suburban lives for sport, independence, and even occasional spasms of abandon. The latter revealed itself one Saturday morning when my dad and I were scheduled to meet his regular golfing buddy at the course about twenty miles away from our St. Louis suburban home, except we got up late that morning. It would horrify my mother to this day to know this, but we hauled down the interstate at something close to ninety-five mph to catch our tee time.

We didn't make it in time, but it was a great try. Who cares, anyway, about golf when you can be a fourteen-year-old in a '66 Mustang at dawn streaking down an empty freeway at nearly ninety-five mph, sticking your arm outside the open passenger side window, sluicing and carving your hand through the cold air as if it were an F-4 Phantom jet fighter.

That Mustang sat in our garage taunting me for another year and a half before I convinced my dad to let me drive it by myself to the edge of the curb, then in reverse back to the garage. Just to the curb—not one inch further. As I learned to stop that car within an inch of the curb, I was almost soaked with anticipation of what it would be like someday to actually take it out on the road. So on a Sunday afternoon, you would see this yellow Mustang pacing back-and-forth, back-and-forth on our driveway, to the curb back to the garage and back to the curb, for hours, like a tiger trapped in a cage.

I had to get my license.

I enrolled in the mandatory driver's education class, and given my time-tested agility at shifting from first gear to reverse and back from my driveway warm-ups, I passed the class easily. Cruelly, Missouri required a "cooling off" period between graduating from Driver's Ed and actually getting your license. That made no sense to me at all; I think it is far safer to slip right behind the black, knurled steering wheel of that Mustang within minutes of your last driver's ed class before the flush of responsibility and training wears off. Plus, as anyone knows, you don't tell a teenage boy to cool off.

It was already late spring. Teenage guys were starting to ditch class early on Fridays to drive down to the local hamburger stand where they could preen and troll the parking lots in their father's cars, or in the case of my filthy rich neighbor's kid, a GTO that his father bought for him. Convertible. Dual exhaust. Hurst shifter. I still hate him.

I hit the bottom rung of the teenage social ladder when I asked a beguiling blond girl on the next street over if she would be my date for a concert by the Turtles at Kiel Auditorium in St. Louis. When I met her at her front door and walked her to the driveway, her eyes widened when she spotted the yellow Mustang. Her eyes then pinched to a pained, scornful glare when, instead of inviting her into the passenger seat, I hustled us both into the back seat and my mother turned around to look at us from the driver's position.

"Well, don't you two look so cute!" My mother beamed as she reached back to shake the girl's hand. "I'm Paul's mother."

The girl slumped sullenly in the seat and stayed in that stony posture through the entire Turtles concert, even when everyone else was holding hands and wrapping arms around waists during the finale, "Happy Together" ("*Imagine me and you, I do … *").

I had to get my license.

Just a few days after my Driver's Ed graduation, I was at the kitchen table plotting my first solo flight in the Mustang when my parents nervously announced at breakfast that they were moving the family to California the next month—a job change for my father. I sulked off to my room and pulled the covers over my head, only to hear the muffled rumble of Jay's brand-new '67 GTO cruising past my house. Lucky jerk.

A few weeks later, I arrived at our new home in Northern California to discover that the Missouri-issued driver's education certificate I had labored so hard to earn was somehow *inadmissible* in California. I would have to take the driver's ed class all over again, and the next session didn't open up for six weeks.

School was starting in five. The three-mile route from our new house to my new high school was a serpentine, two-lane stretch of road without any sidewalks. As well, the asphalt was crumbling at the edges, so riding a bike meant either a teeth-chattering, spoke-bending adventure in steering or the more perilous game of chicken from competing for the smooth roadway with oncoming cars.

I was left with the Faustian choice of riding my bike to school or having my mom drop me off in her car. For those first few days, my mother may not have known *exactly* where my high school was located because I always had her drop me off at a park about a block away.

"Are you sure you want to walk the rest of the way, dear?" she asked.

"Yep, Mom. I'm fine. You're the greatest."

There is a certain curiosity associated with being a junior-year transfer from out of state, but not much. By the time you hit high school, you had to be on your toes, pick your spots and blend in, or stand out in a good way. Without a driver's license months after my sixteenth birthday, I did none of that. Like right after the last class one day during the first week when a group was hanging around in the hallway, rendezvousing for a motorcade to a local hamburger stand.

"Oh, you don't have your license yet? Really?" Then, again, they would walk away.

I finished the California version of Driver's Ed, and within days I checked off all the right boxes, made all the right three-point turns, and demonstrated my prowess at parallel parking to the examiner and got my license. I needed just one more thing.

A car.

My dad had sold his Mustang—*why he sold one of the coolest cars around just when he moved to California where I could enjoy it I don't understand*—and replaced it with this ugly, moss-green Pontiac LeMans. His car just screamed *family car*. I wasn't going to get caught dead in it. I was already dead on arrival socially. Mothers being mothers, my mom wanted my dad to buy me a safe, reliable, practical car. My dad was more direct: I could get whatever I wanted, as long as I got it myself. It was the YOYO Plan—You're On Your Own. (It wasn't like I was unprepared—I had stashed two hundred dollars from mowing lawns over the last few months. Not hard to do when you haven't had any dates.)

Scouring the classified ads, I was bewildered about which cars were which and, being new to the area, how far I would have to hitchhike or walk to see them. I circled several that sounded close—a '59 Rambler, a '61 Impala that didn't run, and a '59 Ford Galaxy that ran sometimes—but slunk away from the prospects when I called and found each one was well beyond my two-hundred-dollar limit.

During a recess one afternoon at school, a burly senior with pinched eyes and a tight jaw walked up to me near my hallway locker.

"I hear you're looking to buy a car."

It wasn't so much a friendly inquiry as a challenge. The inquisitor had a thick barrel of a chest, stumpy blond hair, a nose that looked like it had barely failed to dodge a swift left cross, and a chin shaped like an anvil.

I chose my words carefully. "Oh, yeah, kinda. I mean, yeah. Yes, actually ..."

"Well, you can buy mine. I'm selling it."

"How much do you want for it?"

"Two-twenty, cash. I'm going into The Marines after this summer. I won't be needing it."

I kneaded the wad of bills in my pocket, as if rubbing them like an Aladdin lamp would magically create the twenty dollars I was short. "Okay, deal." I felt myself gaining confidence, perhaps as a result of taking my first breath of the last sixty seconds. "By the way, my name's Paul."

"I'm Dan. Most people call me Rocky."

"Okay ... Rocky."

"I said *most* people."

"Right, Dan." I smiled wanly. "Say, if I may ask, what kind of car is it?"

"A Chevy. '57 Bel-Air coupe. See me tomorrow at noon recess in the parking lot." He spun crisply and started to stride away when I called out.

"Does it have any gas in it?"

Even with a neck as thick as a tree stump, he managed to crane his head around to glare back at me, his eyes even more pinched, his jaw set like a vise. "I'm not a gas station."

I traced the tip of my tongue across the front edge of my teeth and under my lower front lip before gamely asking the for the moon, "Well, okay, but think you can spot me twenty bucks for a month?"

He rolled his eyes. "Yeah, okay. One month."

The next morning, my mom dropped me off a block from the school and reminded me she would pick me up that afternoon at 3:30.

"Nah, that's okay, Mom. You just enjoy the day. I'll find some way to get home."

"Are you sure, it really is not a ..."

"Mom, I'm fine. You're the greatest. Really, I already have a ride arranged."

As noon finally came, I nearly ran down the hall and headed toward the parking lot at a brisk trot, slowing my pace so I approached the appointed time and place with just the right amount of cool. Rocky was holding court with several other guys in the parking lot near the gym, braced against a car that was leaning under his weight. The paint was a steel blue, uniformly faded. The body was intact and dentless; the rear bumper hung listlessly on one side; the muffler was sagging in the midsection; and part of the headliner inside fluttered lazily in the breeze from the open window. I was falling in love already.

"So this is it, I take it?" I asked, surveying the mass of metal in front of me.

Rocky stepped away from the car, which continued to lean a bit on its own. By now my eyes were taking it all in. It was beefy and imposing. It bore a front fortress of chrome bumper and grille, capped with twin rubber cone tips. I thought the tail fins, which raked the entire rear quarter panel, were pretty cool. The rear tires were balding; the fronts did not match. It did not leak, and nothing smelled funny. I was smitten.

"Start it up?" I asked, almost apologetically.

Rocky shrugged, stepped into the cavernous front seat, and jiggled the key into the ignition. The engine whined and bucked and then sputtered to life. There was a cacophony of sounds—a harmony of hissing, creaking, thumping, and wheezing—but it was steady.

"Okay, I'll take it."

I unfolded the bills from my pocket and counted off twenty ten-dollar bills into Rocky's meaty palm. When my cadence stopped with the last bill, he crushed the money into his curled fist and then dug deep into the pocket of his Levis for the pink-colored owner's registration form, smoothing it out on the hood and scribbling his signature on the bottom. He handed me the paper but kept it pinched between his thumb and forefinger as he winced at me. "You owe me twenty bucks. Next month." He did not release his grip until I nodded dutifully.

I folded the pink slip into my pocket as I held out my hand to snag the keys he jangled in front of me.

"It's all yours. Enjoy."

That afternoon at the end of classes, I loitered around the commons area until most of the students had climbed into their cars and left the parking lot. Now, except for a few cars over near the football field, my car was alone. I squeezed the door handle and settled inside, noting for the first time the green shag carpet on the floor. The steering wheel seemed proportioned to navigate a New Orleans paddle wheeler, and I had to slide the front bench seat near its forward slot just to touch the gas and brake pedals and see over the dash. Flipping some knobs, the radio crackled to life, the speaker rattling in the dash. I turned the key and was rewarded with a healthy "rrrrhump" as the engine caught and settled into a loping idle. The stick shift wobbled with each vibration, and I wrapped my hand around it as if to calm it down. I gingerly pulled the stick shift into first gear, but my first move as a car owner was greeted by a searing whine and clatter from the transmission as I ground the gears. I jerked my hand away from the stick as if I had touched an electric power line. I pawed at the floorboard with my left foot, finding the clutch pedal, pressed it down firmly with a foot that was now quivering, and nudged the stick shift into first gear. The car moved. That was a good sign.

The speed limit on the road leading from the school was forty-five mph, but I barely kissed forty as I shifted through the gears, wary of urging the engine higher until I had a chance to check it over. On the three-mile drive home, it occurred to me that I hadn't a clue how to check over an engine.

Our new home was in a country-club community—maybe picking it was a statement by my dad that he was stepping up in class or maybe was just a convenience so he was close to a golf course. The homes were predominantly rambling California ranches or two-story stucco Spanish villas with rounded tiled roofs. Most had concrete driveways, some of them circular, with brick accents on the sides. The front doors were mostly hidden behind fortresses of shrubbery and all-too-perfectly-placed granite boulders. Now rumbling into view in front of this cultivated landscape was a faded twelve-year-old Chevy coupe with a leaky exhaust and mismatched wheels and tires. It had to have been a head-turner, even if not for the reasons I imagined.

I rounded the turn from the clubhouse, hearing and feeling the engine reach a deeper timbre as I climbed the hill of our street, and then eased it down the other side into our cul-de-sac. I stopped short of our house, one foot pressed firmly on the brake, the other cramping from holding down the clutch. My fingers clasped and unclasped the steering wheel as it dawned on me that I had no inkling about *exactly* where this car was supposed to fit at our house. We had a three-car garage, but the third bay was home to my dad's golf clubs, a lawn mower, and some bicycles. So I just pulled it to the curb in front of our house, shut down the engine, and walked inside.

"How did you get home, Paul?" my mom called from the kitchen.

"Car ..." I murmured dismissively, heading toward the hallway restroom.

"Okay, good." There was a pause. "Whose car?"

I hesitated, took a deep breath. "Mine," I said brusquely and then shut the door and flushed the toilet to discourage any further interrogation.

An hour later, the house shuddered as my dad slammed the garage door, clicked open the latch on the back screen door, and tossed his briefcase on the kitchen table. I was sitting stock-still in the family room, my math books cracked open on my lap.

"Hi, dear," my mom called out, a bit nervously. "How was your day?"

"Fine," my dad brushed off the question and got right to the point. "Who parked that piece of junk in front of our house?"

My mom turned on the kitchen faucet and began to furiously scrub the vegetables for dinner. After a half minute of pensive silence my dad connected the dots and stood in front of me, his thumbs hooked into his belt, glaring down at me. "What did you pay for it?"

"Two hundred," I replied. "Two hundred and twenty, actually … eventually."

"Does it run?"

"Got it home …"

My dad eased ever so slightly. "It's your dog. You feed it. You take care of it. When it dies, you bury it."

The next day, the Chevy fluttered awake at my first turn of the ignition key, lumbered back up the hill, and made it to school, with the only distractions coming from some last-minute twitches from the temperature gauge and a slightly sweet smell curling from under the hood as I walked away from it in the parking lot.

Now, with classes ended, the small crowd watching my every move, and this Mark guy bouncing on his toes and poking his head inside the open window, I was finding myself more at the center of attention than I knew how to manage. As much as Mark was making a show of it, I did not feel like he was trying to make a spectacle of me. Maybe it was his offer to help—an offer that struck me as misdirected, until he pointed toward the front of the car.

"I think you're leaking." He laughed, but it was not one of those derisive laughs; if anything a little sympathetic. Sure enough, an oily stain was snaking its way from under the car, trailing off and soaking into the dirt patch in front of the car. I got in the Chevy, more gingerly now, and turned the key, grateful that it started, but with most of my confidence draining right out of the green carpeted floorboards.

The crowd began to drift away as I eased the car out of the space. I nursed the car home, my eyes now riveted on the temperature gauge as it crept toward the red zone. The earlier sweet smell of the anti-freeze now turned acrid. As I turned down the cul-de-sac, the thought of working on the car out on the street seemed both impractical and rude to the neighbors. Idling the car in the driveway, I hurriedly shoved the bikes and lawn mower to the side of the third bay of the garage and then eased the now-lurching Chevy into the space. I turned off the ignition, and the engine sputtered a bit and then fell silent except for a muffled wheezing and pinging sound from the radiator.

Reaching under the grill with my fingers, I grabbed the latch and hoisted the hood as it groaned in protest. I might have well opened the bilge of an old cargo ship. The compartment was filled with the stench of fluids—oil, water, brake fluid, anti-freeze, all in various stages of decay. The battery was coated with grease; little peaks of grayish corrosion surrounded the terminals. Hoses snaked around into the darkness. Rivulets of vapor curled around the engine.

"It's probably okay," I assured myself as I eased the hood back into place.

That night, the garage door closed with a sharper thud, the screen door whirled on its hinges, and the briefcase hit the kitchen table with a smack.

"What is that piece of junk doing in the garage!" my dad bellowed.

My mom stood at the kitchen sink, gripping the edge of the countertop, and turned to him. "Ed, it's just for a few days. He just has to fix something. A leak, I think." My mother wiped her hands on her apron and walked over to him. "Be patient. Remember when you were a boy."

The shadow of a dark look crossed his face; then he raised his eyes to me as I stood near the refrigerator.

"Dad, I'll be careful. Tomorrow's Saturday and I have plenty of time. I just need to replace a gasket or something."

"Better be," he growled. "And I better not see a mess of the floor. And as soon as it is fixed, it needs to get back outside. We don't have room for *that* in the garage." He had started to turn away for the living room when he looked back over his shoulder. "You do know what a gasket is, right?"

"Oh, yeah," I scoffed. "Who doesn't ..."

# # #

Chapter Two

After reading through Mark's e-mails, Carol leaves my office to putter around the house, and I am rocking gently in my chair, ruminating about her expression of concern about Mark. She's like that, you know—always scratching a bit under the surface, seeing or sensing things that blow right by me, or maybe I just blow right by them.

It has probably been four years now, but I remember almost to the day when I was prompted to find Mark after so many years. Just like the day I first met him, the '57 Chevy was right in the middle of it again. Only this time, the car was not in a garage; it was up on my credenza. Along the back wall in my office, that credenza has been the gathering place for a parade of paraphernalia, each with its own meaning and attachments. There is the hand-painted clown from my older daughter, the canister of golf tees from a legendary golf course in Scotland from my best friend, a coffee mug I bought in Ireland when Carol and I skittered around there for a few days on our twenty-fifth anniversary. And the model car.

It is a gift from my younger daughter Lesley on my forty-fifth birthday.

She hands me this heavy shoe-box-sized wrapped package with this sly grin on her face.

"You'll like this," she declares. I tear through the paper and peel off the top of the box, feeling through the wads of crumpled paper for the lumpy object nestled within. It is carved out of dark, varnished mahogany, but as it comes into view it is instantly familiar: the tail fins, the massive front bumper, the pointed hood ornaments.

"Hey, you got me a '57 Chevy!" I inspect it quietly as Lesley beams and my older daughter Lisa and wife Carol shake their heads in casual bewilderment. Look at that, will you, every detail is exactly as I remember it—the slope of the roof, the ribbed panels on the side of the rear fins, the jutting headlights.

"Mark would get a kick out of this," I say off-handedly, almost to myself.

There are a few seconds of quiet, and then Lesley breaks the silence. "Who's Mark?"

Who's Mark? I toss off a quick response—*oh, he was a good friend in high school who helped me rebuild one of these cars*—but without much thought, I start to ramble on a bit more. Engine swaps, loud music in the garage, double-dates with cheerleaders, the funk band, cruising the Creek on Friday nights, Mark booking bets that my car would beat all the others.

"Sounds like a pretty good friend," Lesley challenges my casualness. "So where is he now?"

Where is he now? Yeah, where's Mark? I hadn't asked that question of myself—or anyone else for that matter—for years, maybe decades. There was the chaos of our last few days together at Fresno State—his worried parents rushing him home to the doctor's, coming back to clean out his dorm room, me visiting him weeks later as he still lay nearly lifeless in his bed—but, yeah, where's Mark?

"I don't know, actually," I say sheepishly. "I'm not really sure where he is."

Lesley shrugs.

"Well, some kind of great friend you are, then."

To: paul
From: mark
Subject: the beast

you didn't know anything when you started ... which way did head gasket go? funny.

Saturday morning, after tossing half the night wondering what might be wrong with my Chevy, before anyone else in my family was out of bed, I gulped down a bowl of cereal and then went outside and quickly lifted the garage door to the third stall. I stared at the Chevy as it stared back at me with the glazed look of a beached whale. Where just the day before

I imagined it alert, poised, it was now hunched over its tires, weary and wasted. The paint looked more faded, the tires more worn, the odd lean a little more pronounced. Fumbling again under the front grille for the latch, I heaved the hood up as the hinges and I both grunted in unison. The engine, which just hours earlier had throbbed with life, now sat cold and dark. More as a gesture of distraction than diagnostics, I jiggled a few hoses and rapped my knuckles on the air cleaner with as much effect as someone kicking the tires of an old Rambler. The car seemed suddenly much bigger than me, or I felt suddenly small.

Standing in that garage on the cold concrete floor I felt the first of the chill. What had I gotten myself into?

I went back into the kitchen and rummaged through the papers on the counter for the high school directory, flipping through it until I spotted the familiar name. When I called, a woman answered. The sounds of dishes clattered in the background.

"Hi, is Rocky there?"

"Rocky?"

"Yeah, well, I mean Dan, really …"

"Oh, okay," she said as I heard the phone clatter to the counter. "*Dannnn!* It's for you." There was a click as someone picked up the phone extension, and then Rocky's nearly familiar voice, "*Got it, Mom! (click)* Yeah?"

"Rocky, this is Paul, the guy who bought your car …" I waited a few second for what I expected to be his acknowledgement, but none came. "Well, hey, I was wondering if you could help me with something," I explained, as off-handedly as if I were asking to borrow a library book. "The Chevy—*your* Chevy—stopped running. Any ideas on what might be the problem?"

My question was met again with silence for a few seconds; then came the answer: "Check the Johnson rods."

"Oh, okay, the *Johnson rods*," I repeated carefully.

"Yeah, and then check the chrome muffler bearings. Good luck." Rocky laughed as he hung up. I strode out to the garage, fortified with my newfound knowledge, and leaned over the engine compartment. I peered around in the greasy darkness and inspected the engine more carefully. It still pretty much looked like an engine to me. Lots of metal covers, wires, hoses, fittings—but nothing that looked like it might be a Johnson rod. Or a chrome muffler bearing.

I retreated again to kitchen and thumbed open the school directory. Having been at school for only a few weeks, scanning through the names reminded me that I knew few people, and nobody well. I took a guess that one of the three "Mark" names was the guy who offered his help in the parking lot the day before. He picked up on the second ring.

"Oh, hi, Mark? This is Paul, the guy you met who—"

"With the hot '57 Chevy. Howzitgoin'?"

"I need a ride … to the auto parts store."

In a half hour, I heard the metallic complaint of worn brakes as a white '63 Chevy Impala glided to the curb and the horn beeped twice. As I emerged from the darkness of the garage, Mark already was standing outside the driver's door of his car, drumming a beat on the hood. The passenger door creaked as I opened it, and Mark held up his hand just as I started to slide in.

"Wait, wait!" he blurted out. He reached behind his seat and he grabbed a can of WD-40 spray lubricant. He spun around the front of the car, pivoting on his hand that he placed on the hood and landing with both feet at once on the other side. He leaned down toward the door hinge, and the can hissed twice. Within seconds, he reversed course and was tumbling into the driver's seat.

"Hate squeaks." He slammed the shifter arm on the steering wheel into drive and smoothly turned his Impala around the cul-de-sac and up the street.

I had not been in many cars to that point, so each one was a study. Mark's was very clean, being only five years old. More than anything, though, I noticed that the dash was spiked with little cuts of paper jammed into crevices. I reached for one.

"Don't touch that, man!" Mark nearly barked.

"It's supposed to be there?"

"It *has* to be there," he explained. "It stops the squeak. This car has all kinds of squeaks." Mark reached over as we drove and flipped down the glove compartment. Inside was a clutter of matchbook covers, many with corners torn off. "I keep a supply handy," he said proudly. "You have to get right on the squeaks the first time you hear them or they'll drive you crazy."

As we drove, I recited my Chevy's symptoms to Mark and he listened attentively, taking mental notes of my halting, tentative descriptions of what I saw and heard from the engine. A few minutes later, we strode into the parts store and leaned on the grimy back counter as the clerk looked at us over his glasses and asked me what I needed.

"Do you have any Johnson rods?" I replied pensively.

The clerk chuckled. "Who said you needed that?"

As soon as I said it aloud like that for the first time to anybody but myself I realized how foolish and comical it sounded. *There's no such thing as a Johnson rod. Which meant there was no such thing as a chrome muffler bearing, either.*

"A gasket," I said with more self-assurance. "I need a gasket, I'm pretty sure."

Mark was snapping a beat on the counter and then leaned toward the clerk and engaged in an intense, staccato repartee about my car's symptoms, acting like he had witnessed them all himself. After a few minutes, the clerk and Mark proudly announced that the culprit was a head gasket, whatever *that* was.

The clerk opened a thick, grease-stained parts book and began thumbing toward the back of it. "What kind of car; what year?"

Mark slapped his hands on the counter again. "An *awesome* car. A '57 Chevy, man. The best!"

The clerk ran his finger down the column and paused. "283?"

"283 *what?*" I asked tentatively.

"The engine. 283 cubic-inch. Is it a V8?"

"Yeah."

"Probably a 283." He disappeared between two rows of shelves bulging with boxes of parts. I leaned one elbow against the counter and turned around to survey the store. It was my first time in an auto parts store. The atmosphere to me as a neophyte was both intoxicating and suffocating. Gray metal shelves on each aisle were stuffed with categorized parts and accessories—fittings, paint, oil, and filters—all in neat rows. Meantime, the clerk had now emerged from the back shelves with a thin, stamped metal gasket plastered to a piece of cardboard, enveloped in cellophane. I looked at it for a few seconds, pretending to be inspecting it and making sure it was correct. I gave up the charade.

"Which way does it go on?"

Mark laughed and tapped out a faster beat on the counter. "This is going to be so cool ..."

The clerk shook his head for a moment and then pointed to the edge. "This side toward the engine. Gotta torque wrench?"

The clerk registered the vacant response on my face and then reached under the counter and dragged out a torn, brown box. "Here, kid. You can borrow this. You'll need it." He handed me a foot-long chrome bar with a dial on one end and a knurled cap on the other, not like any wrench I had ever seen. "And this," he flopped a thick, blue book on the counter. The creased and grimy binding said *Motors Manual*. He told me just to bring it back when I was done. I mumbled an embarrassed "thanks" and headed for the counter. Rummaging through my jeans, I dredged up a rumbled bill and some coins, just enough to pay for the gasket. The cashier flipped the gasket into a bag and looked up at us.

"Got gasket sealer for that?"

I looked over, panicked, at Mark, who pulled his wallet out and slapped a bill on the counter, rescuing me from my humiliation.

Back at my garage, Mark stacked two cardboard boxes atop a small stepstool to serve as a podium and laid the *Motors Manual* on top with all the pomp of a tenured professor placing a giant textbook on a lectern.

"Okay, we're all set!" He rubbed his palms together but then stepped back and looked over at me. I stared back at him, partly beset with panic, partly with puzzlement.

"Okay, what?"

"Okay, let's get going." I was frozen. Mark was not. "You need to be the first one to open the book," he said. "Ceremony is everything."

I gripped the edge and flipped the book open, but I was met with pages of tables and charts, line drawings of engines, and black-and-white photos of car parts.

"What did the guy at the store say? You know, the engine," I was more tense than curious now. "238 or something?"

"283," Mark corrected. "Same as in my car." Okay, so Mark's just messing with me. He does know this stuff. I thumbed through the pages until I spotted the section that seemed to be the one for my engine. Every few seconds I would rise up from the makeshift bench to compare the image in the book with the dark, dreary scene under my hood.

"Mark, what's this?" I pointed at a greasy fitting on the side of the engine, squinting to look back at the open book. Mark's eyes followed my arm and finger to the dark shape, scrutinizing it for several seconds, scrunching his brow and rolling the tip of his tongue around inside his cheek.

"I could tell you, but I bet you can figure it out if you look at the book," he said. "It's all about the *learning*, my man."

Well, okay, then. I finally connected the shape on the engine with the line drawing on the book. "It's the return hose from the radiator, right?" I looked up at Mark as much for approval as confirmation.

"See," he said proudly, "you're a quick learner."

Mark busied himself rustling through the few tools my father had in a wooden crate in the garage and then broke down a cardboard box, laying the cardboard on the garage floor to serve as a mat so he could slide underneath the car.

"Careful," I warned him.

"I'm not touching anything …"

"No, I mean the rattlesnakes …"

"*Whoa!*" Mark used both hands to grip the side of the car and slide out from underneath, jumping up and slapping his hands on his jeans and shaking the pant legs. "*What do you mean—rattlesnakes!? You've got rattlers in your garage?*"

"Sometimes," I explained calmly. "They come in here to cool off. They come from the hillside behind my house."

We turned our attention back to the engine, even if Mark did occasionally slip a furtive glance down at the floor and around his ankles. I leaned over the radiator, stretching deep into the engine compartment as Mark leaned in next to me, directing the efforts.

"Take that off first … okay, now that … just pull on it … *pull harder …*"

One part would not budge, and I was getting ready to find a crowbar to wrench it off when I spotted a remaining bolt in the shadows.

"Hey," I said, feeling a little betrayed. "Why didn't you tell me that bolt was there?"

Mark took on a hurt look and shrugged.

"Hey, these engines are all a little different," he said. "You can't memorize everything."

After a while, this became exploratory surgery run amuck. At Mark's steady directives, I kept pulling hunks of metal off the engine, perhaps hoping that one of the parts would yield the clue—showing a burn mark or a suspicious hole, anything that might give a clue to why the engine wasn't running. Considering I had no idea how an engine ran to begin with, I can't fathom why I thought I could find the reason it did *not*.

Mark stayed with it for a while but eventually patted me on the back with a "You're getting it, my man …" and bounced into the front bench seat, fiddling with the radio. "We need to get an eight-track for this thing," he announced. "And some bucket seats."

We spent most of that Saturday under, inside of, and draped over my Chevy. If anyone had come by at that point, it would have been apparent that we were not disassembling the engine, we were *dismembering* it. We macheteed and clawed our way through the engine compartment, taking off anything that could be dislodged. Within the first two hours, the garage floor was covered with the flotsam of our toil; bolts, screws, hoses, belts, valve covers were strew everywhere, along with a wide smear of oil and grease.

"My dad's going to kill me," I groaned. Before I could stop him, Mark grabbed a towel from the shelf where my dad stored his golf supplies, sweeping it across the slop on the floor with his foot. He held it up like a dead skunk and then tossed it in the aluminum trashcan in the corner, turning toward me with a mischievous grin.

"So one of these weekends," he grinned, "your dad will be in here going, 'Now where the hell is my gold towel that I won in that tournament last year?'" I ran past Mark and stuffed the towel deeper into the trash.

"Mark, don't you *ever* do that again …"

"Okay." Mark made no effort to cloak his hurt. "Be cool."

Mark announced that he was going to head out and bring back some burgers, jumping into his Impala and squealing the tires as he whipped around the cul-de-sac and disappeared over the hill, leaving me alone with the disemboweled Chevy.

I turned back to the *Motors Manual* and found the section that described the *cylinder heads* and the suspect gasket the clerk agreed needed to be replaced. I had stripped enough stuff off the engine so that it was easy for me to figure out that there were two of these things called *cylinder heads*, capping each bank of the engine. But they were battened down with a dozen or more long bolts, cranked and cinched down so tight that all of my feeble attempts to loosen them by beating on the wrench with a hammer only succeeded in peeling flesh from my knuckles. For once in my life applying the physics I learned in grade school, I slipped a four-foot steel water pipe over the end of a socket wrench and just hauled on it. There was a satisfying *crack* as each bolt yielded to my ingenuity, and before long the grimy engine block heads were upturned on the garage floor.

I turned back to the now-decapitated engine with a mix of awe and anxiety. Looking at the inside parts of the engine—the pistons and cylinders—had to be like a surgical intern for the first time sawing open the chest of a heart transplant patient. It's one thing to study it in a book;

it's quite another to be staring at the real guts of it. Oh God, maybe I killed him.

Just then, tires and brakes squealed in harmony, announcing Mark's triumphant return, and he strode into the garage brandishing the bag of burgers.

"Hey." He surveyed the clutter of parts on the floor. "You're making progress, my man." He reached in the bag and tossed me one of the burgers. Ignoring the oil and anti-freeze glaze that my hands had just smeared on the bun, I wolfed the burger in three bites, and Mark launched himself back on top of the workbench behind me as I returned to the cavern of the engine compartment. I laid the gasket over the exposed engine block, running my fingers around the edge and peering with a flashlight through the holes stamped in the gasket to see if they lined up with the holes drilled into the engine block. They did not. I anxiously flipped it back and forth, turning it every way I could imagine to get it to line up. I did not know much more about gaskets that afternoon than I did that morning, but one thing I did know: this was the wrong gasket.

"Should fit," Mark assured me. He inspected the cardboard backing of the gasket, affirming that it was for a "283 Chevrolet." Tossing it to the floor, he leaped up on the bumper, pointing at the dark abyss of the engine compartment as his eyes widened. "Man, what is in this beast?"

I just stared at the mass of hoses, wires, bolts, and oil-caked iron, not knowing really what else to do. There was a serial number stamped on the engine block, so I scribbled that on a piece of paper, hoping it might offer some clues. We raced back to the store before it closed.

The clerk matched the serial number to a list in one of his massive three-ring binder books and looked up at us puzzled.

"What kind of car did you say you had?"

"A '57 Chevy. Two-door." I stopped at the limit of my knowledge.

"Well, somebody dropped a different engine in your car then, fella, 'cause those numbers are for a bigger engine—a 348."

I was getting ready to ask what it would take to get the right engine back into my car when he stopped me.

"I'd keep this engine if I were you, kid. It's a stronger engine than the 283. It can crank out a lot more horsepower if you know what you're doing." I was pretty sure he had already deduced that I did not know what I was doing, but he didn't ask if I had brought back the torque wrench or *Motors Manual* yet, so I figured he was still on my side. "Do yourself a favor," he said. "Bring the heads in here first for me to look at before you start putting everything back together."

On Monday, Mark glided his Impala to my front door—brakes wailing in protest—and beeped the horn twice. He took me to school and then to the parts store that afternoon with the two cylinder heads wrapped up in newspaper in the trunk. The clerk rolled them over on the counter, scraping at them with his penknife and holding a straight edge against one side.

Mark leaned in and engaged in a hushed conversation with the clerk, something about *burned valves, warped heads;* but it was all blurry to me. He and Mark shook hands, and Mark wrapped his arm around my neck and starting dragging me to the door.

"Mark, what about my cylinder heads?" I looked back as the clerk stowed the masses of cast iron under the counter.

"It's cool," Mark smiled back. "He's going to get them fixed. Probably only fifty or seventy-five bucks." I ran the math: that was one-fourth the cost of the entire car. I had known Mark all of one day and already he had cost me more money than I had any idea of how to raise, I was probably on the verge of getting grounded by my dad, and I was most certainly condemned to riding my bike to school probably until the day of my senior graduation.

Mark and I sat in his car for a few minutes in silence.

"I need to get a job," I declared.

For the next week, I hitchhiked around town, beseeching store owners to offer me a few hours of work a week—just enough scrape to pay for repairs on my car and not do any more serious damage to my already compromised study habits.

The first job lasted a day. It was a family-owned hamburger stand. Within an hour, I had mastered the art of burger flipping, cheese slapping, bun flaying, and condiment spreading. The task of cleaning and closing was left to me and the owner's moody, petulant son. He left—*in his car, geez*—to cruise or neck with his girlfriend an hour before closing and never came back, which also meant that the closing keys in his pocket never came back either. The owner did not leave his phone number anywhere, and by 1:00 am on a school night, my parents were nearly frantic and insistent that I come home, even if the hamburger joint was left unlocked. I alerted the cops to keep an eye on the place and called it a night, walking three miles home.

I slipped out at first break between morning classes the next day to call the owner and make sure he was pleased with the extra measures I had taken to safeguard his business amid his son's obvious neglect.

"You're fired," he hissed.

"But ... your son had the keys ..."

"Nobody leaves my place unlocked," he growled.

"What was I supposed to do? Sleep in the refrigerator until morning came?" A bare note of sarcasm crept into my tone now that I knew the argument and the job were lost anyway. "Are you going to fire your son, too?"

"Smartass." Click.

I never did come by to pick up my five hours of pay. I still had my commitment to pay Rocky the remaining twenty bucks, and I was unemployed. With a scar on my record.

Two days later, on a Sunday after church, my family piled into a Chinese restaurant for lunch. Midway through the meal, my dad nudged me to ask the owner if he needed me to work. The owner took a step back and surveyed the prospects—nice clean church clothes, combed hair, shiny loafers.

"Come back to kitchen."

I glanced back at my parents, who shrugged their shoulders.

"Let us know how the interview goes, dear," my mother called out to me in a hopeful tone.

I had never been in a commercial kitchen, much less the cacophony that is a Chinese restaurant kitchen. Five people—almost as many people as were sitting at the tables in the dining room—were scampering about, flinging pots and epithets with equal velocity. Flames billowed from oil-slathered pans, steam roiled over two large vats, and the floor glistened from a stew of peanut oil and chicken fat.

"Here!" the owner appeared in front of me and thrust a stained apron into my chest. "Put on. Get to work. Wash!"

Too stunned to stammer out an explanation that I didn't *exactly* mean I needed a job that very minute, I ruefully slipped the apron over my clean, pressed white shirt. I pushed open the swinging doors to the dining room and called out to my parents:

"I've got a job. See you later today."

The owner's dark, bony fingers curled around my upper arms, and he pulled me back from the doors and steered me toward a pair of deep stainless-steel sinks with snake-like water hoses and spray nozzles dangling above like bats in a steam-drenched cave.

"Wash!"

That meant wash as fast and as hard as I could. Wok pans as large as hubcaps on an eighteen-wheeler semi were flung at me from across the room, clattering against the wall and bouncing into the soapy water. Little fragments of dismembered squid, chickens, pigs, and shrimp twirled lazily in the wash water. I determined quickly that there is no way to spray a round wok pan with water nozzles—set at a level that could extinguish a fire on a forty-story skyscraper, at a temperature that could peel paint off an engine block—without exfoliating most of the skin on my arms and forehead.

"Wash better!" the owner admonished me as he clanged a still-sizzling fry pan with a ten-inch cleaver.

I washed better with every passing hour, and I had plenty of time to improve. Squinting through the fog of the steam rising from the vats, I saw the clock ticking toward 9:00. It had been an eight-hour shift with no breaks.

"How late are you open?" I asked nervously.

"Just close." He grinned. "Now we clean up."

My mother used to tell me that it would take less time if I just kept my room clean all along rather than letting it go to waste and then trying to clean it up all at once. My mother did not raise the owner of this restaurant.

By 1:00 am all the animal parts were crammed into trash bags, the stainless steel sinks and counters gleamed softly, and the floor again was clean enough that you didn't slide without trying. The balance of what was cleaned from the kitchen was firmly depositing on my clothes—my slacks were sopping and streaked with colored sauces, my shirtsleeves were mangled and stained, shards of chilies and clam shells were entwined in my hair, and my shoes were curled up from the steam and hot water.

"You go home now." The owner tugged the apron from my shoulders and pushed me toward the back door.

I grasped the door handle like a pilot grasps the ejection button of an F-16 that just had one wing blown off by a surface-to-air missile but gamely turned around and asked the only question I had not asked that day: "Do I get paid?"

A scowl shadowed his face; then he yanked open a metal drawer and pulled out a twenty-dollar bill.

"You very good," he grinned. "Good job for you. You come back tomorrow."

I did not go back the next day. I am a professional student, not a kitchen slave.

"Wow, where have you been?" Mark surveyed my reddened hands and the steam-burn marks on my face and arms when he picked me up for school the next day.

"Mark, we need a job—I mean a real job."

"I got a lead on a gig for us!" he bubbled the next morning as he sprang out of his car door and thumped on the hood. "Corner drugstore needs a stock boy."

Stock boy is singular, and not a collective singular, like *deer* or *moose.* So this was one job. Now what, Mark and I compete for it? Nonetheless, after classes that afternoon, Mark and I peered up over the top edge of the drugstore counter and coughed to catch the attention of the wispy-haired, bespeckled pharmacist who towered above us on a raised platform.

"What can I do for you fellas today?" he said cheerily without looking up as his trembling, liver-spotted hands herded pills on a blue plastic tray.

"We're applying for the job as stock boys," Mark announced confidently.

The pharmacist lifted the tray and slid the clump of pills into a narrow amber plastic jar, twisted on the cap, and looked up. "Stock boy," he said. "Only need one of you. Four afternoons a week and on Saturday."

Mark was undeterred. "I'm Mark. This is Paul. And you are …?" Mark stretched his arm over the tall counter to shake the pharmacist's hand.

"I'm Mac," he said, amused at Mark's ebullience. "McMurphy, but everyone calls me Mac."

"Mac it is then." Mark shook his hand and then drummed his fingers on the counter. I watched in some awe as Mark adroitly negotiated his way through the interview, convincing Mac that we were a better value as a duo; we would come in on the same days and could get more work done in half as much time as one person, because "we've worked together before." Within a few minutes, Mac was shaking his head in admiration and shaking Mark's hand at the same time. It was a deal.

"Mark, geez." I cornered him at his Impala as we walked out to the parking lot. "Where did you come up with the bright idea of us working on the same days?"

"So you don't have to walk to work, man," he said chuckled. "You don't have a car, remember?"

# # #

Chapter Three

Despite my daughter's retort about my neglect of a friendship, the notion of tracking down Mark has faded over the last few days since she said it, replaced by the more pressing matters of running my consulting business here in Louisville. Where's Mark? Answer is, I didn't know. It's not that I don't care—I mean, you have to care, right?—but it's hard to figure out where to start something like that. Or maybe it just doesn't add up to go looking for something only to find out it's not what you thought it was. Or just maybe isn't the same thing now.

So several weeks later, I'm fidgeting impatiently as Carol and I stand in a long line at the local KFC. I hate lines, but I also hate to watch people eat, so I'm looking anywhere else I can, including the ceiling. The Musak "music" droning out of those ceiling speakers in most retail stores or fast-food joints is nothing more than white noise—you don't even hear it really, and you rarely listen to it. It's just *there*. So why, then, in the middle of a milling lunchtime crowd at this KFC, do I catch myself actually listening—no, *hearing*—the washed-out instrumental cover of "Mustang Sally" drifting down from the overhead speakers?

All you want to do is ride around, Sally, ride, Sally, ride ...

For a moment the clatter behind the counter and the chatter from the booths falls away and I am humming the bass line and nodding my head to the same beat that echoed off the walls of my garage nearly thirty years before.

I have to find Mark.

The voice in my head is that clear, that insistent. I repeat the directive to my wife as we creep closer to the counter to place our order.

"I have to find Mark."

She turns to me, puzzled. "Okay," she says carefully. "But what does that mean? Do you even know where he lives?"

Not really, no. Not now. Mark and I had only been attending Fresno State for a semester after graduating high school back in 1971 when I noticed Mark had been uncharacteristically absent from the regular weekend Frisbee-tossing on the commons lawn in front of our adjoining dorms. I went to Mark's room on the second floor and knocked on the door. No answer. For some reason, I knocked again. This time I heard what sounded like Mark's voice, but it was weak and cracked. I tested the handle, but it was locked. I now pounded on the door as I heard Mark moaning in the background. The dorm advisor heard me punching the door and came by with the master key. We found Mark sprawled on his bed, white, sweating, nearly delirious. We didn't know what was wrong, but Mark kept telling us to take him home. The rest was a blur; I called his mom and dad, and they were on campus within a few hours. I crammed a few of his books and record albums in a box as they carried Mark into their car. With Mark laid out in the back seat, sweating and shivering, they barely said good-bye and then drove off to their home, to the place they knew, to the doctor they could trust with their son.

All you want to do is ride around, Sally, ride, Sally, ride …

I pumped quarters into the pay phone in the lobby of the student union each of the next few days to call them for updates. They told me that Mark had contracted encephalitis—an infection of the brain and spinal fluid—and was in a coma. They blamed a mosquito bite, since Mark had been at his grandmother's farm near Fresno just a few days before the illness hit. Weeks went by; I pleaded with the dean not to drop Mark from the rolls, that he would be back soon, but too much time had passed. One weekend, his parents came down to Fresno one more time to pick up Mark's remaining clothes and his record collection. I remember visiting Mark later, but it was so strange seeing him lying still and silent in his bed at home. I barely had enough money to pay dorm dues and cafeteria food plans, and it was not long before I simply could not afford to make the trip. Then my '59 Opal Kadett quit on me, and Mark seemed very far away.

You been running all over the town now. Oh! I guess I'll have to put your flat feet on the ground.

Whether it was due to the distractions of young adulthood or the exigencies of studying and keeping up in college, I never visited the Bay Area again. I transferred to Long Beach State, started a career and a family in Southern California, and then moved to five different states over the next few years. I can't say I thought about Mark a lot; maybe that was to avoid the inconvenience of realizing I had lost—no, honestly, abandoned—a friend who would never have abandoned me.

Mustang Sally, now baby ... think you better slow that Mustang down ...

I have to find Mark.

To: paul
From: mark
Subject: bedlam

---

lot of late nights in garage, neighbors hated radio blasting. you kept going

"What's the best guitar lead ever?"

I was under the Chevy, staring up into the greasy shadow of the engine, and all I could see of Mark were his sneakers tapping a beat on the concrete garage floor.

"Mark, I'm concentrating."

"So am I," he replied, undeterred by my retort. "Like I said: What's the best guitar lead ever?"

"Okay. 'Crossroads' by Clapton when he was with Cream." I traced my hand across the cold floor to find the socket wrench amid the clutter of other tools. "So what's yours?"

Silence prevailed for at least a minute. A genius mind at work cannot be rushed.

"Santana. 'Evil Ways.'"

"Okay, that's up there. But it needs more time. You can't call it yet; it's only been out for a few months."

"True," Mark conceded. We were only two weeks into the work on the car, and I was learning Mark's routines. He would often pull his Impala up to the opening of the third garage bay, roll down the windows, and turn up the volume of his eight-track to lay down a good soundtrack for our dialogues or work routines. It was both a backdrop and a distraction. More than once, Mark would drag himself out from under the Chevy at just the right moment to scamper back to his Impala and turn the volume even higher.

"*Oh man!*" he would shout above the din. "*Check this out!*" I accepted that it was part of our symmetry for me to stop what I was doing and at least lean in his passenger window. "Listen to the stereo separation on this," Mark would instruct. With the Beatles' *Abbey Road* worming its way through the eight-track, Mark would twirl the balance knob to one side and the other. "John and Paul on one side and Ringo and George on the other. You can pick out their parts. Amazing!"

Mark was fanatical about the Beatles and particularly the oft-overlooked virtuosity of George Harrison, who could carve crunchy lead lines that summoned the sound of early southern blues as much as any rock patterns of the day. John Lennon's sometimes ethereal, nasal whine would bark through the speakers in Mark's car when he turned the balance to the left; Ringo's steady, understated drum rhythms would thud throughout the car when Mark turned the knob right. Mark's favorite was *Abbey Road*'s infamous B-side medley scorcher "Carry That Weight" (*"Boy, you're gonna carry that weight, carry that weight, a long time …"*) where he would twist the balance knob so violently and regularly that it was months before I would have a moment alone to hear how the song was supposed to sound with John, Paul, George, and Ringo playing together.

"Hey, my man." Mark would bounce into the front seat of the Chevy and slap the steel expanse of the dash with his palm. "I'm serious—we have to get an eight-track for the Beast." Mark volunteered that he knew a guy who does car stereo installs and has a big box full of discarded stereos. I think if I had told Mark I wanted to mount a pair of elk horns on the hood of the Chevy he would know a guy who had a rack in his attic. Sure enough, two days later when he picked me up from school, Mark reached around to the back seat and flipped open the flaps of a worn, stained cardboard box. There, tangled in a clump of wires and plugs, was a Craig eight-track.

"How much do I owe you?"

"Twenty-five bucks."

I looked the eight-track over one more time to make sure it looked like it would work and then put it up on a shelf in our garage—my reward someday soon for getting the car running. Meantime, we had work to do.

"Gimme a nine-sixteenths box-end," I would call out from under the chassis. There would be the metallic shifting sound as he sorted through the wooden box and then slapped the wrench into my upturned palm with as much authority, precision, and purpose as an operating room surgical assistant.

"Channel locks." (*rattle, smack*)

"Five-eighths socket …" (*rattle, smack*)

It became a routine, a ritual—me consumed by the work; Mark cheerfully assisting yet so easily seduced by the slightest distraction, especially mental. He never fully immersed himself in the task. His real absorption, even obsession, was in other areas—funk music, stereo-system specifications, dashboard squeaks, or his infatuation with some cheerleader.

"We need to start a band," Mark pronounced one day as he sat on the workbench, banging the back of his shoes on the cabinet doors and rapping a screwdriver on the counter.

"You're nuts. We have to get the car running. Hand me a half-inch socket …"

(*rattle, rattle, smack*)

"No, man, I'm serious. A band. Everyone is all stuck on acid rock and Fillmore West, but there needs to be a band where people can still dance to the music—like *Sly!*" Sly and the Family Stone was a Bay Area band hitting it big—"Dance to the Music" and "It's a Family Affair" were sitting proud on the charts and thumping out of the stereos of cars every Friday night like a shared heartbeat. Theirs was an earthy, gritty, even drug-tinged funk sound—but you could dance to it. You could hardly not.

"Mark, get real. You play trumpet and I play folk songs on a six-string acoustic guitar."

Folk music was not something you admitted to knowing much about when you were in high school in the late '60s or early '70s, at least not without some qualifications and clarifications. Folk music was Woody Guthrie, but it was also Bob Dylan. It was the Kingston Trio but also, in some ways, Crosby, Stills & Nash. It was Peter, Paul & Mary, but also Simon and Garfunkel. Better yet, James Taylor. The importance of the distinction was that owning an acoustic guitar could be a badge of coolness or dorkiness, depending upon what you played on it.

I had taken piano lessons since I was four years old and had rocked the house and the staid sensibilities of most of the parents of fellow students when I played—and sang—"The Legend of Davy Crockett" at a piano recital at the age of seven. It was a pretty heady experience for a kid my age; still I soon tired of a music regimen where the next step up was just a sheet of music with even more notes on it—notes without words. When I got to Chopin's Prelude in C Minor, I concluded that that was enough for a teenaged guy—it was time for some other instrument that was, to me anyway, a bit more relevant.

A nun at my middle school in St. Louis offered me an old f-hole jazz guitar that had been left in a closet for years. It smelled musty and its strings were rusty, but it took me to another world. I was playing the guitar in our basement, imitating Chuck Berry's duck-walk, when the moldy leather strap gave way and the guitar hit the concrete floor with a crack that ended its life. I was morose for weeks until my dad drove me in his pre-Mustang-era Ford Falcon to a music store in the downtown district. We pushed open the creaky metal doors and entered a deep, vaulted, showroom. There, hanging like angels in the clouds, were dozens and dozens of guitars of shapes and sizes I never knew existed. I would have picked out a Gibson Les Paul electric had I known it would have later become the guitar of choice for Led Zeppelin's Jimmy Paige, the Who's Peter Townsend, and Cream's Eric Clapton. I instead wrapped my eager hands on an acoustic Harmony Regal, which is something of a cult classic today. I went home and practiced chord after chord—no song in particular, but working on my chops with a vague anticipation they would serve some purpose in the near future.

On February 9, 1964, I was sitting in the dim light of our living room in front of our black-and-white TV, coaxing my mom to turn up the volume on *The Ed Sullivan Show*. I remember being annoyed at the screaming girls in the front row; I knew enough guitar by then to appreciate that, more than the prepubescent hysteria, there was something going on musically that was profound. The clean chords ringing out from George's hollow-body Gibson were a level above anything else at that time. Lennon, with his power-stance in front and a black-and-white Rickenbacker electric slung low over his chest, was saying rock 'n' roll was no longer this passing fancy—it was rebellion, an in-your-face snarl, and it was going to shove aside more than a few pretenders to that point. I watched as Lennon slammed the strings with an instinctive rhythm. I went up to my bedroom that night and tried to imitate it—I got the chords right, but the attitude was Lennon's alone.

The attitude was, upon reflection, a lot like the '57 Chevy—sure it had its tamer elements, like the Beatles' collarless suits and neatly trimmed mop haircuts, but it also had a pugnacious streak that was only a hint at first and would need some time to really come to bear. You needed to turn up the volume like you needed to drop a larger V8 engine in there instead of the factory six cylinder. You needed to cut through the shapeless rhythms with a guitar lead that had some bite like you needed to beef up the clutch and bolt on a new differential. You needed to scream your lyrics and let rock 'n' roll rock like you needed to add some headers and glass-pack mufflers.

For now, my guitar-playing "career" was vicarious, taken up with providing some imagined rhythm backup to bands embossed on the forty-fives on my home record player. The Spencer Davis Group never sounded so convincing on "Gimme Some Lovin'" as when I played along with it in my bedroom on a Saturday night. Record players of that era were clunky devices: a turntable coated in felt or rubber and a tone arm that was often so heavy that, over time, the needle shaved off the sides of the grooves in the vinyl records, giving them a powdery cast that was a tell-tale measure of their popularity.

Like must junior high kids in the mid-'60s, I learned the requisite guitar licks that certified you as cool: the three-chord track of the Rolling Stones' "(I Can't Get No) Satisfaction" or the equally simplistic triad of "Gloria" ("*G-L-O-R-I-A ... Gloria!*") by Them, a Celtic rock band that headlined a then-unknown Van Morrison. I could finger and strum my way through the basics of just about anything by the Kinks, early Beatles, Steppenwolf, and the Hollies and even whack a respectable power chord or two to keep up with the wind-milling Peter Townsend of the Who (*"Yeaahhhh!!! We won't get fooled again!" bop-bop—bop-bop—WANG!"*). It just never seemed to have the same visceral impact on my Harmony Regal six-string acoustic guitar.

When you're fourteen or fifteen years old, there aren't a lot of places to take your act on the road. In my case, I was recruited as a freshman to play acoustic guitar for the weekly chapel services at the Jesuit high school I attended in St. Louis. Those were heady days for the Catholics—the Charismatic Movement was sweeping through suburban churches and especially among the more adventurous Jesuits. So each week at our chapel service, instead of hymnals, two or three of us with acoustic guitars would play. Anything. The priests really had no idea what to do with the music during this era but were game for anything that had any mystical tone to it. In my case, I worked out a very meditative—but purely instrumental—arrangement of the Doors' "Light My Fire." The priests thought it was great; my fellow students just about upchucked from laughter at the inside joke. Another guy in our little chapel band played organ, and it was pretty routine to hear him, during a full-stops-out piece, slip in the signature drone from Iron Butterfly's "In-A-Gadda-Da-Vida" *("bay-bah … don't you know I looo-oove you …")*.

In the mid-'60s, listening to the St. Louis rock 'n' roll radio station KXOK, I heard a new genre of music—*beach beat*—but in the landlocked nether land of the Midwest, I had little context to grasp the revolution that was sweeping the shores of California, with Chevys right in the thick of it. The Beach Boys were extolling a 'Vette in "Shut It Down" *("Tach it up, tach it up, buddy gonna shut you down …")*, but the braggadocio extended to the whole line of Chevys that were becoming the darlings of the emerging muscle-car culture.

From my narrow vantage point in the St. Louis suburbs, I had little sense of what the Beach Boys were singing about—it sounded fresh, free, even a bit rebellious. Still, the lyrics spoke matter-of-factly, even a bit in code, about a new phenomenon—the early amoebic stirrings of the muscle-car era. I listened to "Little Deuce Coupe" a hundred times on the radio and knew it had something to do with street-car racing, but *"a flat head mill that was ported and relieved and stroked and bored …"*—what was that all about? Like my dad's Mustang or Jay's GTO down the street, I thought you pretty much took what the factory gave you. Still, there was a language, a shorthand rap coming through the radio that spoke of a different world.

While I sat in steamy St. Louis, with not even a driver's permit to my name, the Beach Boys were calling me in a voice I did not yet recognize. Unknown to me, there was a '57 Chevy out there in California that had my name on it.

By the time I got to California in the fall of 1969, I had a regular thing going playing in churches, at least ones that were ignorant or ambivalent about the more secular underpinnings of my selections for the offertory or recessional. At this stage, some Catholic churches were suckers for just about any kind of drifty, feel-good folk music as evidence that they were relevant and in touch. I could pull off a respectable "Bridge Over Troubled Water," which admittedly does have a nice spiritual metaphor woven in there. Another big hit, usually featured during the collection, was my plaintive version of the Hollies' "He Ain't Heavy, He's My Brother." But my signature *piece de magnifique* was to signal the recessional with a solo performance of Mason Williams's "Classical Gas" as people would spill out of the pews with a little extra bop in their step.

I was in demand with the region's parish priests as long as I stuck with instrumentals or sang insipid, innocuous songs about brotherly love and vague notions of peace that were quite the rage at that time. Woofer, a Willys Jeep-driving wild-man senior who attended our church, was the only other rock-infused member of our little church singing group. He and I would pair up on twelve-string guitars and slyly import a few hits by the Byrds *("To everything, turn, turn turn, there is a season ...")* or some mush-minded peace movement anthems. The church was in a swoon over their newfound freedom in worship styles and interrelationships, so it just seemed suitable that Woofer and I play the Youngblood's misty, utopian "Get Together" *("C'mon people, now, smile on your brother, everybody get together, try to love one another right now ...")* while everyone scampered from pew to pew to give each other a "friendship hug." We knew how to set atmosphere, that's for sure.

The only problem with the peace movement was that it was only a marryin' cousin away from the antiwar movement, which carried a bit more bite. We got a taste of boot leather when we performed Peter, Paul & Mary's "The Great Mandela" *("Listen, Father, I will never kill another. He thinks he's better than his brother that died ...")*. I can't say I even knew at the time who this Nelson fellow was in South Africa or exactly why he was hunger-striking; I just knew the melody was of the same genre as "Puff the Magic Dragon" and a lot of other Peter, Paul & Mary stuff I performed without a ruckus over the years. Maybe it was the satirical part about how Mandela's death would have liberated the oppressed military/industrial complex war machine *("We are free now, we can kill now. We can hate now, we can end the world ...")* that smacked them out of their swoon. Upon reflection, with Vietnam lurking and the embers barely cooled from the race riots of the mid-'60s, my timing was a bit off. Maybe, too, was my sense of location. So Woofer and I were banned from playing anymore at church. It was a shame, too. We were pretty good.

As proficient or clever as I may have been in injecting British and American rock sensibilities into suburban, middle-class Catholicism, it did not translate into playing in a funk band east of Oakland.

"No, wait!" Mark jumped off the counter and knelt down by the side of the car to get my attention. "There's a guy at school who plays guitar who is looking to get something going. I can do trumpet. I know a sax player at the other high school. We have a drummer in our marching band who actually really is a drummer and wants to play ..."

"Well," I said warily, "that's a start. But who plays bass?"

"You!"

"Mark, I've never played bass. I don't even have a bass, and I sure can't afford to buy one."

Mark's gears were already grinding. "We can do this, man," he said, almost plaintively. I slid out from underneath the car and looked up at him. "Mark, if you can find me that bass—and a bass amp—I'm good for it." I knew better than to try to dissuade Mark when he was on a roll. "But I *have* to get my car running first."

And, I muttered to myself, I thought you were going to help.

It was only a few days later at school that Mark rushed up to me in the library, slapped his books down on the table with a crack that drew a scalding glare from the librarian, and rattled off a rapid-fire report of his progress. Grant was on guitar, Davis on sax, Denny on keyboards, Tim on drums, and me—on bass, thanks to a Fender Bassman amp that Mark tracked down from one of the many contacts he had in the bartering world.

"Okay, but who sings?" I asked.

"This is the most awesome part. Remember Denise's older sister?"

Denise was a brown-eyed, brunette gift from the heavens—traffic-stopping gorgeous, charming, affectionate, and logically enough, the cocaptain of our varsity cheerleading squad. A guy could go swimming in the dark pools of Denise's eyes and never come up for air. I did not know she had an older sister, but by the looks of Denise, I was intrigued. Interesting concept: the first funk band in the East Bay with a chick for a singer.

"No," Mark grinned back. "The first *black* funk singer in our area!"

"Denise's sister is *black*?"

"No, dummy. She's not black—but her boyfriend is!"

"Whatever. Can he sing?"

Mark flopped back in his chair as if struck by the question, but his grin never waned. "Yeah, sure. I guess. I don't k-n-o-w! I didn't ask."

So there in the library, in the span of a few minutes ditching some class or another, our little funk band was formed—with the only black singer in a very nearly all-white community. The whole deal started to sound pretty promising, if not adventurous. Except a name. We did not have a name.

"Already got that covered—Bedlam Showboat," he responded with a finality and smugness that simply left no room for debate.

So Bedlam Showboat it was.

The reality of being in our own band playing at dances at local high schools super-charged Mark's interest in music. For the next several days, he arrived to pick me up for school in his Impala, each day the dash more plastered with matchbook covers, and excitedly waved me into my passenger seat while he pumped the volume knob on his eight-track.

"Check this out!" he would exclaim over the sound rattling through his dashboard speaker cones. One day it was Junior Walker and the All-Stars ("Shotgun") and then Percy Sledge ("When a Man Loves a Woman"), Sam & Dave ("Hold On, I'm Comin'" and "Soul Man"), and the omnipresent Wilson Pickett ("Mustang Sally" and "In the Midnight Hour").

The "Memphis Soul" sound that was flowing out of Stax Records' studio on a grimy side street in Memphis was edgier, more soulful, more streetwise than the polished predictability of Barry Gordy's and Holland-Dozier-Holland's Motown. Mark introduced me to the godfather of the movement—King Curtis—whose wailing sax first was heard but unattributed on "Yakety-Yak" ("... *don't talk back*") and later became the main ingredient in "Memphis Soul Stew"—a smoky, laconic soul/jazz/rock fusion that left you feeling you had just hung out for the last three hours in a brick-lined basement blues bar on the wrong side of town, and wanted to go back. This earned King a rare soul-music headlining appearance at Fillmore West, normally reserved for the acid-laced likes of Jefferson Airplane or Isaac Hayes.

While I was lying on my back working on the underside of the car, Mark brought into the garage a new world of music, and I gradually became convinced I could learn it on bass. I found myself humming the tramp groove of "Shotgun," the stalking bass lines of "Green Onions," or anything by Booker T. and the MGs. The biggest difference between Stax Memphis soul and the glossy R&B of Motown was that you *sang* Motown, but you *felt* Stax.

So in the third-stall garage of our home on the cul-de-sac of our country-club neighborhood, if you drove by our house you would have heard Wilson Pickett's gutsy scream, King Curtis's howling sax, and the pump-action "Shotgun" of Junior Walker and the All-Stars wafting out onto the street. Add to that rhythm the glistening clatter of wrenches dropped on concrete, the thud of a dead-blow hammer on a old shock bushing, or the chirp of a torque wrench as you crank a bolt down tight, and you have a curious symphony of sounds coming out of that garage that testified to the emerging harmony between our passions for music and cars. It was a pulse that kept us working, often long into the night on the

Chevy—me, the fledgling mechanic, the occasionally brooding Alexander Graham Bell; and Mark, the slightly frenetic and distracted assistant, Mr. Watson. Whatever the combination, spooned over with some Memphis Soul Stew, it kept us moving.

Maybe it was the music, but I began to sense, even feel, that there is a thing, a place, a state of being called "the groove"—and either you understand it and are in it, or you are not. You can't force it. It just comes on you, I guess, or maybe from within. You have to just ease into it, be cool, work it, go with it, let it take you.

Then before you know it, *you're in it.*

# # #

Chapter Four

Okay, this is not going to be easy.

Mark has a common last name, but the pervasiveness of that commonality is now in evidence with the long scroll of names that comes up on the Internet directory on my computer after I hit the search button. It's predawn in my home office—I'm not sure what stirred me from sleep so early on a Saturday unless it was the thought of the task now before me—and I have a cup of coffee and plenty of time before the family is awake, so I might as well see what I'm up against.

There are dozens of people by that name. I scour the list for clues—maybe Mark had stayed in California all along, but that only shaved the list to a few dozen. Is he married? What about kids? Hey, how about … well, it sure would help if Mark could have at least told me his middle name. I go back to the main search list and scan it again. Has he published anything? Maybe his name will come in a newspaper article, or maybe a message board posting.

The sun is piercing through the open window of my office now, bringing with it subtle ripples of radiant heat. I turn on the ceiling fan—*whump, whump* ("Gotta fix that …")—and turn back to the computer. I scribble some names and phone numbers for later. Not now. It's going to get hot today and I have a lot to do.

I quietly shut the door to my office and go into the garage through the back kitchen door. It doesn't take long before the clammy, stale, hot air of the summer morning starts seeping around the loose joints and side rails of the garage door. A white plastic floor fan, teetering on its warped base, dutifully pans the garage, succeeding only in churning and sloshing the sopping air, making me all that more mindful that the morning and its afternoon to follow are about to get worse. Even the garage floor is hot. Maybe the heat is coming from the earth rather than the sky. It seems to come from everywhere. I feel like a plucked turkey in a convection oven, only dumber—I am here by choice.

Standing upright, I survey my jet black BMW 330Ci, now marooned on four jack stands. Just the week before I had been beaming down Interstate 71 between Cincinnati and Louisville glancing down every few seconds for that magic moment when the odometer dutifully would roll over 49,999 miles and the number 50,000 would appear.

The milestone of 50,000 miles meant my bumper-to-bumper warranty—which included, for crying out loud, replacing your windshield wipers and topping off your oil—had expired. I had just been issued a hall pass for self-sufficiency. With that tick of the odometer, I was no longer forced to sit in a dealership waiting room with a Starbucks thermos and croissants on a tray, nervously pacing like a fledgling father awaiting the oil-stained smock of the doctor to appear from behind the swinging doors. ("Well, it looks like a burnt oxygen sensor, but we replaced it and she should be running as good as new. You can see her now.")

After four years, I can finally work on my car myself, in peace.

In the broiler oven of my garage, I am alone—the fan lolling its head to the growling beat of the Allman Brothers coming from the stereo perched on the top shelf of the back wall. The rhythm is broken by the whining creak of the door from the kitchen.

Carol is standing there in her bathrobe, cuddling a cup of coffee *("How can she drink that stuff in this heat?")*, leaning against the doorjamb more out of resignation than fatigue. Like a surveillance camera, she sweeps the garage with a trained glance, taking it all in: wheels stacked in one corner, disembodied shocks and struts strewn across the floor, the hood yawing open like the maw of a beached whale, canisters of spent oil and fluids standing in their own drool.

She takes a deep breath to signal that she has seriously considered exactly what to say.

"You took apart your new car ..." She pans the room again and sighs. "Why?"

I try my best to adopt the power stance: feet planted resolutely outside the width of my shoulders, hands braced on my hips, chin up, chest out, but it is hard to do so with my sweat- and antifreeze-soaked pants slipping down to perilous butt-crack-revealing levels, like I am some kind of hip-hop plumber, my legs splaying helplessly as my sandals hydroplane on the oil-smeared floor. I muster a look of both sheepishness and defiance and measure my words.

"Because I can?"

To: paul
From: mark
Subject: '57 chevy

---

lots of weekends working the 57 … 105 degrees during day but you never quit. my mom was scared of the mighty 57 … lots of people were, but I was proud of it.

"Man, it must be a hundred degrees in here." Mark plopped a large plastic cup of soda on the roof of the Chevy and fanned himself with the wrinkled copy of *Hot Rod* magazine I had left on the workbench, pinching his T-shirt with two fingers and peeling it away from his body in a vain attempt to dry it out. "And you look like crap," he cackled.

"Is that what you came by to tell me?" Why it was so hot so late in autumn was new to me as a California transplant, but I just knew I was in no mood for his antics. "You sound like my dad."

"Be cool," Mark said, almost scolding.

"About what—this heat?"

"No, your dad," Mark said more thoughtfully. "You're too hard on him."

I was annoyed. I had only known Mark for a few weeks, but he was way out of bounds on this lecture.

"What do *you* know …" I spat back at him.

Mark kept his position. "I don't, man. I just think you're too hard on him." *No I'm not. He's too hard on me,* I defended myself in my head. I'm not mad at him—maybe disappointed, but not mad. We just can't seem to relax with each other much, get into a rhythm, or okay, a *groove.* I wasn't mad that time when I was maybe eight years old and he came home late from a trip, woke me up at midnight, and told me to get my butt back downstairs into the basement and sweep it properly like I was supposed to do earlier that day. I would have jumped right out of bed just because he was my dad, after all, and kids look up to their dad. I guess I just never felt like I understood him very well, and I never felt like he understood me. So, I kept my distance, and so did he. Just over the years, the distance got longer.

Mark got tired of me just standing there, I guess, so he went back to darting around the garage, his eyes peering into the corners and up on the shelves. "You got a two-by-four in here?"

The garage walls were sealed by drywall, but Mark spotted an open row of studs above the garage door. Before I could say anything or stop him, he grabbed a hammer, jumped on the trunk of my car, and pounded out one of the exposed wooden braces between the wall studs, holding up the block of wood like a victory scalp.

"Now we just need a saw." Mark snagged an old Craftsman crosscut saw off its hook on the wall, braced the block of wood on the workbench and started cutting. Within a minute, he brandished two seven-inch pieces of wood. "See!"

No, I did not see, other than two pieces of wood wrenched away from my dad's garage.

"Watch!" he was panting with excitement. He gripped the two blocks and smacked them together, creating an ear-splitting *crack, crack, crack* that echoed off the floor and walls of the garage.

"*Mark! Okay! Okay!*" I hollered with my hands pressed against my ears. "You made your point. Now, what *was* your point?"

"What does that sound like?" He stood there with a wide grin of self-satisfaction and anticipation.

"It sounds like two wooden blocks getting knocked together."

"Noooo," he pleaded. "Listen." He then smacked them together again, harder.

"*Mark!*"

crackkk—craaackkk

"Okay, I give up! What?"

"It sounds like a duck, man!"

"Really ... a duck ..."

"Close enough."

crackkk—craaackkk

"*Fine!* I guess. What's the point?"

"You don't know about the Ducks yet, do you?" Mark's face was creased by a wide grin as he realized that he held a secret that was lost on me. "Let's just call it a club. You have to have the right car, but we're working on that. Someday, my man, you will be in the Ducks."

Someday, *man,* I am hoping to get this car running. I turned back around and all I could see were sockets and bolts scattered over the garage floor and the workbench mounded with parts, wires, and gaskets. I told Mark to put the blocks down; we had work to do.

In just a few weeks, the garage already was becoming my refuge; it was there that I at least knew what I needed to do. It was easier than being at school.

The contrast between me and the rest of the guys at school was painfully obvious. California guys wore bell-bottom jeans; I wore straight-leg—and they were from JC Penney or someplace, not even Levis. Most teenagers in California were sporting tie-dyed T-shirts; I had a closet full of these dopey paisley-patterned dress shirts with button-down collars. California guys wore tennis shoes; I was still shod with Bass penny loafers (with real pennies wedged into the slot on top). California guys had modishly long hair—not shoulder-length like those older hippies I had seen on the TV news, but certainly brushing their collar and looping over their ears as a badge of independence. My hair was neatly cropped and combed and trimmed so far above my ears that the exposed skin looked like white-wall tires mounted to the side of my head.

Everything and everyone around me oozed *California*; I reeked of *Missouri*.

For the first few weeks, I fretted whether other students were casting glances my way, elbowing each other (*"Hey, who's the new kid with the dopey paisley shirt and penny loafers?"*). Every once in a while someone would walk up and say something appropriately polite and ask me where I was from. When I said "St. Louis, in Missouri," they would pause awkwardly for a second or two and then respond with a polite "Oh, that's nice." Then they would walk away. I wanted to run away.

Back in St. Louis, I knew my way within the circles you draw around your world—your friends, the things you like to do, the places you go. Now, in California, those circles tightened and shrank a little more each day; they became a noose. I was not a shy person, but I found myself off stride, wary, and uncertain about what to say and do. I knew better than to retreat—amid the sharks that patrol the ranks of high school guys, you never want to spill blood in the water—but I did not quite know how to engage, how to join, without looking like I was trying. Trying too hard.

My new hometown was tucked into the rolling grassy hills east of Oakland, west of Sacramento, and north of Modesto. It was only defined by three exits on the nearby freeway, a ragged arroyo on the other side and a smattering of weary farms and horse ranches on the north and south. However, by the time my parents moved there the town was already burgeoning with the sprawl of upper-middle-class workers fueled by the explosion of jobs in aerospace and finance in San Francisco and the surrounding lower peninsula. Much like many suburban communities that spidered out from San Francisco and Oakland, the town was carpeted with modest, middle-class homes. However, the longtime owners were now increasingly being crowded by a new breed of hyperaffluent suburbanites willing to trade off a shorter commute for a home with a pool, a view and, most notably, a two- or even three-car garage.

What set our town apart was our high school. It was far from normal. It was best seen as being *paranormal*. The school was founded on a well-intended but psychedelic era–bred concept of an "experimental campus"—the experiment being whether a high school would churn out more socially responsible, intellectually expanded, and culturally balanced young citizens-to-be if they could just have the run of the place.

It was an experiment on a grand scale, a utopian agenda writ large. The classrooms were "pods"—geodesic hut-like learning centers whose nonlinear confines were to nurture our more spatial thinking skills, I suppose. At least once a month we had "open afternoons"—ill-defined periods of loosely organized liberation during which we could wander around the campus and participate in or attend a range of uniquely '60s activities: macramé techniques, tie-dying, organic cooking, Vietnam War draft counseling, and Gothic printing. Some of the less enlightened among us sneaked behind the gym and drank beer.

Some classes were held on the lawn. Or in the trees. We had one wild-eyed student who thought he was a tree person; he would tuck himself into the nook of a high branch and drop acorns on us as we listened to a lecture below.

All of this was embraced, even encouraged, by the teachers. If you look in our yearbook, the faculty pictures mirror the police mug shots after a drug bust at the Rolling Stones' concert at Altamont. Quite a few of the teachers were pretty hairy creatures, including two of the women. Early Grateful Dead was the attire of choice, and during the warmer months of the year, several of them wore sandals or went barefoot. No doubt a few of the female teachers were braless, but their layers of sackcloth tunics did little to stimulate the imagination, even that of a testosterone-infused teenage boy.

There were a few straight arrows on the faculty. There was an intense, nervous drama teacher who would remind you of Dr. Smith in the TV series *Lost in Space*. He wore a pinched narrow tie and pressed white shirt, black-rimmed glasses thick enough to stop the bullet that hit the guy on the massage table in *The Godfather*, and a gray crew cut. He looked like Buddy Holly would have looked in twenty years if Buddy had not augered his plane into a frozen Iowa cornfield in 1959.

More than a few on the faculty drifted about as if this were Walden Pond on hashish. In fact, the whiff of marijuana was the scent for the cultural clashes emerging at the school. We did not nickname the campus "Stoned Valley" on a whim. It was the dawning of the Age of Aquarius, including its drug-infested dark underside and delirious escapism of Fillmore West and the Haight-Ashbury district of San Francisco just across the bay. Our school was ground zero for the gurgling conflict between the fading ethos of the 1950s-era crew-cut generation and what some saw as the looming pathos of the anything-goes 1960s.

The social divide was never more pronounced than with Kent, an all-league tight end on our football team and the self-appointed guardian of The-Way-God-Intended-America-To-Be, which by his definition meant beer, girls who shaved their legs and armpits, and more beer. Pot was not on the list. So Kent set up Kent's Kleen-up Krowd—a swaggering posse of football players, wrestlers, and muscle-car owners whose mission was to sniff out the odor of pot-smokers, kick down the doors of the stalls in the restrooms, and drag bewildered and terrified potheads out of the john and deposit them with pronounced authority against the nearest hallway lockers. Pot was far from mainstream at our school (except perhaps in the faculty lounge) and most of the tokers were skinny, brooding types who wouldn't know how to put up a fight of their own even if they were lucid enough to do so. On a good week of purging the school of the evil weed, Kent would rally his gang up to a nearby hilltop and split a six-pack or two. Righteousness is so self-defining a quality.

As a relative newcomer from the cloistered banality of Midwest St. Louis, all of this cultural turmoil was dizzying to me. Still unsure of where to place my bets in my gamble to establish myself at the school, I had not picked sides in the fight. However, I was leaning heavily toward beer since I had seen my dad drink beer but had never seen him toke up. I figured I would at least have a sporting rejoinder if I were caught a bit drunk but would need a defense attorney if my father caught me stoned. I joined the Krowd quite unwittingly one day when I was in the restroom, blinking through a low-hanging haze of blue smoke, when Kent and his gang burst through the door. They turned a keen nose to a middle stall, where the meaty boots of a pothead were sticking out and a thick pall of marijuana smoke was seeping out around the metal door. A swift kick and the door was down, the pot smoker was out, and Kent was trading high-five hand slaps to mark another victory for righteous living, to the adoring gaze of several cheerleaders. It seemed like an easy choice for me to join them.

The social divide of beer versus pot was not the only line separating the two worlds of our school. In Mark's view, which I was beginning to learn was the only view in his mind, the world of our school campus could be neatly compartmentalized in simple, contrasting buckets:

You either were rich or you were middle class.

You either were a hippie or a jock.

You either supported the Vietnam War or you opposed it.

You either were a brain or a goof-off.

If you were a serious car guy, you either drove a Chevy or a Plymouth/ Dodge.

These distinctions were a binary enough—yes/no, on/off, good/bad— and Mark left even less room for subtlety, nuance, or variance (*"The draft-dodgers are all Commies ..."*). By now, Mark had appointed himself as my concierge to guide me to where I might find some social traction for this awkward misfit from Missouri, who also now enjoyed the reputation of being the guy dumb enough to buy Rocky's dump of a Chevy.

Mark also had appointed himself as my designated driver—squealing around the end of our cul-de-sac each morning, popping a syncopated report from his car horn to announce his arrival. It was part pity over my wheel-less condition, but I wondered if somehow he was taking me on as some kind of metamorphic project (*"Hey, I transformed the dork from St. Louis into a cool dude!"*). All I knew was that I was grateful that my mother was no longer taking me to school.

Each morning as we pulled into the lot, Mark would launch into a regular patter of commentary on the growing phalanx of muscle cars parked three rows deep near the gymnasium or stalking around the perimeter, filling the air with a mixed chorus of throbbing exhausts and squealing tires. The Chevys pulled into spaces on one row, the Plymouths and Dodges ("Mopars") into the other. Even though my car was far from even running, Mark would pull into his space on the Chevy side and point to one of the spaces on either side.

"That's where you go, my man," he said, almost defiantly. "Pretty soon—that's where you and the Beast go." *Get real,* I thought to myself. I'm a long way from having a muscle car. The first step is to get it to just *start.*

My classification as a Chevy guy was pure serendipity (or as Mark would say "dumb luck"). When I had peeled off my meager savings into Rocky's hand a few weeks earlier, all I knew was that I was buying a twelve-year-old car, albeit one that I thought had nice tail fins and an impressive bumper. To that point, I certainly appreciated that there were "muscle cars" pumping around in the parking lot of our school, but it was only when you got close to these seething slabs of steel that you acquired the visceral affinity toward them.

"You know why guys get these cars?" Mark posed the question to me at noon break as he patrolled the line of muscle cars parked near the gym. He did not wait for me to answer; I was learning that most of Mark's questions were semantic straight-men—rhetorical set-ups for the answer he was ready to give.

"It's their *soul,* man." Mark was nothing if not lyrically philosophical. "It's also their *juice,* because it injects them with the *stuff* they can't generate on their own." I had to ponder that a bit.

"Hey, the guy makes the car, or the car makes the guy," he continued with deadpan pontification and earnestness. "It either compensates or expresses. You can't separate them—the *juice* flows one way or the other. Having a muscle car is not a mutually passive state."

I nodded deferentially, but rolling around in my head was a notion in between his two theories—I wondered if the car and the guy are *both* changed by their association; maybe we adapt the car to our sense of self, but at the same time, the inherent qualities of the car rub off on us, like too much Armor All on a seat.

That afternoon, I wasn't sure into which theory I fit. Maybe Mark was asking me to answer that for myself.

While the parking lot before and after school offered plenty of opportunity for parading, there was yet another theater for muscle-car display: lunch break on the circular drive that looped from the main road and draped around a large oval grassy area in front of the school's main entrance. The lawn was Mark's domain; the sheer concentration of so many people meant that he could work the crowd efficiently and with greater impact than he could being a class clown or self-appointed hallway jester. I was not comfortable just walking up to people like Mark, so I would find a place to sit on the grass, observing his antics from a safe distance. He would ricochet off one group after another, touching the bases, checking in, leaving his mark with some quick quip or burst of social commentary before finally coming in for a landing on my spot and pawing through his lunch bag.

It was there and then, each day, that I was introduced to muscle cars. Like bees swarming from a nest, the Cast-Iron Convoy—nearly a dozen Chevys, Pontiacs, Dodges, and Plymouths—strutted their stuff, especially if there were cheerleaders in view. Rams butting horns in rutting season offered no more impressive a display of hormonal-inspired bravado. It started from the lower parking lot, the distinctive *bbrrattt bbbrrattt* of surging engines, followed by a ripple of rumbles as the cars made their way out of the parking lot and out to the opening of the circle drive.

(A movie that came out about then, *Two-Lane Blacktop*, was a melancholy tale of two aimless drifters, curiously enough played by none other than the folk/rock maestro James Taylor and Dennis Wilson of the Beach Boys. They drove a hopped-up '55 Chevy and trolled roadside diners across the Southwest goading other drivers into racing for cash or *pink slips*—the high-drama of turning ownership of your car over to the winner of a two-car race. One of the most famous lines ever in car movies was uttered by Taylor's character when, after asking a potential competitor how fast his car could go and the guy said, "Fast enough," Taylor shot back, "You can never go fast enough." You tell 'em, Sweet Baby James.)

Once Mark got me on the inside track, I started to recognize the "bowtie" hood emblem of Chevrolet and became more aware of the other Chevys among the muscle cars at the school. It's like *after* you buy a car is when you start noticing them on the road or seeing them in advertisements.

I counted two other '57 Chevys at our school. The first was a completely stock, pale yellow '57 Bel-Air sedan. It even had white sidewalls. The car fit the owner; "Bones," was a tall, gregarious senior with uniformly cropped dark hair and long, chiseled sideburns. He was a center on our varsity basketball team—clean-cut, understated in manner, and someone who stood out from the crowd by simple physical presence more than by attitude. He didn't need the car to say anything more.

The second '57 was a rare black convertible. I never really recall seeing the top go up on that car; it's possible that it didn't. Frankie, a slightly distracted, heart-led senior, seemed oblivious to the jewel he had in that car. Polish that baby up, buckle on a set of glass-pack mufflers and some decent wheels, and it would have been a cheerleader-snagging machine. Frankie never strutted the car, thinking that any girl worth dating was one who liked him more than some car. Nuts. Start with a hot car. Let them learn to love *you* later.

Then there was my '57, its faded and oxidized pale blue paint giving it something of a dull steel cast. Rocky had never done much with the car, so it was lacking any folklore or legacy. I was not the only one who was surprised to discover that it housed a 348 engine instead of the stock 283, but a few at school derided the larger power plant as "just a truck engine." I did not know enough at the time to refute the criticism, but whether a truck engine or not, it was the only engine I had—and I had to get it to run.

"You've got the *juice* in your Beast," Mark would reassure me, although I was getting a little confused whether the *juice* referred to the car or its driver. My self-bought, twelve-year-old coupe was a gray hair by comparison with the fleet of new cars that these kids' rich parents had bought for them. Most of the Chevys I was gazing at were the ones you would see on any respectable muscle-car calendar—Camaro and Nova SS being the most legendary. The Chevy engines had a sound signature to them you could detect a mile away. They were screeching eagles in full-attack mode.

I thought Mopar—what most know as Chrysler and Plymouth—was much more evocative in its naming of muscle cars: Road Runner, Challenger, Charger, Barracuda. Their names said *race, hunt, kill.* They looked like they could, too. These cars were bigger, bolder, badass bruisers—lean, tough, no-nonsense street bullies. They were rolling slabs of sheet metal with tires adorned with white or red stripes, exhaust tips flaring out from under rear bumpers—everything said they were all business. Serious business.

There were some eclectic representations of automotive genius or psychosis at our school as well. There was an early '60s Impala like Mark's—pure white, only lowered with deep dish chrome wheels, and airbrushed onto the side panels was a anatomically enhanced rendering of a very lifelike, scantily clad woman draped over a rock in a Mexican sunset. It was enough to make you fall in love. Boomer, a junior who was known for his constant banter and boasting, drove a Vega, which wheezed out an anemic seventy horsepower from a 2.3-liter aluminum engine, a record for flaccid output. Boomer was convinced that it was the sleeper of the decade; every few weeks, he would show up with another performance modification—an air scoop on the hood, mag wheels, dual exhausts—that were all so out of place and stuck-on as to make the car look like a rolling Mr. Potato Head.

Bruce, a tall, quietly thoughtful sophomore, was renowned for having a '50 Ford deuce coupe in recovery in his garage. The previous owner wanted to paint it but lacked the money, so he painted it himself—with a paintbrush. Its brushed-stroked squalor was a nightmare to look at, but it ran like a dream. "Flathead" engines in cars from that era were no more sophisticated a design than you would find in most lawn-mower motors, but Bruce got that Ford purring at idle like a cougar on Quaaludes.

Even though some of the guys at our school were endowed with affluent parents, none of them had hit up the folks for a fastback Mustang, the costar of the car-chase scene in the 1968 move *Bullitt*, where Steve McQueen takes on a '68 Dodge Charger with his own guardrail-scraping stunt driving. Living only an hour or so from San Francisco and absent the legal warnings of today ("Stunt drivers used; do not attempt these maneuvers") the delusional fantasy that we could take our cars airborne on Lombard Street took on a strange reality in our minds. Our propensity for over-obsessing on cars at the cost of other lusts needed no further evidence than the fact that most guys could tell you exactly what cars were in that movie but completely miss the fact that it costarred Jacqueline Bisset.

Brat was another Chevy owner, but on the margins—he had a '65 Corvair. Brat's Corvair was an eccentric creation, but he was fiercely proud of it, even more so after Ralph Nader famously declared the Corvair "unsafe at any speed." We had never seen Brat get his Corvair up to anything that would be considered an unsafe speed; nonetheless, Brat painted up a 1940s-era leather football helmet with the words "Ralph Nader Racing Team" and wore it to class. Of course, at Stoned Valley High, with people humming chants in trees, nobody saw anything out of the ordinary with a guy wearing a painted football helmet to English Lit class.

There was not one car in the muscle-car inventory at school that looked the same. If there was a thread at all it was the T-shirts I saw a lot of the drivers wearing—a simple white shirt with the letters "QQQQ" emblazoned across the back.

"That's what I was telling you about," Mark explained gleefully. "Those are the Ducks." I would see the Ducks hanging out together, usually inspecting each other's latest set of wheels or engine modifications. Hoods were almost always up when the Ducks were around. Most clubs are tribal, their impulses nearly primal—crude, raw expressions of community and exclusion. The Ducks—the muscle-car crowd—projected airs that there was something special about them, at least in their own minds if not my own view. Being in that club was both competition and community. It was a fraternity; yet fire up those V8s in the parking lot and all that community melted in a wash of hot gases and the elbowing would start.

Apart from showing off their muscle cars, the Ducks made their presence known at league basketball games with their own ribald version of cheers, much to the dismay of the cheerleaders. They had, as any self-respecting pep squad ought to have, a mascot—logically, a real duck in a cage that they would suspend from one of the steel girders in the gym. On cue, usually just before the opposing team was trying to sink a foul shot, they would open up with perfectly coordinated clacking of their wooden blocks. The noise was deafening, mind-numbing, and devastating to the concentration of the opposing team.

Most of the time, the Ducks and their muscle cars were more theater than threat. The point was to parade your car by the circular lawn area, punching the throttle in neutral to show off the engine's baritone staccato, but it was too tight and short of a circle for any serious acceleration. Like those rodeo bulls that act tough, throw off a rider, and steam around the ring a bit, it's all for the fans.

Except every once in a while, one of those bulls goes berserk, skewering a rodeo clown or making a leap for the stands. Burnside had a Plymouth Road Runner, a baby-blue monster with a 440 Hemi engine—the sonic equivalent of eight blacksmith fists hammering under the hood—and a rear spoiler that raked the air a full two feet above the trunk deck. Burnside had a pair of the meatiest sideburns of anyone in high school and projected the pugnacious scowl of a Rocky Marciano. In the yin yang of the debate over whether the car made the man or the man made the car, Burnside's *chi* was in elegant balance. His car fit his persona, and his persona was well-fitted to the "Hey, yo, you talkin' to me?" voice of his Road Runner. His car was menacing enough standing still, never mind screaming by the school lawn with its tail on fire. One afternoon, he steered his Road Runner to the back curve of the drive and paused. He rapped the engine, and the car shuddered with the torque like a bull snorting and digging in for its next charge. Then, with a shriek of the engine, the Road Runner leaped forward, hunching down on its rear springs, blue/white smoke churning out of its wheel wells. It was over in a few seconds, but the cloud of carbonized rubber drifted over the student lawn like a fog of acid. Students were coughing, cussing, and holding napkins and shirts against their faces, but an equal number were whooping and hollering in vicarious conquest. Burnside raised a fist outside his window as he spun the Road Runner on a victory lap around the circle and retired to the paddock below.

From our vantage point on the lawn, Mark toked up on the vulcanized vapor, held his breath for a few seconds, blew out the acrid air, and turned to me with a Cheshire grin.

"We have *got* to get your car running."

# # #

Chapter Five

This is going to take forever. Don't let anyone ever convince you that we are only six degrees of separation away from anyone, at least not when you really are trying to find them. I call a few "Marks" from my hand-written list off the Internet, but the conversations are awkward and over in seconds *("I'm looking for a Mark who went to Stoned Valley High back in 1970 ... oh, okay, sorry to bother you ...").* This isn't going to work.

Somewhere down in this basement of ours is a box with packing tape on it and felt marker block letters on the side, something like "Mementos" or "old school stuff." I finally find it atop a file cabinet in back, coated with dust and weary and sagging a bit under the weight of the years. I peel the tape back, inhaling the stale smell of old paper and glue bindings. Inside is an odd assortment of old writings from high school Lit class, a flyer from our high school musical, a bowtie most likely from a prom, and one of those hospital wrist bands they give you so they don't confuse your hernia operation with the guy on the other gurney who is scheduled for testicular cancer surgery.

After some fumbling through the stack, I find what I am looking for, the mascot on the binding still familiar. I crack open the yearbook and thumb to the front where neat little photos of geeky kids are lined up in alphabetical order. I don't pause on any of them; I look for the round-faced kid with the tousled, blond hair—there he is. That's who I need to call.

Brat.

Finding him is easier. His last name is unusual enough, and while there are a few listed on the Internet search directory, I am taking a gamble that Brat has not gone far from his familiar turf in high school. I pick a likely suspect on the West Coast, and more Internet searching brings the name up again, this time associated with a real estate office in Nevada.

His voice is different, and after we exchange the mutual "Hey, how have you been?" he is still not up to gear. His cadence is kept in check by his growing curiosity—even a wariness—about why I am calling him after three decades. It's simple enough, I tell him. I need to find Mark and I thought you would know where he is.

Yes, he knows where Mark is—right back in the same town as our high school. He doesn't know the phone number but he gives me names of two people who might. We both realize that there is not much more to talk about, so I end with telling him that I appreciate his help. He ends the call another way.

"Paul, just be aware—Mark is not really the person you remember. He's been through a lot."

Yeah, haven't we all.

I sit in my office for a while, glancing through the yearbook, wondering how many other people are not the people now that I remembered them to be then. Amid the rows of now-sepia-toned black-and-white photos, there are some familiar faces; others are complete strangers over the years. Like the guy in my photo.

You never really feel as old as you are unless you let yourself—or your body makes you. I'm not sure it is a matter of having a good time or a bad time. It's just *time*. Whether we are reminded or assaulted by the passage of time, we do not come out of that passage unchanged.

Maybe that's why some people seem to get quieter when they get older, to start keeping to themselves. You lose—or lose track of—friends, and it's just a little too hard to make new ones. Take the housing development where my wife and I now live. It's full of empty-nesters and early retirees. People seem to keep to themselves. We're also supposed to keep our garage doors closed. Something to do with preserving the ambiance of the place and protecting property values. Nobody around here works in their garage anyway. For that matter, most people around here don't work—period.

My neighbor across the street is a nice guy, well into retirement years, but he fusses more than a flea-ridden dog in summer. He and his wife moved to Florida a few years ago to, well, you know, retire. Get away from the snow. Let their kids move on with their own lives.

He hated it. Too many old people bumping into each other at the supermarket. Too much heat and humidity. Missed the kids. Nothing to do. So he moved back.

Now he gets all cranked up about the snow again and how there's nothing to do up here either. Good hard-working man all his life; our street looks like a parking lot during holidays with all his kids showing up. He doesn't mean to complain, I don't think. It's just become a habit too hard to break.

He drives this big ol' honkin' Lincoln Town Car. Nothing fancy. It even has hubcaps instead of solid alloy wheels. Has about two hundred and twenty thousand miles on it, and every time something breaks, he fusses about it. He's about seventy years old, and I can only imagine what he'll be saying when parts start falling off him.

He thinks I'm a crazy genius. Most times when I have my BMW up on jack stands in the garage with the door open, he just stands across the street for a while and then blurts out, "*Now* what are you doing?" I consider it a rhetorical question unless he repeats it. I'm usually doing some maintenance, but sometimes I'm just fooling around with some "mods"—a stiffer sway bar, cold air intake, racing struts, just stuff. The whole notion of working on a car is alien to him. Why bother? He says the shocks are still good after two hundred and twenty thousand miles. If they haven't fallen off, they must be good.

Now, though, things are starting to break on his old Lincoln, so he comes across the street and starts talking in this casual, nonchalant way, but I know a guy trolling for free labor when I see it. He's easy to please—he thought it was pretty genius of me that I could replace his windshield wipers and a window switch. But he'll fuss. The other day, he calls me over to listen to this whirring whine from the engine—some kind of bearing starting to wear out is what it sounds like to me. I tell him it could be several things: maybe a water pump, but these usually leak along with whining, A/C compressor, maybe the alternator, but after listening a bit more I venture that I think it's the fan clutch.

He wants to know for sure what it is, and I just say to let it go for a while until the noise gets a little louder or something starts to leak and then it will be more obvious what it is. You don't want to just do exploratory surgery on an engine that has never felt a caring hand for two hundred and twenty thousand miles. At least I don't.

Sure enough the next week, he's across the street, calling me out of the garage. "It was the alternator," he growls. "Had to pull over when the 'check engine' light went on. I thought you told me it was the fan clutch."

Easy, man. I'm not a genius.

To: paul
From: mark
Subject: anticipation

---

lots of guys wanting great muscle cars. only four people: me, kendall, greek and rocky told people the 57 Beast was to be reckoned with.

"You know, everyone at school is starting to talk about our car." Mark breezed into the garage, grabbing the broom like a hockey stick and panning it under the Chevy to sweep for rattlers.

"*Our* car?" I fired back. "How did that happen?"

"Oh yeah," Mark stood up and leaned back against the Beast. "We are on a mission! Everybody is watching this deal."

"Why should they care?" I stretched to reach more deeply into the engine compartment, my shoes scattering wrenches across the concrete floor.

"It's a race," he said. "You and Dotson. Who gets their car running first."

Dotson was the son of a wealthy family that lived in a rambling painted white brick house right off the tenth green at my dad's country club. In high school, you are a little oblivious to the airs given off by the affluent, but Dotson left a vapor trail in his path. It was hard to pin down, but everything about him—his manner, his posture, his language, his attitude—reeked of superiority marinated in money. And who names their kid Dotson without trying to make a statement? Dotson was tall and athletic, with hair carefully combed like some kind of blond helmet. While most of us wore rumpled, faded Levis and plain T-shirts or simple blue cotton shirts from Sears, Dotson was draped in tailored, button-down oxfords and cuffed khakis. Where we wore plain tennis shoes or penny loafers, Dotson was shod with woven leather tassel slip-ons.

Dotson had a Porsche Speedster, or more precisely, most of the parts for one. The car, also known among devotees as the 356, was the signature car for Porsche from the '50s: a squat, rounded, clamshell body powered by a four-cylinder, rear-mounted horizontally opposed (or "pancake") engine—a design that arrayed pairs of cylinders butted up against each other on one plane rather than being aligned in a row or in a V-shape. It was the antithesis of a muscle car—it was light, subtle, agile, and poised to carve through twisted mountain passes. It was pure European in its sensibilities and design: sparse, utilitarian, understated—and expensive. The car would have been unknown to most of the Detroit Iron–bred population in the United States had not movie stud James Dean plowed his super-modified Porsche Spyder into the side of a 1950 Ford Tudor sedan turning left on a quiet road on a late September afternoon outside Bakersfield. Dean earned his place in that unenviable catalogue of fantastic finishes by movie actors, and the Porsche Speedster entered the American lexicon and folklore.

We never saw Dotson do anything to earn money, so we had to assume he had open rights to his dad's wallet. Dotson was proficient at converting paper to steel—he peeled off the bills regularly to secure parts from a lean and tightly knit market for Porsche Speedster parts. These were not parts you could buy on the cheap from a J. C. Whitney catalog, a ubiquitous mail-order listing of aftermarket parts for just about any car made in America. There were just not enough parts around to create any competition or make it easy for buyers and sellers to get together. Whatever spare parts existed were coveted and commanded a price premium. Some parts owners treated their spare control arms, steering wheels, or seats like family heirlooms that needed care and a loving home before they would let them go ("So how far along are you in your restoration? How long do you plan to keep the car? Do you change your own oil? Okay … just this time I'll sell you the spring set, but you can't have the floor mats—I'm not ready to part with them just yet.")

Nobody had to get rid of Porsche parts—all you had to do was wait until some overanxious teenager with an overstuffed wallet and ego came your way.

Just down the hill and over two streets in my garage, it was a different story. I wasn't intent on restoring my car; I really had little idea of what that meant and little interest in having a car that looked like it did in 1957 anyway. I just wanted it to run. If I was going to get my Chevy working, it was going to have to be with a full tank of improvisation.

Mark and I had gotten the cylinder heads out of hock at the machine shop by now with my first couple of paychecks from the drugstore. After a few confirming glances at the *Motors Manual* pictures, we bolted the heads back into place—with the correct gasket and all—within an afternoon. Once I got Mark to stop playing drumsticks with the pushrods, we were able to nestle the intake manifold into position and screw the valve covers down over the whole assembly. Next step: the carburetor.

I was told that you might as well rebuild the carburetor if you are taking it off, so I had purchased a rebuild kit, spread some newspaper on the workbench and went at it, pretending for the moment that it did not look like the picture puzzle it really was at that point. Loosening some screws that held on the top piece, I was met with a confetti spray of springs, needles, and floats that sprang from their nesting places and skittered around on the tabletop.

"Mark, can you help with this?"

He skidded over to my side and scooped the spinning parts into his palm, laying them in a pile in front of me.

"Thanks," I said, holding the carcass of the carburetor in front of me, "but where does all this stuff go back in? It all came off at once."

Mark offered another one of his studied gazes, rolling the tip of his tongue around on the inside of his check before answering.

"Hard to say, my man."

I spun around on the tool and looked at him with a mixture of pleading and annoyance.

"Mark, have you *ever* worked on a car before?"

Mark stepped back from the parry, bobbing his head to his internal beat, and forced a smile.

"Well, no, not really," he said. I had barely let out a sigh that spoke both to my frustration and my relief at finally having the charade bared before Mark rallied himself.

"You needed the help, man," he said. "That's what friends do."

It was the first time he called me a friend, and it startled me into silence. Here I was getting testy with the only guy to that point who had offered to help, as helpless as that aid might be. What mattered more—competence or companionship? Efficiency or empathy? Oddly, as much as I understood the answer to be the friendship, what tore at that was the sheer task before us. As much as a teenage guy even *thinks* that hard about what a friendship means rather than simply what it does, I at least understood that it had to be based on *something*, right? There is a transactional component, an equilibrium at play that means both parties sign on with some visceral or subconscious sense that they either will gain from the deal or come out even-steven, but at least not lose. Can't we just get the car done and then decide, hey, that was great so I guess we can now say we ended up being friends?

If Mark wasn't going to be the able guide in this, then I was going to have to recalibrate. Either he needed to step up a bit or I needed to back off.

"We can do this, man," Mark said more quietly, with a determination that belied his hurt. I looked at him for a few moments, drawing a blank at that point about what to say or do. As exasperated and lost as I was at that moment, somehow this stupid grin roiled up from deep underneath my carefully controlled face muscles and just erupted. Worst time in the world, right when I really want Mark to know how I felt.

That's all it took. Mark lit up with a wise-cracking smile.

"Told yah, my man," he roared. "We can do this."

Maybe so, but I needed someone on the side who at least knew what they were doing. I could not seek out a member of the Ducks for two reasons that seemed clear enough to me even at that early stage. First, you just don't ask. As a junior transfer from out of state, you don't bare your ignorance that early or that easily. Second, the Ducks did not work on their cars. They *bought* their bragging rights. I had to *build* mine.

I knew there were two '57 Chevy owners at our school—Bones and Frankie—but they didn't know me. They were seniors; I was a junior. When you need wisdom, though, you have to move up, not down. It was a gamble, but I was desperate.

Bones was finishing a basketball scrimmage in the gym, a towel wrapped around his neck and still breathing heavily, when I walked up to him.

"Hey," I stuck out my hand tentatively, and he grasped it easily and smiled.

"You're the guy who got screwed with Rocky's car," he said.

I wasn't sure how to respond to that, but my head was nodding mindlessly, since it really was true, even if hard to admit.

He planted his hand on my shoulder.

"You can use some of my tools if that helps. We'll be around on Saturday. "

I knew where he lived; I had passed the house often on my way back and forth to the drugstore—the yellow '57 four-door could be seen through the trees, parked in the gravel turnout, over to the side next to the garage. The "house" itself was really a haphazard cluster of cottage buildings and a main building that, at one time a few decades earlier, may have been a farm or ranch before suburbia swallowed the acreage around it. It was oddly out of place amid the upper-middle-class homes sprouting up all around it. The trees all around the property, its gravel driveway, and the burnt umber color of the wood siding of the houses all added to a sense of mystery about the place.

That Saturday I rode my ten-speed bike down the main road from my house to the Bones enclave, gripping my handlebars as the thin tires chattered down the gravel of his driveway. I slid the bike to a stop near the front of the open garage door and peered into the darkness. A pair of yellowed bulbs hung from cloth-wrapped electrical cords, casting an uneven, muted glow on the poured concrete floor. On the right side of the garage, tools were suspended on pegboard hooks, with felt pen outlines behind them so there was no doubt about the proper location for a crescent wrench or pry bar. The whole room was dank and moody but clutter-free and clean. Everything was old—even the wood studs and ceiling beams had that dark, weary patina of age—but everything was in its place and everything in that garage had a job to do.

The yellow and black convertible '57s were dozing on the side gravel area, but there was no sign of Bones or Frankie. I was about to go to the front door when I heard faintly a Marvin Gay song seeping through the walls of an out building near the back edge of the property. I walked up to the rust-colored wood door and rapped on its panels. The door creaked open, and Bones reached out of the darkness in the room to shake my hand and wave me in.

Like the verse from "Momma Told Me Not to Come," I ain't never seen a place like this before. The walls were covered with posters of all sorts—Jimi Hendrix, the Oakland Raiders, Easy Rider, Ali/Frazier, Rigid Tool calendars—all seemingly vibrating with a surreal purplish/white glow coming from a pair of fluorescent tubes on the ceiling, which was draped in black fabric tacked up with staples.

"Black light. Cool." I feigned common knowledge but actually had never seen one in action.

"He came by to ask for some help on Rocky's wreck." Bones turned back to Frankie, who was perched Yoga-like on a bar stool. Frankie nodded readily and smiled back, revealing a picket-row fence line of purple/white teeth. He slipped off the stool, shook my hand, and then followed Bones out the door into the bright—*and natural*—sunlight.

"First rule," Bones said, "is that any tools we use get hung back up, clean." I learned that Bones's father was a jumbo jet pilot for one of the major airlines and took it personally when his ship was out of shape—whether on the tarmac or on his property. So I was instructed that every time we worked, we would always finish off with a strict checklist to ensure that tools were restored to their proper resting place, not unlike surgeons making sure they hadn't left behind a clamp or scalpel in a newly sutured patient. The neatness standard also applied to Bones's '57—his father banned it from the garage to thwart any chance of an oil stain on the floor, condemning it to the back edge of their gravel driveway, where the sun, wind, and temperature extremes had their way with its paint and seats.

"Second rule," Bones said sternly, "is that there are no rules." He said it with such a straight face, it took a moment to sink in. "You got a question, ask it …"

"If we don't know the answer, we'll make it up!" Frankie popped off on cue.

I had no more of an admission slip to be there than the registration paper attesting that I now owned a '57 Chevy, but that seemed enough to enter their sanctum. It was a pragmatic affinity at first—guys with similar cars tended to hang together to trade parts, working knowledge, and bragging rights. These old cars don't run on their own.

If Mark was restless and distracted, Bones was all *groove*. There was a calm about him, a quietness and a gentle humor that I found a welcome counterpoint to Mark's more mercurial impulses. I also found I could ask a question and get a straight answer, and I had lots of questions.

"What's this thing next to the battery?" (*That's the voltage regulator. It distributes the electricity to different parts of the car.*) "What's this cap for?" (*It's the engine blow-by vent.*) "What's this other wheel for on the engine?" (*That's the crankcase damper.*)

I never took notes—in class or in the garage—so more than once the newfound knowledge slipped out of my memory, usually later that night when I was back in my garage by myself. It would be convenient to my ego to think that I did not have moments of severe doubt, but the reality was that more than once panic or despair was the Rasputin on my shoulder, pricking my confidence with insidious counsel that I was way over my head and my adventure was folly. This whole thing started with a head gasket and just seemed to devolve from there into this mass of cast iron, steel, and rubbers hoses now lying lifelessly in the engine compartment. The calendar on the wall of the garage was a constant nag that any chance I had of getting the car in shape to take to the fall homecoming football game was slipping away.

When Mark was not with me to provide distraction or encouragement, the task often overwhelmed me. It was the chaos theory in motion. I would take off one thing or turn something around and only realize hours later than I had done it wrong and now it had wreaked more severe consequences somewhere else. Maybe a washer that seemed so insignificant one moment was the reason that at some later point another part would not tighten down properly. As simple as a Chevy V8 engine is by today's standards, back then it seemed like a puzzle—a costly, greasy puzzle.

Rebuilding an engine, I soon recognized, is not an exercise in spatial creativity. To keep the chaos in check, I started to gather up shoe boxes, cigar boxes, or anything that would hold parts and labeled with them a black Magic Marker—*intake manifold bolts, brake parts, radiator hose clamps, strange clip that came off the steering linkage.* It was not any real breakthrough in project management, but it reined in just one more thing that seemed, to that point, out of control.

One of the epiphanies you can have in rebuilding an engine is realizing that it is made up of parts, all with a job to do. That may seem evident, but you would be surprised at how many people choose to see an engine as this big, metal *thing* that just runs and ought not to be meddled with. For me, my self-education was acquired in degrees by taking off parts and looking at them, comparing them to the pictures in my trusty *Motors Manual,* and not putting them down on the workbench or the garage floor until I was satisfied I understood what they did and how they did it. In particular, I remember figuring how the clutch worked (*Okay, so you press the clutch pedal and this thing squeezes the spring fingers that hold this other disc up against the flywheel and then the shaft is attached to that … Ohhhh, I get it!*).

Deciphering the working code of the distributor was a real challenge. I knew something about coils from Bopper, our electronics class teacher, and realized the hard way that the coil stores up to about twenty-five thousand volts—a dose that can numb your arm and knock you on your butt if you're dumb enough to touch the wire attached to it, which I did. (As I sat dazed on the garage floor, I imagined walking around school with a flaccid arm flopping at my side and kids looking at me, clucking to each other, "Idiot touched a coil …") I knew from *Motors* that the distributor somehow *distributed* all that voltage to the spark plugs, like flipping the circuit breaker in your house as fast as you can. I remember taking the distributor out of the engine, gripping the geared shaft, and turning it slowly—back-and-forth, back-and-forth—and discovering the little cam on the shaft that would force open these two little electrical contacts and close them again—the light switch! All this is dreadfully boring to someone who, again, thinks engines ought to be left well enough alone, but for me, sitting there for an hour in the garage with that distributor and figuring out how it worked was a flush of accomplishment that I had not experienced in any way to that point.

Pretty soon, I was not just *looking* at the line drawings in the *Motors,* I was *studying* them, animating them in my imagination, visualizing the engine turning, parts moving up and down, in and out, around and around in a beautifully symmetrical mechanical ballet. With the image churning in my mind, I then would recreate the movements with the real engine—gripping the front pulley and cranking the engine slowly by hand like those old Model T newsreels, all the time watching the real parts move in their synchronized routines.

The revelation did not come all at once, nor easily, but stretched out under the hood of my Chevy, with a bare-bulb trouble light dangling overhead and with the oily sweat of the engine soaked into my arms and streaked across my face, I learned how an engine worked.

———————

"So you got a date tonight?" Mark was stacking rolls of toilet paper and cans of hair spray on the stockroom shelves of the drugstore one Friday afternoon when he posed the question, as if it had no more consequence that asking me about the weather.

Actually, I did not. I had pledged myself to self-imposed monasticism until I got the Chevy running. No wheels, no cash, no dates. Every once in a while, I would try to position myself in the bleachers at a football or basketball game next to some cute girl so people might think we were on a date, but my cover was blown each time when she would leave to buy a soda and not come back. Sometimes I would get invited to join a crowd going out for pizza after the game and I would just ride shotgun in their car—but despite my obfuscations, most everyone knew I did not have a car that ran. Yet.

So Mark's question about whether I had a date that night was uniquely timely and equally painful.

"You know I don't," I sighed. "Thanks for asking."

"Well, then I have just the plan." Mark always did. The plan was to "cruise the Creek"—a regular Friday-night foray where guys driving just about every muscle car imaginable would form a bumper-to-bumper convey on the main drag of nearby Cedar Creek and just cruise. I had never done it but had heard about it. We got off at eight, but that wasn't the problem. I delicately raised the issue.

"Mark, your Impala is about as stock as a Jersey cow. It hardly qualifies as a cruiser."

"Got that covered," Mark said, without a hint of hurt. "We're going in Greek's Goat."

Now, Mark my man, you're talking sense. Greek was a towering all-league offensive lineman on our football team who drove a burgundy '64 Pontiac GTO, colloquially referred to as "the Goat" in the folklore of the muscle-car era. Greek was an imposing figure—barrel-chested, nearly six-and-a-half feet tall, a growl of a voice, piercing black eyes, and loading-dock pylons for arms. Even in the boundless culture of Stoned Valley, he had earned legendary status as the only guy in high school who had a full beard. He looked like Brutus in *Popeye*. The GTO fit Greek—it was stout, muscular, and had a pronounced "I don't take crap from anybody" look about it that often convinced contenders at stoplights to limp away without so much as a tire chirp.

That evening, just as we were closing up the front doors to the drugstore, there was a squeal of tires and an echoing roar across the parking lot. Greek spun the car around a bay of shopping carts and jolted to a halt in front of us. Up close, in the shadowy lights of the parking lot, the GTO seemed meaner than ever. It was lowered, the windows were tinted, and chrome exhaust tips flared out beneath the chrome rear bumper. Mark opened the door and announced to Greek that I was joining them—a statement met with a shoulder shrug and a baritone "Get in then."

I sat in back and Mark rode shotgun as we lumbered down the highway toward the main exit for Cedar Creek. As we exited the freeway to Main Street, suddenly the scene from my vantage point in the back of the GTO came to life, an explosion of lights, sounds, and action. We fell into line behind a trail of taillights that streamed up the street for blocks. On each side, most stores were brightly lighted, showcasing front windows of merchandise, with strobes and pulsing music spilling out from their front doors. A few stores, like those selling high-end jewelry, a dentist office, maybe an insurance office, were battened down against the din like an Amish maid is buttoned high and tight. But for every other store, especially the pizza shops, the Army-Navy surplus store, and the clothing shops, this was a party to be joined.

The sidewalks were teeming with teenagers—a boy and girl walking hand-in-hand, a gaggle of girls giggling and pointing or, often, casting a scoffing, indifferent glance at a car of guys hooting and honking their horn at them. Most of the guys were in cars, and most of the girls were on the sidewalk, as if this were an awkward junior-high dance where the boys and girls stood on opposite sides of the gymnasium with no one really wanting to make the first move but wishing someone would. In this case, it was a primal ritual—the guys could act out their seductions and avoid the disgrace of a refusal by calling out from a moving car. If they did not get a response they wanted, they could always look like they were moving on anyway. The girls could volley with a suggestive wave or blown kiss but easily retreat into the crowds if things got too serious.

Within a few minutes, we had edged up to the first traffic light, with Greek never really releasing the clutch fully but teasing the car forward in first gear at a pace you could easily outwalk. Mark was into it, rolling down his window, wolf-whistling, and calling out, "Hey, baaaaby!" When he elicited a grin back he would laugh; when he drew a mocking glare, he would laugh. The whole deal was to just get some reaction. When you are thundering down Main Street in a lowered '64 GTO, even if it was not your own, you just did not want to be ignored.

Greek was not one to holler out the window or even race his engine at the lights. He had a sense of himself and his formidable presence and did not have to inflate it. He had a quiet boldness to himself, much like a Brahma bull might give you a bored, benign gaze when you first step into the field—one of those "Do you understand I can kick your butt into the next county or do you *really* need me to get up and prove that point?"

What added to Greek's air of confidence was the fact that his seats seemed to be lower than usual—either he put in some aftermarket bucket seats that just came out that way or his heft had sunken them. Either way, if you drove past Greek, you would get an immediate sense that you were about to have a close encounter with Earthquake McGoon.

We were on our third light, with Mark taunting and teasing out the passenger-side window and me just taking in the scenes from the backseat, when there was a subtle *bump* that shuddered through the car. It was like the first time the shark elbowed the boat in *Jaws*—something that caught your attention as being out of the ordinary but you didn't know what it was. At the next light, there it was again—*bump*—only sharper and more insistent, as if trying to get our attention. Greek glanced up into his rearview mirror and then down to his side mirror to peer back at a lowered '61 Impala that was tight on our tail.

"I think he bumped me," Greek said firmly and calmly. "I think he bumped me," he said again to himself, as the bull lumbers up from his sleeping position to take a closer look at the fool still standing in the fenced pasture.

"Oh, yeah, he bumped you!" Mark stirred it up. "Who does he think he is? You gonna take that, Greek?"

Greek didn't take anything he didn't want to take, including advice. He flicked another glance into his rear-view mirror and then rumbled away as the light turned green. A block later, we came to another red light, and as Greek slowed the GTO, he watched in his mirror as if to gauge the distance. The car behind us stopped, and then, even as I watched twisted around in the rear seat, the Impala crept forward and bumped Greek's GTO again.

Mark and I didn't need to say anything; in fact, a dark blanket of foreboding settled in over us as we watched Greek's face twist into a scowl. "Okay," Greek announced in a low, matter-of-fact voice. "Now this guy has pissed me off." He raced the engine, popped the clutch, and lurched ahead four feet, chirped the tires again, and slammed on the brakes.

Greek rolled out of the GTO and rose up into his full persona as a towering, bearded, all-league defensive tackle with arms like flank steaks and a build like Brutus. He walked to the front of the Impala and stood there for a poignant second. Then, as calmly and with as much effort as you would punt a can down the road, Greek kicked in one of the headlights. Satisfied with his technique and the effect it was having on the now-terrified Impala driver, he shifted over to his left and kicked in the other headlight.

As a final gesture, Greek reared back with his fist and—with all the authority and force of a mason chiseling a Roman numeral into a granite tombstone—planted it right in the middle of the Impala's hood, leaving a fist-shaped dent. Then, as if he had done nothing more exerting than just scraping a dead possum off the road, Greek calmly sat back in the GTO and muttered, "I don't like people screwing with my car."

It was an impressive display of sheer force but done with such controlled fury that I was in awe of Greek from that moment on. Greek *was* his GTO. The '64 and '65 versions started as a Pontiac Tempest, a simple, pedestrian family car that was beefed up with a more powerful engine and upgrades to its drive train and suspension. That's all. Other than the engine insignia on the side, something of a tattoo on the upper arm, most laymen would not easily be able to delineate a GTO from its weakling little brother—until it lit up at a green light or roared past you on an open road, its engine howling and its tires clawing the pavement. The GTO officially inaugurated the muscle-car era but did so with a certain reserve. You knew the car had some righteous power under the hood, but as you looked at the car, you did not fully appreciate its capacity for mayhem. A lot of people who drove early GTOs, in my experience, did not have much to prove. They knew what they had (and preferred that the cops did not), and any expression of superiority was better felt than seen. The GTO did not need to lower itself to every street fight. If you were dumb enough to take one on—to walk into that pasture without carrying one heck of a big stick or a plan to escape—you could walk away with more than your ego bruised. If you didn't know what a GTO could do, there was one stupid way to find out.

All you had to do was tick one off.

# # #

Chapter Six

My fingers pause over the button on the phone, the last digit of the number. I really want to do this, right? Will he remember me after all these years? Will he wonder why I have waited this long to call? Am I fooling myself that guys tossed together in the transient years of youth would even care enough at this point to pick it all up again? Even worse, what if he just doesn't give a rip if I do call, after somehow me not finding—you know—just a few minutes over the last thirty years to do it? Who's doing whom the favor here?

The phone rings several times, and I'm about to call the whole crazy idea off when there is a click and a voice-mail message starts. The voice is low, measured, and precise, as if it is a struggle to get it right: "You've reached the voice mail of Mark. Thank you for calling. Please leave a message after the beep." I take a breath, not sure what to say, and then blurt out, "Hey, Mark, I heard you're still looking for a bass player for Bedlam Showboat. If so, call me back." I leave my number and hang up.

This is really stupid. You don't leave messages like that after thirty years. Then again, I'm not sure what you do say.

Two days later, Mark calls back. His voice is thin and strained, but it is Mark. He is exuberant. We talk for an hour—about what I can't begin to recount, but we catch up on a lot of years.

"I finally got ahold of Mark," I tell Carol that evening.

"Oh, okay," she says. "Good, I guess. Did you have a good talk?"

Oh, oh. I know what that means. So did you just talk, or did you *talk?* Yeah, we actually did have a good talk. We talked like we had never stopped talking, actually. It was weird—you would think we would shuffle and dodge a bit, trying to get some traction, grab a gear in the conversation, certainly wondering if it might stall. It never did.

"So do you think you'll be talking to him again?" Carol seems to know the answer herself but is checking to see if I do. She doesn't like to stir people for no reason, create expectations that you have no intent to fulfill. She knows I'm not great on the phone—just get through your list and be polite and all, but you don't go deep on the phone. Too weird. You can't see how people are reacting on the phone. Or if they are reacting at all.

Carol is in a different hemisphere than me when it comes to the phone. She is what I would call an *active chatterer*; she is perfectly comfortable curling up on the couch with the phone and a cup of coffee and talking to some friend about—maybe this is a chick thing, but, geez—cancer, divorce, bad husbands, clothes, drapery fabric, poopy diapers, kids, phobias, God, a little politics; whatever. Actually, not that she talks about it—she *listens*. Hard. I mean, listens in a way that the other person knows they are being heard. So they talk. Then, somewhere along the line, at the right time, she asks some question that not only shows that she has been listening but makes the other person realize that they need to listen to themselves. Most often, she says, they know the answer. You just have to listen, and then you have to just ask the right question.

It's why people call her.

I call Mark again the next week and we fill in a few more blanks. Then I call again a couple of weeks later. Carol would be proud of me. Mark and I are talking just fine—not running to the end of our list of topics, but still it is odd. He seems to get pretty excited about almost everything—maybe too excited—and yet behind all of that there was this other mood. It sounded like maybe *sadness?*

I don't know everything, but what I'm hearing so far is not fitting into any frame I had assembled. He's talking about having gone back to college after he woke up from his coma, getting a job, and then another, and then none. Getting sick again and not getting better, a divorce, an estranged daughter, going on disability, living in an apartment. He doesn't sound morose about it, but I can tell that all this has not left him emotionally unmolested.

There is a fine line between empathy and sympathy and between sympathy and just plain pity. I can't empathize authentically; I have not experienced much of anything he has these last thirty years. I also refuse to resort to pity. You pity people you see in those pictures trying to raise money for charitable missions. You pity people you don't know. You don't pity your friends. Not if they're friends.

So I sympathize. I listen a little more than usual, even if I never land on those million-dollar questions that Carol comes up with all the time. But I do listen. Hard. Then I realize that it's still just a phone call. You can't do this on a phone.

"What about if I have Mark come out here to visit us for a week?"

Carol is surprised by the question I pose that Saturday morning at breakfast but far from flummoxed.

"I think that's a good idea."

I do not ask her if that means a good idea for me.

Or for Mark.

To: paul
From: mark
Subject: the wait

---

beast was built almost top secret. people would drive by your house and report back to the school. people asked me when it would be ready but could never say because problems kept occurring; this only fed the speculation that people better get ready; the wait drove people crazy.

Mark never turned the radio down in the garage. Never.

Except one Saturday morning.

"What's up with you?" I looked over as Mark flipped the volume knob hard to the left and glanced nervously outside to the street.

"Shut up; be cool," Mark said nearly under his breath. I followed his eyes to the house across the street, the home of Dr. Turner, a wealthy and high-strung surgeon. He was standing in the driveway with the morning newspaper in one hand, the other curled into a fist braced on his hip as he glared at us. After a few seconds, he threw his hands up in disgust, spun on his heels, and stormed back into his house.

Mark was the first one to speak.

"Your dad's taking a lot of crap from people about the Beast," he said. I started to respond when Mark cut me off with a raise of his hand. "A lot more crap than he gives you."

We locked eyes for a few seconds, waiting for the next exchange, but strangely Mark looked like he was ready for a fight on this one.

"The Beast would not still be here unless your father had some reason to let it stay," he said firmly. "Be cool."

We worked in awkward silence for a half hour, me under the car and Mark reading a *Hot Rod* magazine while sitting on top of the workbench and banging his sneakers against the thin, plywood doors underneath.

"Mark, you there?" I called out.

"Always, my man."

"I need the brackets for the shift linkage. They're in the box on the workbench."

"What do they look like?"

"Just get the whole box and slide it to me."

I heard some rustling and the muffled clanking of parts shifting around inside the box, but then the garage fell silent.

"Mark, did you forget about me?"

Silence.

"Mark?"

"Paul ..."

"What?"

"Paul ... oh man ..."

"What!"

"C'mere ..."

Annoyed, I slid out from under the Chevy to see Mark standing stock-still halfway between the workbench and the car, the cardboard parts box pulled up tight against his chest. He was staring wild-eyed at something on the floor, so I followed his gaze to the caramel-colored mass just a few feet away.

The rattlesnake was tightly coiled, its head waving gently from side to side, lacing the air with its tongue and eyeing Mark with a sinister fixation. I couldn't calculate the serpent's length, being wound up like a garden hose, but it was as thick as one of our forearms. Everyone, including me, was frozen in place for a few seconds, sizing up our respective defensive and offensive positions, when the snake broke the stalemate by leaning its head forward toward Mark and tensing its tail, sending the chatter of its rattlers reverberating off the walls of the garage.

"Mark, don't move!" I hissed.

"Easy for you to say!" Mark's eyes were saucers, his mouth agape, barely breathing. The snake shifted again. "Oh crap, man." Mark's voice had developed a tremolo by now. "He's locked on to me! Do something, man … get a shovel!"

The shovels, rakes, and whatever else might be considered a snake-killing apparatus were against the back wall of the garage, and I would have to angle in front of the snake to get to them.

"Golf club!" The pitch of Mark's voice was rising by the second as the snake stepped up the volume and the duration of its next round of rattles. "Hit him with a golf club."

I looked over at my dad's clubs, gleaming, polished, and neatly arrayed in the brown leather bag, carefully and proudly stationed by itself against the sidewall.

"No," I called back reluctantly. "Think of something else."

Mark did a perfect James Brown-style toe-heel move with his feet, sliding back a couple of feet, but the snake matched the move. "I'm gonna die if you don't do something!" Mark flicked a glance my way and then trained his eyes back on the weaving snake.

That's when I came up with the big idea. I slid back underneath the Chevy and pulled myself through to the other side, where the bicycles and lawn mower were clustered against the wall. I grabbed the red metal gas can and ran to the open garage door behind the Chevy to where Mark's Impala was parked in the driveway. I flung open his passenger door and punched the chrome button to the glove compartment, pawing through the stacks of paper until I found one of the books of matches with the torn covers. The hot fuel of sheer survival instinct had flooded whatever part of my brain is dedicated to reason. Upon reflection, my big idea was probably not among one of my best, but these were desperate times.

I doused the snake with a frantic splash of gasoline, and before the rattler had a chance to whirl around and redirect its assault, I flicked open the matchbook cover and, in an impressively fluid motion, tore off a match, scraped it against the igniter strip, and tossed the flaring missile at the glistening snake.

To this day, it stands right up there as the most spectacular pyrotechnic display of my lifetime. The snake erupted in a yellow pillar of flame, writhing and spinning, spewing tongues of fire in all directions. Mark screamed and dropped the cardboard box, scattering springs and sockets in all directions as he hurdled onto the top of the workbench. *The Wizard of Oz* witch-melting scene seemed tame by comparison as we stared in awe as the snake swayed through the flames and then slowly sank into a crumpled, charred lump. A sickly steam rose from the carnage, and flickers of flame were still spitting out when Mark slowly slid down from the workbench perch and leaned over the immolated lump.

"Awesome!"

I surveyed the rafters to make sure there was no collateral damage as Mark nosed the broom handle underneath the still-smoking coils of the snake. I followed Mark as he carried it outside to the backyard and suspended the crispy critter over the steep drop-off to the arroyo below. He broke into a mischievous grin as he looked at the barbequed reptile.

"Wonder what this tastes like."

"Gasoline," I replied. "Shut up and throw it away."

Mark swung the broom handle in a slow arc, hurling the charred carcass into the brush far down the hillside. He peered over the ledge for a few seconds.

"You know," he chuckled, "a couple of snakes are going to see that later today and say, 'We warned Norman that he needed to stay away from all that serious dope.'"

Mark was still laughing as he went back to the garage. I found a bucket, a bristle brush, and a canister of Bon-Ami cleanser and got down on my hands and knees to scrub away the burn marks before my dad spotted them. Mark scooped the spilled sockets and springs back into the cardboard box and then leaped back onto his throne on the workbench.

"Dotson's getting worried."

"So," I said. "We're not even running yet."

"Well," Mark said mischievously. "He ought to be worried." Mark saw this toil not as a race on the street but a race in the garage; the battle of wits against wealth. Who shows up at school first under their own power—the son of privilege with the exotic German sports car or the working-class hero with the classic muscle car?

"So I guess I should at least ask—what's the betting line?" I asked.

"Oh, I don't know, but maybe it's about even," Mark said in a low voice. "Maybe a few points on the side of bucks against guts." I watched Mark's eyes rocking and rolling under his eyelids and knew he was calculating.

"Mark?"

"What?" he said, turning toward the workbench and rifling through some wrenches.

"You know, don't you? You're the one taking the bets, aren't you?"

Mark stopped shuffling in the toolbox and turned around. "Well, it was time to get everyone to put up or shut up."

I sighed from fatigue but asked anyway, "And what do you think?"

Mark paused for a second and looked down; then a massive grin streaked across his face. "I think you're going to kick his butt—and I intend to be there when you do."

With the twenty-dollar bill I had kept in my dresser drawer from my one-night stand at the Chinese restaurant now wadded up in my pocket, I spotted Rocky in the cafeteria at school and held the bill out to him.

"Here you go. Close to on time, and on budget," I declared proudly.

Rocky stared at the rumpled and limp currency, stained with soy sauce and pork grease. "Yuck. Where's that thing been, a toilet?" Rocky surveyed the sordid currency one last time and chuckled. "Keep it. You'll need it. Get yourself a set of chrome muffler bearings."

This time, I set my jaw, looked him in the eyes, and laughed back. "Nope. Don't need 'em. And I already got the valves reground on the cylinder heads." Rocky shot me a surprised but knowing grin. It was the first time I ever saw him smile at me.

It had now been several weeks since I began the open-heart surgery on my '57; it was time to take stock of my situation and my goals. I had been flipping through enough issues of *Hot Rod* magazine to know that there were things you could do to boost horsepower and torque, tighten up the suspension, improve the tonal quality of the exhaust, even dress it up a bit for show.

More than that, it was the Ducks. Every time I saw them gathered in their huddle in the parking lot or on the lawn, I wondered if I could just walk up and, well, pretend that I was supposed to be there. I did not have some urgent need to belong; I was just tired of not fitting in. I was not a jock; I was not a doper; I was not some drifty literary dreamer; I was not a math geek. I was a bit of a musician, but it's not like I was going to sit on the lawn playing John Denver's "Rocky Mountain High" and hope some cheerleader would come up and say, "Hey, that was beautiful. Can you play another one for me?"

So that left *car guy*. The problem was, of course, that I did not have a muscle car. The Ducks all had muscle cars, and everyone of them was new or nearly new. They were muscle cars right out of the factory. The whole ethnology of the Ducks was centered on the muscle cars churning out of

Detroit over the last few years—not just a car with a hot engine but a *new* car with a hot engine and a name to match. "'57 Chevy Bel-Air" seemed to lack some grunt and *gravitas*. Still, there was no way I was ever going to be able to buy my way into the Ducks. I was going to have to build my way in.

It was, in my mind, incremental rationalization—as long as you were doing something anyway, why not take it up a notch? Sure, it was more money, more time. But it was only *incrementally* more hours and dough. In my own somewhat distorted view, I could build a muscle car on the margin, repairing an engine as the core task and just—well, you know— adding a few touches along the way. While my meager drugstore stipend kept some limits on my impulses, I pushed it at every opportunity. The Beast did start to take on some meaty bulk—slowly, often incidentally, but inexorably. The cash continued to flow from my drugstore paycheck right into the register of the auto parts store, or to a local junkyard, or to a shop in Cedar Creek that sold second-hand performance parts. My purchases were first impelled by the need to simply get the engine to run: gaskets galore, new air and oil filters, hoses and hose clamps, a rebuilt radiator, battery cables, and about a gallon of some kind of parts cleaner solvent. (If the EPA had been around then like they are now, the amount of solvent I spilled out onto our driveway over a year would have had my street declared a SuperFund site. But man, could it clean parts.)

When I got bored or overwhelmed with the mechanical work on my car, I would turn to aesthetics. The Beast's front wheels were stock steel rims. The hubcaps were missing, so the lug nuts stuck out like bad teeth on a bridesmaid. I bought two new front tires, repainted the front wheels black with two cans of spray paint, and bought a pair of chrome moon covers to crown the transformation. I must have used two jars of naval jelly to clean up rust here and there. The stuff works. So did the mineral oil on the black rubber weather stripping. Frugality is the mother of improvisation.

Meantime, my real passion for performance parts started to seep into my logic and take on a rationality all of its own. When the new issue of *Hot Rod* magazine appeared with the monthly shipment each month at the drugstore, I would slip a copy into the back storeroom and read it on lunch breaks. I was steadily building a new vocabulary with each page I turned—solid valve lifters, ported and relieved intakes, leaf springs, compression rings. With it came a satisfaction that I not only knew now what those things were, but even knew how to install them. Sure beat Johnson rods and chrome muffler bearings.

I decided early on not to buy "hot" parts—stolen, if you will—because it just didn't seem right to me and there was too much chance for the word to get around the small community of gear heads. However, if I heard about someone blowing up an engine or running their uninsured car into a ditch, I was a hyena picking over the remains. Even if the parts did not fit my car, I knew they were currency for trades later.

What money I could not make in buying and trading or selling parts I made doing brake jobs. I'm not sure where I developed the knack for doing drum brakes, other than staring at the *Motors* book for a while and figuring out how the brake parts went together. After a while you could safely conclude that *brakes are brakes*—there was not that much difference between the brakes on a Chevy and those on a GTO or a Dodge. Once I got the knack of it, I became proficient at it, good enough to where several students from school would stop by when their brake drums would start howling. I even did a few sets of brakes for my father's friends at the country club. Just because somebody's rich doesn't mean they're not cheap.

I was becoming determined, even at times passionate, about the work I was doing on my car. I took some measure of pride in having advanced from crippling ignorance of what a gasket was to at least being able to match the pictures in the *Motors Manual* with what I saw in the dark bowels of the engine compartment. There was a long, grimy, oily path ahead before I would ever feel like I knew *how* to do things on that engine, but I at least was getting an understanding of *what* had to get done. My vocabulary was evolving; parts that before I would simply call "that thing" were taking on their own etymology—carburetor, journal bearings, intake manifold. I probably knew most of the bolt torque settings on the car, had most specifications memorized. In my own way, or at least in my own mind, I was beginning the metamorphosis from a blockhead to a gear head.

Even though Mark never really did work on the car, I found that my work seemed to go faster and easier with him around. Maybe he was my muse, the guy who would pick me up and inspire (or goad) me into moving to the next level, even if I had neither the skills nor the budget to do so. Maybe it was the sheer distraction of having someone who was perfectly satisfied to talk about whatever was on our minds that day. More likely it was because he represented the world out there, outside the garage, where people actually played pickup basketball on the net-less hoop that drooped on the old flagpole behind the gym. Or the world where friends would head down to the hamburger joint and stand around or sit on the hoods of their cars and talk about the prospects for winning the homecoming game. Or the world where teenage guys would just hang out and argue who had the best stats—sometimes talking about the starting pitchers on the Oakland A's, other times those of our varsity cheerleaders.

My world was awash in engine oil, transmission fluid, and anti-freeze, plastered with grime and grease. My weekends and often some weeknights were spent in the garage, focused on the task at the moment, never allowing myself to add up whether it was worth it all, because on too many days the calculation would have spoken to my foolishness. I would get into this *place* where I could work for hours—how I found enough to do is baffling to me, unless it was simply a function of my relative incompetence—until my absorption was interrupted by a sharp rap on the side door of the garage and my father's voice demanding that I get inside and do some dishes or finish my homework. I was convinced inside myself that I could get the car to run, even run fast, but I also simply could not honestly confront the prospects of failure. It was not merely bruised ego; it was the economic and social consequence of having devoted so many weeks of my fleeting high school years to getting to know bolt torque valves rather than lifelong friends, spending money on parts rather than on parties. And as far as my father was concerned, far too much time studying engine specifications rather than multiplication tables. As much as that car might have represented something special, it was also a symbol of something far more pedestrian, far more utilitarian. I just wanted a car of my own to drive.

Mark, without knowing it (or did he?), represented a conscience in the midst of my obsession, a reminder that there was a life outside the garage, but he also accepted that my life for now was in the garage—under a car instead of around friends. He really never talked much about cars. Most of his banter revolved around funk and blues bands coming into the fore in the East Bay area, whether he thought he could "make weight" on the wrestling team for their match the next week, and all the latest dating flirtations, fixations, or confrontations at school.

There was an ebb and a flow about our time together—when I was down, he was up; when I was up, he was down. Whether that was a conscious response to each other or just dumb-luck timing, all I know is that it worked. The only difference seemed to be that his ups and downs were more extreme.

That was just the way Mark was.

During the weeks of rebuilding and modifying I was reduced to the most humiliating state for a sixteen-year-old with a driver's license—hitchhiking. We now live in a more perilous era where the notion of just jumping into the car of a stranger is alien to our sense of safety and common sense, both for the hitchhiker and the driver. But back when I was in high school, you could find hitchhikers spread out along just about any road. It was a communal exchange, a mutual understanding of our need to get from one place to another—a trade-off of the kindness of strangers with the courtesy and deference of those who need the ride. You did not insist or contrive to secure a ride by jumping out in the road; you simply spun on your heel when you heard a car approaching and stuck out your thumb and hoped for the best.

I was trudging up the main road from town to my home after a few hours at the drugstore, spinning and thumbing hopefully at the dozen or so cars that passed me by, when I heard a sound behind me that was quite unlike a car. It was a resonant pounding, like someone striking a metal drum with a thick rubber hose. I kept my thumb curled inside my fist and simply turned around to assess whether this was a ride worth taking. Closing in on me were the glistening front forks of a motorcycle, chopped, with handlebars arching up far past the point of reason or utility. You would have expected Dennis Hopper to smile back at you, but instead, with no helmet over his crew-cut head, wearing torn jeans and a white T-shirt, was Rocky.

"Hey!" *(bop-bop-bop)* Rocky yelled over the pulsing exhaust of the bike. "Got that *(bop-bop)* crate of yours *(bop-bop)* running yet?" He shut down the bike, and it loped to a halt.

"Close," I said. "What's this—a Harley?"

Just about any motorcycle that looked big and sounded loud was a Harley to me. My parents would not let me see the movie *Easy Rider ("We heard there was a lot of drugs and violence in it ...")* so I saw it one Saturday afternoon when my mom thought I was at the library. There was a lot of drugs and violence in it.

Rocky's Harley was not as impressive as Dennis Hopper's or Peter Fonda's chopper, but it was louder. Rocky had taken a grinder and cut off the muffler and was running straight pipes out the back. I followed the headers from the engine to where they angled up to a tall stack of pipe that ran behind the backrest of the seat (dismissively called a "sissy bar" for passengers who felt they needed extra support). The Harley was far away from its days in a showroom—it was Spartan, shorn of anything ornamental, not even a Harley insignia on the side of the gas tank. The seat leather was worn, and the chrome around the engine and the exhaust pipes carried the purplish patina of too much heat over too many years. Still, it was a Harley, in all of its primal power.

As we stood there, a police cruiser came up behind us, a little too fast to suggest it was a casual stop. The officer stepped out of the car and walked over to us, shaking his head and pulling out a spiral pad. "This thing got a muffler?" he asked.

"It has an exhaust pipe, sure," Rocky replied.

"It's too loud," the officer declared in a low monotone. "This is not the Arizona desert. This is a neighborhood. The next time I see this bike, it needs to have a muffler on it." He surveyed the bike, noting its nearly naked appearance, the scuffed back frame, the greasy chain and yellowed chrome. "We do have some standards around here."

There was no write-up, no ticket, no warning in fine type on a torn-off form, just a cold look over the sunglasses that made it clear that the next time the officer saw Rocky's bike, it had better have a muffler on it.

"Want a ride?" Rocky shook off the encounter and thumbed to the space behind him on the seat. I gingerly swung my leg over the lower back of the bike, making note of exactly where the hot exhaust pipe was in relationship to my ankle, and leaned tentatively against the sissy bar, choosing to hook my thumbs into the side belt loops of Rocky's jeans. I had no idea what you were supposed to hold onto when riding shotgun on a Harley, but I was not about to wrap my arms around some guy who was weeks away from marine boot camp, no matter how fearful I might be of falling off.

Rocky kicked the engine back to life, and I jerked instinctively as I felt as much as heard the pipe behind me begin its machine-gun pounding. Without warning, he gunned the bike in first gear and we angled back onto the road amid a cacophony of whirring gears, spitting gravel, and the now *rhump-rhump-rhump* of the hollow exhaust pipe just inches from my head. It was exhilarating and terrifying.

Rocky wove through the last half mile before the country-club main gate and then leaned the bike hard into the turn and opened the throttle as what sounded like a spatter of M-80s firecrackers spit from the exhaust. He seemed to take delight in knowing that he was drawing stares and scolding looks from some of the neighbors and the golfers along the route and made a point of giving it a little more throttle than needed. We coursed up and then down the winding street to my house, wheeling the Harley into the driveway. I slipped off the back and stood next to the bike as the pulsing exhaust rippled the fabric of my jeans.

"My money's on you to get that Chevy running," Rocky called out above the din from the pipes. "It can be a real machine in the right hands." With that, he edged the Harley backward out of the driveway with the heels of his boots and then roared up the street with the blasts from the engine echoing off the houses.

# # #

Chapter Seven

I scan the faces of the people coming into the main airport terminal from the gate areas. Mark is not as hard to spot as I thought he might be. He is taller than I remember and walks with a nervous gait, but he still has the restless energy I always saw. He is wearing loose jeans, cowboy boots, and a black Grateful Dead T-shirt. His hair is longer, down to his shoulders, and his face is lean. He looks like Mark, just older. Maybe a lot older.

We shake hands and then do one of those awkward guy hugs that start with a tentative wrap of an arm around the shoulders followed by a couple of good, healthy slaps between the shoulder blades. I look older than he does, I think, but he looks more worn. He is thin enough to be accused of being gaunt; he seems uncomfortable with everything around him and says he wants to get to my house. I wonder if he just wants to get away from the crowds.

Back at the house, Carol greets him with a warm but careful one-armed hug, and our daughter Lesley shakes his hand politely. The first hour is filled with the normal graces of showing him the house, getting him something to drink, narrating the family pictures on the hallway wall. *That's us when we got married, that's our older daughter Lisa who is in college; yep, that's my dad and mom.*

That night at dinner, Carol and Lesley listen, bemused, as Mark and I retell our stories—Chevys, the Ducks, the Creek, Greek, and a few adventures we gloss over to retain our standing as responsible adults. Lesley is a Beatles fan and soon is trading trivia with him. He schools her on the fine art of baseball-card collecting. Carol and I have left the table long before to wash dishes, but Lesley and Mark stay at the table for another hour.

The next morning, we drive all over town, ending up at Louisville Slugger Museum, where he traces his fingertips—like a blind man reads a Braille letter from home—on the wood-burning metal stamps used to sear the signatures of Babe Ruth and Mickey Mantle on their bats. He rattles off statistics—batting average, earned run average, home runs—with encyclopedic precision. He is not talking to me, maybe not even to himself.

The next morning, Mark fails to emerge from the guest bedroom. I knock on the door a few times, but there is no answer. I edge open the door and call out into the darkness, "Hey, Mark, buddy—time to get up."

I hear him stir and then mumble something about not wanting to get up, not being *able* to get up. He must be kidding. Right? Okay, maybe I'm being a little intrusive in insisting that a guest get out of bed, but I also feel a mood in the room that makes me persist. I grab the heel of his foot through the blanket and shake it. He draws his legs up against his body and curls into a lump under the covers.

Now I am worried. There is something more at play than just the need for extra sleep. "Hey, don't do this, Mark," I say firmly. "Time to get up."

"I can't." His words are muffled under the covers. "You don't know what it's like." He curls up tighter and falls silent.

Now, suddenly, I am back in Fresno State, pounding on that dorm room door. I have to keep knocking. "C'mon, man." I shake him more purposefully. "You're not coming all the way out here to go into a funk." I pull the covers back and sit him up on the edge of the bed. He tries to lie back down twice, but I flip on the lights and toss his jeans and shoes on the bed. "Coffee's on. Let's go."

Carol is at the kitchen table, her cereal bowl scraped empty, her coffee cup drained.

"Sorry, hon," I say. "I couldn't get Mark up." I try to explain—maybe he just gets in a mood, maybe he's being stubborn, maybe he's just tired. I'm sorry.

"I'm fine," she says. "Really. Just keep an eye on him. Take him out again for the day."

Mark is sheepish when he comes into the kitchen, staying over near the sink, drinking some water. He wants to head out now. It's easier than standing here.

He'll like today, I think as we head for the car. Mark had told me during one of our phone calls that he had worked the concessions at Golden Gate park racetrack after college. Bruce, the owner of the Ford deuce coupe in high school, worked at the track with his father and set up the job for Mark. In his spare time away from concessions, Mark served as an exercise rider, taking thoroughbreds around the track to keep them warmed up. So this morning I have worked out an arrangement with Churchill Downs, one of my clients, to get Mark into the jockey area and barns on the backstretch of the famous Kentucky Derby venue. Mark spends an hour just breathing in the earthy aromas of the horses and the sandy track. Mark is sick this day—he says it happens a lot—but when he walks back through the barns, inhaling the greasy smoke of the bacon frying at the jockey's clubhouse and hearing the riders clucking at the horses as they trot them out to the track, he is renewed.

There are no races this day, so we are able to just walk back to the clubhouse and sit on the aluminum bleachers that ring the backstretch. It is a cool, clear morning, and you can see the horses' flanks glistening in the morning sunlight as they round the famous turn. The riders' chatter blends with the snorting breaths of the horses into a harmony that Mark knows by heart, like the lyrics of an old Otis Redding song.

I'm ready to leave after a while, but Mark is not. We sit there on the cold aluminum planks of the bleachers for another half hour, as if Mark really has nowhere else to go. I sense that in his mind and at this time in his life, he doesn't.

To: paul
From: mark
Subject: garage

---

your dad used to scowl at us when he came in the garage to get his golf clubs.

Garages are the most fascinating places in a home. You can go into a home and get a cursory sense of a person's or a family's style and tastes— the selection of furniture, whether the frames on the walls hold artwork or simple family pictures, whether the rooms have a casual, inviting feel or stand off or away as if some kind of display.

But garages are like an MRI, sonogram, or x-ray, revealing inner conditions that are not always seen or are intentionally cloaked in the more exposed environments of the living quarters. A box of photos still in their packets—does it mean the family is too busy to relish its memories, or has something happened that makes those memories better left tucked away where they cannot punish people with images of a better time? A dusty pair of ice skates—are they just remnants of a passing fad or are they the dashed dreams of a girl seeing Olympic gold draped around her neck? An old pipe wrench, its metal coated with the patina of decades—is it really there to fix a leaking pipe or to make sure someone doesn't lose memories of working alongside a kindly grandfather?

Garages are a bin for the castoffs of daily life that we just can't or don't quite cast off fully—the raft that never seemed to stay inflated, the tennis racket with the peeling grip, the stacks of board games with the missing pieces, the family pictures that have been taken down but are still attached to our hearts.

I'm surprised after all these years just how vivid are my memories of what our garage looked like when I was in high school. The house was new when we moved into it, so the garage did not have the musty, weary look of most older garages—exposed two-by-four studs, spider webs in the dark corners, or gummy, dusty lumps of debris on the base of the walls. Its painted drywall interior was a benign backdrop to the assortment of tools, toys, and flotsam that reflect the accumulated years of a family.

Shelves on the back wall were stocked with moving boxes labeled with felt marker scrawls—pictures, books, dishes, important papers. One box in particular was familiar to me. It cradled a three-ring binder and lumps of newspaper clippings—sepia-tinged photos of stunned crowds in Dealey Plaza, the limousine outside Parkland Memorial Hospital, the stern detective holding aloft the Mannlicher-Carcano rifle in the police station hallway, the grimacing face of Lee Harvey Oswald as the balding strip-joint owner Jack Ruby blasted a .38-caliber bullet into his gut, little John-John saluting the casket of his father as it was carried up the steps to the Capitol Rotunda. Every time I looked at the box it seemed to open and reveal its memories to me. I remember sitting stunned and puzzled as my mother wept in front of a black-and-white Motorola TV in our living room, staring at the flickering images on the screen of a blood-spattered Jackie stepping off Air Force One. My mother clipped newspaper columns and entire pages from *Life* magazine, carefully laying them out in the binder, a Scotch-taped testament for the ages. Over a few weeks, the project moved to a desk in a backroom, then to a box, and finally, much like the consciousness of a nation getting on with its life, to the garage shelf.

Another box bulged with S&H Green Stamps—gummed stickers that were ubiquitous back in the late '50s and early '60s, offered by nearly all merchants and redeemed over time for merchandise from a catalogue. My brothers, sisters, and I would spend hours on Sunday afternoons licking those stamps and plastering them into the books. Most of the merchandise was utilitarian—a toaster, a cheese knife, a boot scraper for the front porch. We often complained that our work never yielded anything that we could use as kids, something frivolous and fun. But our complaining often triggered a sharp retort from our dad: "Appreciate what you have. Not everyone has had it so good." I found it odd that in the face of such frugality, the box in the garage still held so many unredeemed books.

My dad never imagined a third car in the family when he bought our home with a three-car garage. If anything, he was relieved that he had some storage space. All of our previous homes had basements and attics, and much like work expands or contracts to the time allotted, so too does junk to the space allowed. Within weeks of moving in, he had hammered nails and hooks into the walls and used them to impale or suspend decades of *stuff*—bicycles, duffel bags, some aprons and work clothes, yard tools, some mops, and oddly enough, a tree trimmer, even though the most statuesque tree we had on the property was a dwarf flowering crabapple tree stuck near the front walkway like an awkward, skinny kid.

The wall of the garage nearest to the house, the wall most accessible if you were in a hurry, was reserved parking space for golf clubs, pairs of golf shoes draped over hooks, and a long wooden shelf stocked with an assortment of golf balls, tees, gloves, and towels. It was something of a shrine to golf.

I never imagined from the day my Chevy coughed its way into what was to become an emergency room and rehabilitation center in our garage that anyone would be helping me—not Mark, and certainly not my father. It may have been my own naiveté or bravado in thinking I could handle it myself, but I suffered no illusions that my dad would appear in the Norman Rockwell frame of the scene around my car and chuckle, "Here, son, let me show you how to do that ..."

When you're a teenager, particularly one preoccupied or obsessed with cars or other passing points of passion and distraction, a lot of life's subtleties and nuances slip past you without notice. Most of us guys in high school only caught fleeting glimpses of the family lives of our friends, and even those passing views were often cloaked and veiled. We did not have self-help books by Dr. Phil or any other psyche-probing resources—not that would we have used them anyway. Back in the '60s, we just took everyone for who they were, without picking them apart or mapping their psyche to some roots within the walls of their home—or the shelves in their garage.

Bones, for example, seemed confident, always willing to engage and be involved in things. Yet, as I reflect back on it, his independence may also have been imposed on him to some degree since his pilot father was often away on transatlantic flights. And now that I think about it, I never did see his father stopping by in the garage to lend a hand.

Frankie, the other '57 Chevy owner, was quiet, gentle, and avoided conflict like deer running from crunching leaves. He abhorred crowds and loud groups; if we were at a party, Frankie was never in the thick of it. He often could be found having a quiet conversation with just one other person off to the side, or even on the back porch. He never drank and seemed quite settled with his position, despite the ribbing he took over that on a Friday night. It was only many years later that I learned that his parents both had drinking problems. Getting out of the house was his escape, and he wasn't about to ruin it by repeating the scene he lived at home.

Just a couple of houses away from my home lived Kendall, the son of a corporate executive. Kendall had a modest dignity about him that went beyond his years. By any measure, he could have been the cockiest guy at our school—captain of the football team, studly good looks, smart, born of a relatively affluent family—and probably could have run up some good odds in tagging a date with most of the cheerleaders. Yet, as regal as his presence was at our school, it was never overbearing. He was a guy who had it all but never really had anything to prove. He was the Rudyard Kipling poster boy—he kept his head when others all about him were losing theirs. It was a calculated detachment, almost as if he had some kind of transcendent perspective on the silliness and transience of our high school years. What we didn't know then, that might begin to explain his balance and reserve, was that his mother—at a time when mothers are supposed to go to your football games and let you bring your friends over to raid the refrigerator on a Saturday afternoon—was nearly consumed by chronic depression.

So it is one of life's mysteries and contradictions—we want to believe that our home life is the reason or the cause for who we are, and yet there is as much evidence to resist that notion. What is true is that, when you are just sixteen, you really don't know that it is affecting you quite the way it is. Most often, all you want is for everything to be normal, to be safe, and to be something that is within your capacity to manage and accept. It is a dance of degrees—some people emerge from horrific backgrounds and are perfectly normal; others are nurtured in caring nests and yet devolve to beasts. Most of us, in my observation, simply carry subtle blessings and curses from parents who carried the same from their own.

———————

It was an early Saturday morning and I was stretched under the car trying to unbolt and lower the transmission to the garage floor. I don't know how much the transmission weighed, but even for a healthy teenager on the high school wrestling team, it was proving to be a match for my weary arms. Another set of fresh hands would have served me well.

As I lay under the car, I heard the side garage door open, the shuffle of shoes on the floor, and then some murmured cursing. The voice got louder.

"How much longer do I have to put up with this mess?"

It was not a question that was really in search of an answer, and I had none. I remember lying against the cold, concrete floor, still trying to suspend the transmission with my now-quivering arms as tears burned in the corners of my eyes. I waited until I heard his golf clubs clatter as he took the bag from its post on the wall, the thump as they were tossed into his trunk, and the squeak of the tires as his car pulled out of the garage and disappeared over the hill. I lowered the transmission back to the floor and crawled out from under the car, occupying myself with cleaning some tools and organizing parts.

Mark came by about an hour later, and we were able to slide the transmission into place. We then moved to an even more difficult task—removing the front springs. I had figured out from reading the *Motors* book that my Chevy's ball joints—knuckle-shaped pieces that allow the wheel to move up and down without splaying out—were dangerously worn. To remove them, the coil springs had to be removed first. Even when a car is perched on jack stands, the front springs are compressed to the point where they have plenty of bruising energy stored up if they are allowed to pop loose on their own. We lacked a real spring compressor, so I rigged up one of my own—a stack of washers on the top and bottom of the pieces holding the springs and a threaded rod that ran through the middle. This way I could compress the spring by tightening the nut, remove the other suspension parts, and then loosen the nut slowly to release the spring in a controlled way.

Right as we were about to finish, my father's car pulled into the driveway. I heard the door open and the sound of his golf spikes crunching on the concrete driveway. Just then, our threaded rod snapped and the pent-up spring released with a loud whack, spiraling for a moment under the car like a toy top out of control and then skittering out from under the car and ricocheting across the garage. We scooted out from under the Chevy in time to see my dad glaring at the whole scene in disgust; then he turned and kicked the still-vibrating spring out onto the driveway, where it spun circles and came to rest against the curb.

Mark and I stood frozen as my father walked toward us. He looked right at me with piercing eyes and spat out, "You and your fancy friends ..." and then paused, as if he didn't quite know how to finish the sentence, or chose not to. He brushed by us, hung his clubs up on the rack, and turned to the side door. As he reached for the handle, he looked back and shook his head one more time.

"What are you—stupid?"

Mark and I waited for what seemed like several minutes until we heard the back door close. Mark turned to me with a pained look. "I'm really sorry, man. Maybe I need to go home."

I looked at Mark, the frustration and sadness in his face, his hands covered in grease, his hair matted, and his pants stained with oil. "No, it's cool," I said. "It's not you."

Mark wasn't convinced. "He said 'fancy friends' ..."

"I know, but it's not you. He's said it before to others."

Mark sighed quietly but then stared down at the floor.

"Okay, but the 'stupid' part. He's said that to you before, hasn't he ...?"

I turned away and slid back under the car.

"Yeah," I replied quietly. "A few times."

"And what do you think?" Mark bent down and peered under the car so I could not escape his gaze.

I waited a few seconds before responding.

"Sometimes I think he's right."

Several years after I had graduated from college and gotten married and my wife Carol and I were visiting my parents, we were sitting around the kitchen table recounting some of our childhood days in New Jersey. When the discussion drifted toward my grandfather—my dad's father—I laughingly mentioned that my fondest memories were when he would put us on his lap in the big rocking chair and make Donald Duck noises.

My dad snapped his head up and looked at me, puzzled. "That's what you remember about your grandfather?"

I shrugged my shoulders. "Yeah, in fact, that's about all I remember."

What had been to that point a loud and boisterous conversation fell silent. My father gazed down at his placemat, fingering the edges. "Those are good memories," he said quietly. "You should keep them."

The kitchen was awkwardly quiet for a while, and then I broke the stillness. "Dad," I asked tentatively. "What are your memories of your father?"

My father didn't look up for some time; then he leaned back in his chair. Reluctant at first, the story then tumbled out, like marbles rolling out of an upturned jar. He told us about growing up as a boy in the Irish slums of Jersey City and Hoboken, his family crowded into a cold-water flat off a cobblestone alley. His father drank—a lot of poor Irish did, especially when swimming in the depths of the Depression; but he drank a lot. He drank when my dad pushed a fruit cart around on weekends and came home with change in his pocket that went into a jar that was empty again the next day. He drank after my father's three-year-old sister reached for the handle of a pot of boiling water on the kitchen stove and died a few days later from the burns. He drank when my dad's older brother was diagnosed with brain cancer and my dad left high school at the age of sixteen to work in the Civilian Conservation Corps and sent money home in a desperate but failed quest to save his life with better medical care. He drank enough to think it was okay to push my dad's mother—my grandmother—down the stairs, where my father would hold her until she stopped crying. He drank when she developed tuberculosis and wasted away in the upstairs bedroom.

A lot of people drank hard during the Depression. My dad's father drank real hard.

What really riveted me about what I heard was not the grisly truth of it but that my father had never told me. He was a stoic man. He clawed his way out of the Irish slums, helped fight a war, danced until dawn with and later married the most beautiful woman he had ever seen, and didn't look back.

A few years after I had left for college, my youngest brother decided he wanted to spend a year or two after high school working at a surf shop in Hawaii. It was every bit unrealistic, and my dad made that clear in both tone and volume when he heard of it.

"But Dad," my brother protested. "Didn't you ever have dreams when you were my age?"

"Yes, I did," my father shot back. "I just couldn't afford to have many of them come true."

My father struggled a lot more than I knew when I was in high school. He had a grueling job as a chief financial officer at a major international corporation, but things were not going well. All I cared about, I am embarrassed to admit, was whether I would be able to go to college. I also feel ashamed now years later that, all the time my father was living in a small apartment in San Francisco while we stayed in St. Louis until our house was sold, I never wrote him a letter, even after he told me how much he would like to hear from me. A few years after that, when again he was struggling to get his footing as an unemployed executive in his mid-fifties, he was away from the family for months taking on odd jobs in accounting and living in inexpensive apartments. I was playing guitar regularly in restaurants while going to college at the time. He bought a cheap six-string guitar at a pawnshop and asked me if I could teach him a few chords so he could have something to do when he was away from home alone, in the apartment. I was busy—too busy to do more than give him a lesson or two. I remember particularly him wanting to learn the Beatles' "When I'm Sixty-Four" (*"Will you still need me, will you still feed me, when I'm sixty-four? ..."*).

My father went to a Billy Graham Crusade a few years later, walked up the center aisle during the call, and never looked back. His life was redeemed, transformed. He worked at being the husband he always meant to be and the father he never was and became the grandfather than any grandchild would love. He died when he was sixty-five.

He made it to sixty-four, after all.

I only wish, as I stood there in that garage that day with Mark at my side, that I could have seen that man. The only thing that was clear to me that day was that if you were going to be Ed Heagen's son, you were going to have to work at it.

# # #

Chapter Eight

"What's different?"

It's Mark's last night with us during his visit. Lesley has gone upstairs to do homework, Carol is in the kitchen cleaning up after dinner, and I am sitting across the table from Mark as he leans across and bores down on me with one of his intense looks.

"What do you mean different?" I ask, taken aback by the directness of his probing,

"You are different," he says. "You and Carol are so—what's the word—*peaceful*. So settled," he says. "You weren't that way when I left Fresno," he says almost ruefully.

"My life has been a junk pile," he mutters. He rocks back in his chair, almost as if his own words have slapped him. It spills out over the next few minutes, the blanks filled in on the story of his life I had only imagined to that point.

It was after he got the infection—the first semester at Fresno State—when he went home and got lost. That's the best explanation. All the guys—the Ducks, the guys in Bedlam Showboat, were all on to other things. He woke up one day and was trying to find something to do, but there was nothing to do. He could go back to the drugstore, he thought, but that seemed weird after telling everyone he was going to college, getting on with his life. He would drive up to Fire Mountain, this time by himself, and just sit there by the rocks at the peak and just look at Stoned Valley below. The view seemed better the day he brought the dope with him and seemed better each time he brought more. He could go up to Fire Mountain by himself and not have to wonder where everybody was, including himself.

There were other drugs and some drinking, lots of drinking. He tried to pull himself out—got a job and then another, went to some classes at San Jose State and finished out his degree, found a girl who seemed to accept his antics and streaks, got married, had a kid; then everything started going dark again. She got tired of his drugs and drinking; he wanted to believe she didn't just get tired of him. She went back to her rich parents in New York, and he never saw her again. She took his daughter with her. She might as well have ripped his heart out and taken that too.

By now, he was desperate to hear that scraping sound in your soul that signals that you have finally hit bottom. Except the spiral took its own sadistic course. Sitting at the table now, looking at the ceiling and sometimes down at the floor, he admits what now is apparent to me—he is on disability not just because of his vulnerability to infection or his screw-ups, but because he has a serious dose of a manic/depressive bipolar condition with a chaser of obsessive/compulsive disorder. It is a toxic brew. You don't always have a grip on reality; even when you do, you rarely know how to deal with it. Mark contends that the encephalitis triggered the conditions. I want to believe that, too, but I start recalling the madness of the matchbook covers stuck in his dash, the wild seesaw from ebullience to despair over every hint of a turn in his relationship with some girl, the way he was so easily distracted from our efforts in the garage by just about anything that crossed his path or his mind. We just thought it was Mark.

"So," he says now, more of a plea than a protest, "what happened to you? Why are you so different?"

My story comes more easily, but it is not as if I have practiced it; in fact, I am not sure I have even told all of it to anyone at this point, other than Carol.

The memory is still fresh—me sitting at the scarred, wobbly wooden study desk in my fraternity house in 1972, thumbing through a crisp new paperback Bible I had purchased that afternoon after a good hard night of beer drinking with my fraternity "brothers" during my sophomore year at Cal State Fresno.

Anyone who had known me at that time would have been totally taken aback to see me with a Bible in my hands. To this day I wish I could fully recapture whatever senses and sentiments converged in my head, or maybe in my heart, that drove me to the shopping mall to actually shop for a Bible. Perhaps it was a stew of curiosity, frustration, exasperation, and yearning that just boiled over, like a pot of oatmeal that one minute is comfortably simmering along and then the next minute has bubbled all over the place, leaving a real mess.

One day, I was fine; I had friends, was starting to figure out a direction for my college degree, was working part-time playing guitar at a local pizza joint, and had a girlfriend—and one on the side as a spare. The next day, I was a mess—I was tired of the parties, tired of pretending I had it all together, tired of wondering where the frenzy of activity was taking me.

So whatever it was, all I knew is that on a perfectly sunny Saturday afternoon I was, of all places, in a JC Penney store looking for a Bible. I had no idea where to buy a Bible, and JC Penney seemed as good a place as any to start looking. Raised an Irish Catholic, I perceived Bibles as mysterious and awe-inspiring fixtures in the homes of my family and our relatives. My parents had one big gold-leafed monstrosity of a Bible on a wooden stand in our living room—easily three inches thick. The massive book smelled of oily, aging leather, ink, and hide glue. The cover was a deep brown, pebbled, thick leather with gold-embossed letters that were so ornate as to be nearly unreadable to the modern eye of a small boy. The pages were a fragile parchment; chapters were punctuated every few pages by half-moon cutouts than ran down the length of the side and listed strange Hebrew names like Ezekiel and Nahum. The book was laden with oil-painted portraits of white-robed men with fiery eyes and flowing hair—shattering stone tablets, slitting rivers down the middle, coaxing animals into arks, and, in the front part, a slender, milky-skinned man and woman standing ashamed with figs leaves over their groins in a garden with a sinister-looking snake draped from a tree limb. The pictures of Christ were majestic—he had blue eyes, a tanned face with a neatly trimmed beard, light brown hair that shimmered to his shoulders, and silken robes and was usually carrying around a lamb or patting some kid on the head. The pictures of God were ominous: the white hair and beard did nothing to soften the annoyed, stern look on his face. I had heard the admonition to "fear the Lord," and as I gazed at the fearsome images on those pages, it seemed like good advice.

I never actually read that massive Bible as a child; I assumed you would get in trouble for accidentally tearing the delicate pages. I remember I used to grab the cover with both hands and flop it closed so I could hear the deep thump and watch the wooden stand shudder under its burden. That book was a monument, an edifice, but not something that invited inquiry.

I had no idea where Bibles came from. Our family just always had one, like you always knew you had a grandma or had that rocking chair in the living room. I just imagined that these testaments somehow found their way into the family inventory of heirlooms and endured the passage of time and generations.

So with little precedent to guide me, there I was in JC Penney buying a paperback Bible—it had a light blue cover and plain paper pages—for something like three bucks. I asked the clerk to put it in a bag so no one would see me with it at the mall, took it back to my fraternity house, closed the door to my room, and sat down at the desk and just starting reading.

Some people read magazines from front to back; I read them from back to front. Always have. So when I started reading the Bible, I read all about how things were going to end or did end, not where or how they began.

I know where I stopped reading that day. It was near the end of one of the Gospels, where Christ was in the olive garden, where he went to agonize in prayer before being arrested and crucified the next day. His buddies were all falling asleep nearby, so he was down on his knees by himself.

Weeping.

That's the part that got me, for some reason. Even at that stage of my life when the whole notion of God and Jesus and everything attached to it was pretty far from my mind and my life, I was mesmerized by this scene in my mind where Christ was slumped on the ground weeping. It just did not fit. He could have just snapped his fingers, I imagined, and gotten out of there before the mobs with the torches showed up, before Judas fingered him as the troublemaker, before all his friends ran for cover in the confusion.

I remember saying out loud, "Why are you crying? You don't need to be crying. After all, you're God."

It was the first time I called him that, or realized fully that he was exactly who he said he was. That he was God on earth, here because there was no way we could grasp or get our heads around the idea of God and who he was up there in heaven if he just stayed there and hoped we would figure it out on our own. So he became one of us, somebody we could understand and relate to. God did not want to be the varnished, distant painting in my parent's big leather Bible—something you really were not supposed to approach and touch. He wanted to be more like that little, easy paperback Bible I bought at JC Penney—where anyone who wanted to could just come in and get it. Read it. Understand it.

The revelation that came to me that day—quietly, unobtrusively, and even logically—was that God wanted me to know him by getting to know Jesus. Not the guy in the old leather Bible artwork, gliding through the chaos of earth with a white robe, combed hair, and clean sandals, but somebody who might come to our high school homecoming game, somebody who might have put up with Mark's antics. Probably somebody who might have stopped by the garage and grabbed a wrench and said, "Hey, need help?"

This Jesus now seemed like somebody who knows what it means to be tired, lonely, angry, funny, sometimes scared, and, well, human.

Just like me.

Just like Mark.

To: paul
From: mark
Subject: burnout

---

the day you picked me up for school the entire class was outside watching and you layed 30 ft rubber. i was very proud to be in your car. i will never forget

Mark and I hated VW Bugs.

The drugstore had one—dark green with white lettering spelling out the name of the store and the tagline that seems so wryly absurd today: "We deliver your drugs."

Mark and I *really* hated that car. It had the smallest engine you could buy in a Bug and was fitted with—*get this*—an automatic transmission. The seats were some kind of horrible fake mesh plastic that would impress tiny checkerboard patterns on your shirt on a hot day. The worst thing was the sound—no, the noise, the racket. Stand behind an old Volkswagen and listen to the exhaust and you are listening to the sound of marbles rolling around in a coffee can or a piece of rebar being dragged across a picket fence. When Mark and I drove it to deliver prescriptions, we would crouch behind the wheel to make sure none of the Ducks saw us driving this miserable wretch of automotive engineering. Whenever I drove it, I just floored it and was rewarded with the same sensory satisfaction you get at the amusement park when you drive one of those go-carts with the governors on the carburetor—lots of spitting noises from the back, but you are not going anywhere faster.

Mark's contempt went deeper into destructive tendencies. He would intentionally shift into reverse while driving forward—*whump*—trying to get the transmission to spill its guts out onto the pavement so Mac would have to buy a new car, a *real car*. The torque converter was so pathetic on that car that it would just whine and moan a bit when Mark rammed it into reverse, then it would just slow to a halt, the exhaust chirping away as if it was ready for the next command. Herbie on a sugar high. Mark's next ploy was to drive it with the parking brake fully engaged, hoping against hope that the heat alone would warp the wheels, sear some bearings, or just exhaust the engine to death. He would whirl into the parking lot with the back wheels smoking and the engine heaving, but still the Bug endured the abuse.

Whether it is cockroaches after a nuclear blast or a drugstore VW driven by Mark, there are some bugs you can't kill.

Delivering prescriptions is a quaint feature by today's standard. Even with the meager gas consumption of the Bug and the meager wages he paid us, it was hard to imagine that Mac made much money having us run those long white sleeves of pills all over town, but he was insistent on it. After a while, Mark and I followed a pattern each week: nitroglycerin tablets to the old farmer north of town, ulcer medicine to the janitor who worked at the local courthouse, and far too many pain pills to the woman who sat on the back porch of the large, under-kept house in the woods near Fire Mountain. This was before the FDA and DEA starting getting wise to the underworld of prescription narcotics. I guess she had a legit prescription for all those pain pills—Mac was not one to break rules—but if you're an old lady who has nothing left in her life but to sit on a back porch alone at the base of Fire Mountain every day, you can at least understand how she might have rationalized anesthetizing herself from her condition.

I had one run that I knew by heart. You would go out the back entrance of the parking lot and turn right onto another main road. Three blocks up, there was a white clapboard house set back from the road, with a separate garage and storage building behind it. One of the first times I had Bug duty, I was delivering some orange-colored pills to that house. No one answered the front doorbell, so I had crunched along the gravel driveway to the back and knocked on the rear screen door. Still no answer. Mac wanted us back quickly on these drug runs, so I tucked the envelope of pills behind the screen and trotted down the steps. It made sense to check to see if there was a car in the garage, just in case. The doors were wooden, paint peeling, caulk cracking; the small window panes on the top row of panels were coated with years of grime, dust, and cobwebs. I could barely see through the glass, but as I peered in, the shadows inside seemed to lift and I began to make out the shape of a car.

It was a '56 Chevy Bel-Air. No doubt about it. It was a convertible, white with a classic red panel on the side. It did not look old at all; in fact it looked like someone parked it there about ten years ago and just never got back to it. I heard a noise behind me and saw the inner door opening and the screen door protest on its hinges. Through the screen, I made out the outlines of an old woman in a wheelchair, her hand gripping the screen doorknob as much to steady herself as to open the door.

"Sorry, ma'am. I was just looking," I called out sheepishly, running up the three concrete steps and retrieving the envelope just out of her grasp. She nodded her head in understanding, her face crinkling into a grin. I helped her back the wheelchair into the living room and perched the sleeve of pills on a dining room table. The table was draped with a musty fabric anchored by an old set of gold-trimmed, floral plates, as if she was expecting company at any time and wanted to be ready.

Our job as pharmacy drug runners was to drop off, smile big, and leave—not to go inside and, least of all, not to strike up conversation. Still, it seemed rude not to do so after she had basically invited me in anyway and I had been caught red-handed peeping into her garage. She told me her name was Dolores; the pictures of her on the fireplace mantle were of generations of family who knew her as Aunt Dolly. The pictures had not been dusted for years. They were out of reach of her wheelchair. But they were not out of her sight.

I was sixteen years old and had never been that near to someone that old. As she reached out for the package of pills I could see that her skin was parchment, a thin translucent veil over the tendons and veins in her hands. She thanked me for the delivery, and I stammered a "you're welcome" as I stepped out the back door, easing the screen closed behind me. I cast another glance at the garage but resisted the impulse to steal another look.

I dropped off those same orange pills at Aunt Dolly's every two weeks. As much as I hated that Bug, I didn't mind bouncing that car into her gravel driveway to peek inside the garage each time before rapping softly on the screen door. I could not imagine what it would be like to have a Chevy like that—all clean, everything working, ready to roll. As much as I came to see the car, I came to check on Aunt Dolly. I never saw any evidence of family or friends visiting, yet the house was kept neat, if not always clean. On a hot day I would get her a glass of water; on a cool day a blanket to drape over her shoulders. And then, as I left, I would always sneak another lustful peak at her '56 Chevy.

"I see you like looking in the garage, young man." She startled me one day; then she eased my embarrassment by wrinkling her face into a smile. "It was my Donald's car." She pointed up to the mantle and the gold guild-frame photo of the young man in an army officer uniform. "He's been gone eight years now."

Hmm, so that '56 Chevy had not been driven for eight years. Had to be low mileage. Had to be in great shape, even if nobody had drained the fluids and set it up for a long sabbatical.

"You can have it, if you want it." She seemed delighted in the shocked look on my face when she first said it. "Not yet—after I've passed on, of course. Let's not rush anything."

Each time I dropped off the orange pills I took even longer to peer inside the smeared windows and inspect the car—*my car*. It did not have the same aggressive stance as my '57; it had one of those family-friendly color schemes rather than my raw steel blue, whitewall tires instead of my meaty Firestone 500s, a Powerglide automatic transmission instead of my Borg-Warner four-speed manual, and it probably just had a six cylinder in it. But, hey, it ran, right?

It was a Saturday morning when I pulled the Bug into Dolly's driveway and knocked on the screen door. It was unlocked, and the inner door was ajar. Within a few seconds, a man I didn't recognize came to the door and asked what I wanted. No, he was not Aunt Dolly's son, or cousin, or friend. He was an attorney, the executor of her estate, doing inventory. The pills would not be needed, but since I had made the trip, he said he would pay for them this time. But make sure to close out her account at the drugstore.

I took one more look around the living room as he sat at the dining room table, writing the check. As I surveyed for the last time the photos on the mantle and saw the wheelchair folded up in the corner of the room, it sank in that there would be no more "you're a fine young man" compliments, no more "tell Mac hello." As he handed the check to me, I paused for a second to muster the courage and then asked the question only a sixteen-year-old would think to ask under the circumstances:

"Did she happen to say anything about who should get the car in the garage?"

He said something about all the assets of estate and probate and auctions and a lot of other legal things I did not understand. One thing I did understand. Dolly, bless her heart, forgot to tell anybody I was supposed to get the car.

Shake it off, I convinced myself. Really, I didn't need her car.

I had one of my own.

Leaky was not a member of the Ducks. Not even close. He did own a Plymouth, but to my best recollection it was a '61 Plymouth Fury, like the one I would own later in life when I was out of money. That name Fury is evocative enough, hinting at a rage of unbridled power, a car that would decimate any other challenger, one that would explode into a frenzy of screaming gears and smoking tires at the slightest provocation.

The fact was, the only thing that screamed on Leaky's Fury was the alternator, and the only thing that smoked was his exhaust. It is fair to realize now, even if I did not then, that Leaky did not choose his Fury; it was imposed on him in the same way that just about everything in his life was imposed on him. The imposition was, as much as we did not fully understand the word back then, simply something awfully close to poverty—at least as measured against the growing affluence of the area.

Most of the homes in our town were comfortable, middle-class houses, and nearly all of the rest were sprawling, massive testaments to wealth. Yet tucked into the hillside creases were remnants of another life that was alien to most of us. The curbs were not adorned with brick-pillared mailboxes. The driveways were not granite-lined runways that swept up to the front of the home. The roofs were not trendy cedar shake or even costlier slate. It was the side of our town that was out of sight and largely out of mind, especially when you surround yourself with the likes of yourself.

I'm not sure how Leaky and I first met, other than we had a mutual friend in Matt, who owned a Jeep and was prone to ditch his homework and chores whenever he could to take his shotgun and deer rifle to some open fields north of town to blast away at empty beer cans and tree stumps. Leaky said he wanted to just meet us at the shooting site, but the location lacked any real definition, so we insisted on picking him up at his house, despite his pensive protests. One Saturday morning, we rolled the Jeep up a light gray gravel road and pulled up to the house. There was a sagging metal awning over the front and some handmade wooden steps leading to the screen door clinging to its hinges. There was little or no grass around the property, and the only thing that separated it from a field nearby was an old slat fence with several missing boards. Leaky jumped in the Jeep, tossed his .22-caliber rifle in back, and waved us out of there. At the shooting site, and on any typical day at school, Leaky was just like any other decent guy—a decent-enough shot, a decent sense of humor. He just did not have a very decent car.

Our school had its share of venerable wrecks—Ramblers, several VW Bugs, a hand-me-down Buick, and several other cars that simply lacked enough distinguishing elements to remember what they were, other than being affordable and reasonably reliable transportation. Nobody's car was the object of scorn or ridicule.

Except Leaky's.

He ran a paper route, mostly up the main road from our school, but also through the winding, carved, and sculptured streets of the country-club neighborhood where I lived. Leaky usually had someone helping him on the paper route; I was never sure who it was—some said it was an older brother or a younger brother, even his father. Leaky never said much.

But, for whatever reason, that day Leaky was lacking a shotgun-seat partner. I was not working at the drugstore that day and was weary for the moment of working on the Beast, so I volunteered when he asked if I could help.

The passenger door creaked and groaned as I opened it, the rubber insulation sticking to the frame and releasing with a *pop*. The seats were grimy, sunken, and torn. There was no carpet or even rubber mats on the floorboards. A shimmering crack in the windshield sparkled its way across the glass and disappeared below the dashboard. Some old newspapers were strewn around the seat, mingling with Leaky's schoolbooks.

"Sorry; just make some room," he said apologetically. He waggled the stick shift mounted on the steering wheel and slammed it into first gear as I heard a crunch from underneath my feet and we rumbled out of the school parking lot. Within a few minutes, we pulled in behind a building I had never seen before. There, stacked by itself near a metal door, was a pillar of newspapers, harnessed with twine, listing to one side and teetering on a wooden palette.

"That's ours," he said as he juggled the gearshift and jerked the car into reverse, backing up to the stack of papers. He forced a key into the lock and whacked the trim of the trunk with the heel of his hand. He pulled the trunk open and used a wooden broom handle from the trunk to hold it open. We hoisted the bound stacks and stuffed them into the trunk, the car's springs protesting the burden. The Fury's engine labored and stuttered with its new load as we pulled away. We drove to a quiet road that, while close to my country-club home, was not one I had ever seen before.

"This is where we go to work," Leaky announced as the Fury sighed to a stop on the gravel. Leaky leaped from the car, unlocked and popped open the trunk, and sliced through the twine binding the papers. He dragged a plastic bag out from the shadows of the trunk and held it high like a trophy.

"Here, this is yours." He tossed the prize my way. It was full of rubber bands. "Stand there," he instructed, pointing to the rear fender of the car. "I fold, hand to you, you put the rubber band on it and then throw it in the backseat." By the time he finished the sentence, he was already rolling the papers into cylinders and handing them to me in rapid fire mode. My first few tosses into the backseat missed their mark. Within a few minutes, we gained our rhythm, Leaky tossing the rolled papers to me, me snapping a rubber band in place and twirling the paper into the back seat. After a half hour of the routine, the backseat was piled with papers. Leaky slammed the trunk shut, and we lumbered away from the parking spot and headed out to the main road.

"Okay, kneel on the seat and grab papers out of the back and then transfer them to your other hand. I call out the numbers and you toss," he said above the screech of the water pump belt and the rattle from the windows. "Get them on the driveway, not the lawn. Don't miss or I have to go back tonight and don't get paid." He laughed as he pressed the accelerator and the car coughed forward.

Wherever you were supposed to be when your dad or older cousin taught you how to throw a baseball, I must have been somewhere else. My first few throws were in the dirt or on the lawn or sailed high and out of sight, but after a few misses, I relaxed and adopted the rhythm of Leaky's call.

"1270 ... *(thump)* 1274 ... *(thump)* Let the next two go. Cheap bastards. Okay, ready ... 1286 ... *(thump)* Watch out, narrow driveway ..."

After he covered the main road, Leaky slowed down and wrenched the steering wheel hand over hand to make the left turn into the curbed-brick entrance to the country club. I saw a flash of red on the dash.

"Whoa, Leaky, oil light! Pull over!"

"Nah, always does that. Running a little low on oil, but it's fine as long as I don't take the turns too hard. Okay, get ready … 1505 … *(whack)* 1510 …" *(whack)*

"Why don't you get a quart of oil for this thing?" I insisted more than asked.

"Oil's too expensive."

Leaky's Fury sputtered up the road that passed through the back nine holes. We passed Hobson's house, and I hurled the paper onto the roof. We covered most of the country-club streets and were just tossing on the last road when a woman pulled her luxury sedan out of the driveway right into the path of Leaky's Fury. He cussed, punched the clutch pedal, and stood on the brake as the Fury ground to a stop. The woman looked over in alarm as the Fury shuddered to a halt just a few feet away from her side door and then looked up in surprise when she saw me through the Fury's cracked, bug-spattered windshield.

"Paul, what are you doing … I mean, what are you doing in … *that* …" she fumbled. She was a friend of my mother's and a well-known member of the club.

"I'm delivering papers," I quickly said. A twinge of embarrassment shot through me. "I'm just helping today. It's not really something I'm doing all the time …"

She looked back for several seconds, puzzled, still scanning the old Fury, and then drove off.

"Sorry," Leaky mumbled as he wobbled the stick shift into gear.

"About what?"

"You know …"

We drove the rest of the route with an awkward silence filling in the gaps between Leaky's mailbox call and my window tosses. "2230 *(thwack)* … 2250 *(thwack)* 2270 … 2270—hey, you missed it …"

"Sorry. I wasn't ready for three in a row."

Leaky ground the car to a halt, lurched the gearshift into reverse, and started to back up, but the Fury sputtered, jerked, and stalled. He turned the key, and the engine wheezed several times as I heard him pulsing the gas pedal to the floor.

"Don't worry; it *always* starts," he pronounced as the engine backfired, bucked a few times, and then lumbered to an uncertain idle.

"Leaky, do you do anything to this car—I mean, like change the oil, the spark plugs, air filter, anything?"

"Nope," he replied with some satisfaction. "That's okay. Me and this car, we understand each other."

Leaky dropped me off at the drugstore so I could pick up my paycheck and my schedule for the next week. I walked the rest of the way home. Going into the garage, I studied my '57 Chevy as it rested quietly in the third stall, like a horse napping. I remembered feeling resentful that Leaky and his car seemed to have such a metaphysical relationship. So that's it? The reason you don't run yet is because we don't understand each other? In some ways, that was true. As much as I had learned over the last few weeks, I still stumbled over my ignorance. It was certainly clear to me that this '57 Chevy did not understand me. I wanted a car—sure, one that was built up a bit and might turn a few heads—but right now I just wanted a car that would run. I was beginning to think the smart money was on Dotson after all.

That Saturday, with my dad out playing golf and Mark pulling his shift at the drugstore, I was near the end of everything I could do before starting up the engine for the first time since the Chevy lugged its way into our garage. Perhaps nervous about reaching that seminal juncture, I found myself checking and rechecking things I knew I had done, a calculated distraction from the failure that I suspected lay ahead. Sure, maybe I better check the cam timing one more time. You just flick the key to kick the engine over a bit, just enough to position the crankshaft so the first cylinder was at the top of its stroke. I scraped the key from the workbench, slid into the front seat, pulled the gearshift into neutral, and jammed the key into the ignition. I thought I just held it for a second, but instead of the engine merely answering the call of the key with the mechanical "clank" of the starter motor solenoid, the sound seemed to grow from a sharp pop to a low rumble. I let go of the key as if it was electrified. The engine stuttered and lugged and then began to get its breath, settling into a throaty idle. I watched the tachometer as it wobbled and then pointed straight to the 750 rpm mark, just like the book said it should. My seat gently rocked under the torque of the 348 as the sound of eight 4-1/8-inch diameter cylinders thundered in the garage.

I felt like Alan Shepard inside his single-seater Freedom 7 capsule when he blurted out "Light this candle!" not knowing if the Redstone rocket was to propel him to infamy as the first man in outer space or simply corkscrew him right into the side of a warehouse somewhere in Pensacola like we saw on all those old NASA newsreels. The only difference is that I didn't wet my pants.

I wanted to wrench that key out of the ignition and turn everything off, just get my breath, see if this was really happening. Meantime, my right foot was ready to test if the engine had the stomach for about 650 cubic-feet-per-minute of air/fuel mixture. My foot won out as I pressed down the gas pedal and the engine surged in its approval. Against the hard walls of the garage, it sounded like a locomotive—deep, resonant, powerful, and loud.

Our dog Cindy, a high-strung Weimaraner who was tied up in a dog run on the side of the house, started to bark and whine over the thunder. My mother rushed from the house and flung open the back garage door and stared in shock as the car swayed slightly with each pulse of the gas pedal. She held her hands to her ears and mouthed something to me, but I couldn't hear it, or didn't care.

"Mom, it runs! Hurry, get in." I scurried around to the other side and yanked open the door. She eased into the seat and braced her hands against the metal dash.

"You're not going to go anywhere in this, are you?"

"Yes we are!" I pressed down the clutch, wriggled the stick shift into reverse, and glanced in the rearview mirror. The car had gained a few pounds of muscle working out in the garage all these weeks, and as I let out the clutch, the rear wheels squealed in delight and the Chevy lurched out of the garage. I did a perfect backward turn out of the driveway, slipped it into first gear, and pressed myself back in the seat as the 348 easily hauled the Chevy up the hill from our house. I shifted into second at the top of the hill as my mother sucked some fresh air in through clenched teeth. "Well, it does run, doesn't it?" she admitted with a mixture of relief and terror.

We made the turn around the thirteenth hole as four golfers looked up from their putts to see the steel-blue Bel-Air carving around the corner and bellowing deeply as we accelerated away. We drove around the wide street that girdles the country club, past the manicured shrubs, the pristine driveways, the brick-pillared mailboxes, and the sedate luxury sedans lounging in garages. The Chevy was a streaker at a tea party—bold, flashy, indifferent to social graces; its exhaust notes were the obnoxious party guest who gets a little too loud at the end of the night.

My mom settled down after a while and looked around the car as we drove, running her hand across the metal dash and looking down curiously at the green carpet, but never so long as to take her eyes off the road ahead, which was slipping under the car at a rate a bit beyond her comfort level.

"Well, that's enough showing off," she said hopefully. "I'm glad you got it running. Let's hope it stays that way." We pulled up to the house, and as I swung the wheel to begin the turn into the driveway, my mother touched my arm gently. "Paul, how about if you park it on the street, okay?" I nodded and steered the car to the curb. "And," she said, a little more firmly, "it would really be nice if you could go ahead and clean the garage a bit before your father comes home." I tossed the tools, and a few spare parts, into a large cardboard box, swept the detritus out onto the driveway and down into the curb gutter, and went inside to call Mark at the drugstore.

"You know we're not supposed to take personal calls at work." His voice was low, and I could hear the cash register in the background.

"Mark, you don't need to take me to school on Monday."

"Why, is your *mooootherrrr* taking you?" he teased.

"No, I'm taking myself. And I'm picking you up. See you at 7:30. Look for a blue '57 Chevy, buddy." I could hear Mark whooping as I slammed down the phone in triumph.

On Monday, I wiped some morning dew off the windshield, tossed my books into the backseat, and slipped behind the wheel. With a twist of the key, the engine, just as reliably as on Saturday, rocketed to life. I rumbled up the street and out of our country-club neighborhood, rolling down the window to hear the exhaust notes bounce off the homes and fences as I pulled out onto the main road. Within a few minutes, I was in front of Mark's house. I was about to tap the horn when the front door sprayed open and Mark bounced down the walk.

"*Oh yessss!*" he beamed. "The Beast *lives!*" Mark pranced around the car, rapping on the hood, fenders, and trunk. He hurled himself into the passenger seat and thumped a drumbeat on the metal dash, bobbing his head to the beat only he could hear. We slipped into the parking lot at school and let the car coast to a stop on the backside of the gym.

"Let it out! Let 'em know we're here," Mark pleaded.

"Not now; not yet."

Mark and I rushed out of Mrs. Brandywine's geometry class just before noon and slinked down to the parking lot. We did not even check to see if there were any faculty or deans staked out at the circle; we were on a mission. I cranked the key, and the 348 thumped twice, caught, and idled expectantly. I cleared the engine's throat with a punch of the accelerator as several people near the gym turned toward the sound and pointed. We cruised at a bare canter to the back exit of the parking lot and turned right onto the main road and then again right onto the circular drive. By now, several students were standing and pointing, some applauding, some laughing, but all looking a bit surprised.

Taking my cue from Burnside, I coasted to a stop at the top turn. Mark rolled down his window and thrust his hand forward as if to signal the charge. Holding in the clutch a little more firmly than ever, I clicked the Hurst shifter into first gear and gripped the shift knob like a bull rider clenches the saddle rope.

"Let's not screw this up," I told myself as much as Mark.

"Light it up," Mark ordered.

I pressed the gas pedal and peered at the tachometer until it kissed three thousand rpm and then, without finesse or hesitation, popped the clutch while I stabbed the gas pedal to the floor. The Bel-Air leaned back, and the torque of the 348 rolled us gently to one side, pouring its heart and horses through the eleven-inch clutch as I gripped the steering wheel. The back tires scorched the asphalt; then the heat-softened tires found their footing. The Chevy lunged forward, slightly fishtailing as it wormed its way across the top lane of the circle. We had only surged forward two or three car lengths before I backed off the gas and engaged the clutch, but by then the Bel-Air was smothered in white smoke and cheers. Mark let out a war whoop and raised his fist outside the window. Then he turned to me and gave off another one of his Cheshire grins. "Awesome! Absolutely awesome!"

I was feeling a bit sheepish at this stage, but as I turned the Chevy down the backside of the turn, Mark jabbed his finger out my window. "Look!"

There on the lawn, filled with students cheering, waving, and clapping, sitting stunned by himself, looking out from under hooded, furrowed eyebrows, was Dotson. Mark leaped from the Chevy while it was still rolling and sprinted across the lawn. The last glance I had of the lawn before turning down toward the parking lot was Mark leaping around Dotson in a victory dance and waving a few dollar bills like a bloody scalp.

# # #

Chapter Nine

Having your phone number on speed dial is some evidence that a relationship has evolved to one of familiarity, convenience, perhaps even urgency. I have other speed dial numbers on my phone: Carol, my daughters, some close friends, and I just added Mark.

It's certainly a decision of convenience; I find that we either get or make a call to Mark at least once every two weeks now since his visit. He had asked me before he left if he could have that same peace that Carol and I had. I said it was his for the asking, his for the taking. He didn't seem ready.

I wasn't there when he asked; it must have been a few weeks later in his apartment back in California—knowing Mark, it was probably late at night, sitting up alone on the couch. It was probably a funny conversation with this God he now wanted to know, but it was certainly direct and honest. Maybe it was good that I was not there for it—maybe best that the two of them hash it out.

He called me the next morning to tell me, with a lilt in his voice that I had not heard since senior year. He asked me what to do next. I told him I would send him an extra Bible we had and that he should start reading it—front-to-back, please, not back-to-front—and call me so we could talk more about it.

It's been nearly a year since that call, so it's time to get on with it and assign a number to him rather than keep punching in those same ten digits each time. The delay carries no greater meaning than the simple fact that sometimes I put things off. My ceiling fan in my office is still going *whump whump*, as long as we're making the case for pure procrastination.

We talk a lot about what he reads. He starts calling God his "Father-God" and wants to make sure he gets all the interrelationships right: God is the head guy, Jesus is the right-hand man, and the Holy Spirit intervenes at times but mostly keeps an eye on things and makes sure everything keeps moving in the same direction. Mark needs the simple clarity of that as he dives deeper in passages, often coming up with insights and questions that had never occurred to me in twenty-five years of reading the same sections. He accepts like a child but pushes and probes like a seasoned investigator. I start to again see so much of the Mark I had known in high school—alive, stirring things up, in the middle of it all.

Still, over this last year, it is becoming inescapable to me that, just as Brat warned me, Mark is not really the same person I remembered. Sure, he still has that fierce energy and interest in things, but his mood shifts are sharper and deeper, his already fleeting attention span more easily whisked away to be replaced by an entirely different line of thought. Other times, when he gets on a topic, he stays on it long after the discourse has outlived its usefulness.

Mark is a virtual family member now. He can tell you what year my older daughter is in college and what her major is. He knows the name of our dog, what church we go to, the name of Carol's mother, and where we went on vacation, but mostly he can tell you about Lesley.

Our youngest daughter was quite taken by Mark back during his visit. Maybe it was his fascination with the Beatles. Lesley had the Beatles *Anthology* and several books on the group and could recite many of the lyrics of their songs. She told Mark that one of her favorites was George's Harrison's "Here Comes the Sun," with its legendary opening guitar riff.

They drop notes and greeting cards to each other a lot—he signs his "Cowboy Mark," and she addresses his to "Uncle Mark." There is a deeper element for both of them. Lesley knows that Mark is important to me and that he is a personification of some of the stories of my more reckless youth that Lesley needs to know were there. Yet I think she also sees a vulnerability, even an innocence, with him that needs a safe place to be expressed. From my view, I feel that Mark, at least in the early days, needs a daughter, albeit a substitute, to salve the pain of his own estrangement. Mark is effusive in his encouragement of Lesley as she finishes college and later law school. He never fails to check on her progress or mail her one of his hand-written cards.

So Mark has adopted Lesley, but Lesley, too, has adopted him.

Carol's growing attachment to Mark is different. She has taken more than her share of phone calls from him, and in some ways almost looks forward to them—at first for the sheer novelty of his stream-of-conscious conversations and later because she starts to see a purpose in it. Sometimes she just smiles and hands the phone to me; sometimes she just takes the phone herself and curls up on the couch with a cup of coffee and does her *listening* thing.

The speed-dial decision is also one of urgency, as modest and even manufactured as those urgencies may be at times. It is now clear to me that Mark is in poor health. The encephalitis had done its damage over the years since college, and while Mark recovered from his coma and went on with his life, the physical and emotional residue of the disease never leaves him fully alone. Sometimes when I call him or he calls Carol, the weariness in his voice betrays him. He has another infection, or the doctor has changed his prescription yet again. He is also so chary of the moods in his head that he has begun to distrust his ability to, well, be *normal* in anything as simple as going out with friends or holding a job. His isolation, dictated by his fragile immune system, slips at times into reclusiveness, an absence of the perspective and balance that normally is honed by regular interaction with others. Little things seemed to matter too much and big things not enough.

His obsessive/compulsive drives carry with them some tragic comedy. He told me once that he could not read road signs clearly while driving, so I cajole him into getting eyeglasses. Now he's calling us every other day to complain that the eyeglasses don't fit, that he has been taking them back to the shopping mall eyeglass store to get them adjusted. He is now calling me after a month of this to tell me he has thrown the new eyeglasses in the dumpster behind his apartment.

"Mark!" I am baffled. "Those were three-hundred-dollar glasses. Why did you throw them away?"

"They were making me crazy."

To: paul
From: mark
Subject: '57 chevy

The Beast was awesome ... man ... the best ... nothing like it

Now what? After you do one burnout and get cheers for it, if you do another it looks like you are pandering, playing to the crowd. I wanted my car—and me—to be defined by more than just a tire-smoking exhibition. Plus I couldn't afford to buy new tires.

Even more serious: failure was not an option. I mean, what if I failed to rev the engine properly, dumped the clutch, and *stalled out* right in front of Dotson, the Ducks, or even worse, in front of the varsity cheerleading squad practicing their skirt-flipping somersaults on the front lawn? What if I really poured the horses through the drive train more than I expected and fishtailed right into the curb? What about the dreaded backfire—not all that unusual if you are running a hot camshaft—when the engine just isn't quite ready for that chaser of air/fuel mixture and upchucks it all right back up into your carburetor? Or, the nightmare of all, and the greatest fear of anyone who has beefed up a car in stages: what if the driveshaft or the differential looks at all the horsepower and torque being drilled at them and drops to the pavement in protest? Evel Knievel could have stopped at the record nineteen cars he drove over in his motorcycle in 1971, but noooo ... he had to try to jump the Snake River Canyon and almost drowned when his rescue chute deployed early and dumped him in the creek. I've got more sense than that.

Events become legends when you just leave them well enough alone. No, it is far easier, albeit cowardly, to allow the folklore to take on a magnitude and reality of its own. Rarely do stories diminish in time; more often, they grow—sometimes beyond normal proportions. For days after my debut, I simply would pull into the parking lot, punch the accelerator teasingly between gears (*bbbrat ... brattt*) like a boxer feigning a left jab, and then pull into my now-assumed space as if I had nothing else to prove.

Except to Mark. With his stock Impala, my car became his expression, his extension. I was also a sucker for his prodding.

"C'mon, buddy, light 'em up," he would chide me after I picked him up from his house and pulled into the lower lot. Mark mattered to me—he had stayed with me during the whole ordeal, talked it up when we were down, slapped down a bill or two on the craps table in my favor, and even now was taking a perverse pride in having picked the right side in this dogfight.

"Okay, but I'm not taking off three months worth of tread," I conceded to him one morning. "I'll do it in reverse just to kick up a little smoke."

I slapped the shifter hard left and up, throttled the engine to the three thousand rpm mark, and popped the clutch. There was only one thing I did forget: there is a lot more gear in reverse than there is in first gear. So when my 348 swift-kicked the drive train with its monstrous torque, the rear wheels roared to life. Within what seemed a mere second, the Beast had reared backward, throwing my body forward into the steering wheel and taking me out of range of the rearview mirror. Mindlessly, I braced myself backward with the only leverage I had—my foot, which was firmly planted on the accelerator. Before I could recover, a crunching thud shuddered through the car and the rear of the car hiked up a few inches as the engine stalled out.

I sat there frozen as Mark piled out of the passenger side and walked around to the back of the Chevy.

"Wow," I heard Mark exhale more than say. "Wow, Oh, wow …"

"What?" I leaned out the driver's window. "*What!!!*"

"Oh, man. Wow."

I flung open the door and gingerly stepped around the back, thinking maybe I had run over the school mascot. It was worse.

"Oh, man," Mark kept saying to no one in particular. "Wow."

The object of his verbal paralysis was the scene before us of the massive chrome rear bumper of the '57 creased squarely into the middle of the hood of a VW Bug. The bumper had scraped up the entire curved front of the hood and came to rest just short of the windshield wipers.

"Wow," I said and then gathered my thoughts. "Well, it can be fixed."

Mark whirled around, his eyes molten with terror. "No, it *can't* just be fixed! This cannot just be fixed!"

"Okay, I'm sorry. It was an accident. What's the problem here?"

"You don't know whose car this is, do you?"

The VW was not exactly a specimen of pampering. The dull orange paint was blistered and chalky. Rust pockmarked the lower door panels, and the rear tires splayed out like a crippled dog taking a piss. I felt bad about hitting it, but was pretty sure I could manage the discussions with the likely owner, probably one of the hippie potheads who would be glad to shake it off for a twenty-dollar bribe.

"This is Dirk's car," Mark hissed.

It took me a few seconds. "Dirk? Like as in 'Dirk Wilson'?"

"Yeah, like exactly like Dirk Wilson." Mark pushed his hands to the side of his face and dragged them down, pulling most of his face with them. "We're dead," he declared. "No, we're more than dead. We wish we were dead. He's going to kill us."

Mark, this time, was not exaggerating. Dirk Wilson was the meanest, toughest, angle-iron-bending, rock-chewing, bicep-bursting hard-ass at our school; an all-league defensive *and* offensive tackle on the varsity football team who could have single-handedly removed the goalposts each year at the end of our homecoming game and planted them three feet deep at midfield without breaking a sweat.

And while it was never exactly written down anywhere, I was pretty sure you don't hit his car.

By now, a small crowd had gathered, all murmuring and clucking, offering me little more than pitying glances. I got back in the Chevy, put it in first gear, and eased it down off the hood of Dirk's car, taking more paint, the chrome center strip, and a headlight along for the ride. Dirk's hood was popped up at the latch, so we raised it. Mark started punching the backside of the hood with his fist, trying to flatten the dent.

"Mark, let it go," I said. "You need to stay out of this. It's my fault."

Mark stopped his pounding and looked back at me. "I made you do it, but, yeah, you're screwed."

"I'm screwed?"

"Royally."

"Don't rub it in …"

"Wait!" Mark's entire face crinkled into a deep thought. "No, we're not. Trust me. I've got an idea."

With that, Mark rocketed up the walkway and into the back door of the locker room as I stood lamely next to Dirk's car, brushing my hand across the crumpled hood, maybe hoping it might levitate back into shape. The crowd drifted away, and I was alone.

I wandered up to the main building and slinked into a rear seat in my history class. A few people elbowed each other and looked back at me, but I stayed cool. It is essential to stay cool on the day you are going to die. Or get killed.

When class ended, Mark was practically bouncing outside the door.

"Were have you *been?*" he pleaded.

"Hiding. No, actually, Mark, I come here to go to school. Learn. Take tests. That stuff. You?"

"I've been workin' it," Mark said proudly. "It's fixed."

"The hood is fixed?"

"No, the hood's not fixed. It won't get fixed. Dirk doesn't care."

By now, students were elbowing past us to get to the next class and Mark got swept up in the tide. As noon break arrived, I headed out to the front lawn and was making the final turn around the administration building when I came face to face—or more accurately, face to chest—with Dirk.

"Hey, howzitgoin?" I choked out.

"You've seen better days," he said.

"Yeah, hey, I'm really sorry. It was an accident, and Mark said you were cool, so ..."

"So where is it?"

"Where's what?"

"My eight-track," he scowled. "Mark said you were going to give me your eight-track. A Craig, as I recall."

"Oh. Okay. Sure." I shrugged. "Sounds good. I'll bring it tomorrow."

That afternoon, as Mark jumped into the Chevy for the ride home, he was jubilant.

"Pretty cool, huh?" he bubbled. "Did I fix that or what?"

The next morning I stuffed the Craig eight-track box into a shopping bag and delivered the bounty to Dirk at break.

Mark never suffered from too much self-awareness, but I could tell he was a little melancholy about the whole exchange. He had fixed it—his pride in that accomplishment was undiminished—but he actually felt a little bad about giving away my eight-track, at least without telling me. He tried to make up for it.

"Hey, you need some tie-dyed jeans," he said later that week.

"I don't have the money for that, and my parents are not about to buy me tied-dyed jeans, Mark. They're from St. Louis, remember?"

"You don't buy them," he said. "You *make* them." He told me to bring in a pair of jeans to school the next day and he would do it himself. He was an expert at it.

A couple of days after I delivered the spare jeans to Mark, he tracked me down after class, holding up a shopping bag.

"You did it?" I grabbed for the bag, but Mark backed away.

"No man, you need to try them on here at school, you know, so I can make sure you like them." We went into the boy's restroom and I closed myself into one of the stalls while Mark stood outside the metal door holding the bag.

"Okay, Mark, give me the jeans," I called out as I hung my old pair on the coat hook.

"Give me your old jeans first," Mark called back.

"Why?"

"So they don't fall on the floor and get dirty. Just gimme them."

I tossed my jeans over the door, and a second later I heard the rustling in the bag and the tied-dyed jeans arched over the door. They looked pretty good—blue and green and red psychedelic designs down each leg. Maybe Mark was an expert after all. I pulled them on and was inspecting his workmanship—my first pair of tie-dyed jeans as a California high schooler—when I looked down at the patch of yellow dye, all by itself, in a carefully selected region of my crotch.

"Mark!!"

The only sound in return was the rustling of the shopping bag.

"Mark—you jerk! Give me my jeans back! Mark!!!"

His cackling laugh echoed off the walls of the restroom until it faded away as the restroom door closed behind him.

It was raining that afternoon when I finished my last class, bundled my books under my jacket, and made a run for the parking lot, pulling my jacket down a bit more over my jean zipper to shield Mark's handiwork. To the car. Damn—left my windows open. We never locked our doors back then; nobody went into your car. But leaving the windows open—that was stupid. I slammed the door and swept my hand around the seat to squeeze off the puddles of water when I caught sight of the unexpected white bundle that somebody had placed on the passenger seat. I did not have to unfold it all before I spotted the telltale "Q-Q-Q-Q" on the back. I inspected it for a few seconds and folded it back neatly on the seat.

Mark at work. Always looking out for me.

I'm glad I didn't have to ask.

I'm in.

The burnout on the front driveway and the growing legend of the Chevy's attack on a Bug assigned a certain legitimacy for my '57. Whether it was only imagined on my part that there was something to prove, I no longer felt it was needed.

I wore the Ducks shirt for the first time the next week, and the transition was noted with a reserved nod from a few other Ducks during noon recess, but that's all that was said. Pace yourself. That's the trick. Don't just barge into the next Ducks' huddle in the parking lot like some guy who won the lottery joining an old-money country club. Don't force it.

Friday of that week, a bunch of the Ducks were prepping for their routine convoy up the winding road of Fire Mountain to their hangout on the rock formations near the peak, maybe grab a beer, maybe just sit there until the sun went down. The Ducks were in the parking lot, revving their engines. I got into my Chevy and turned the key, and the 348 caught quickly, settling into an idle with the baritone exhaust notes echoing off the brick wall of the gym. I eased the Chevy out of its space and slowed down near the end of the parking lane, watching the line of Chargers, Novas, 'Cudas, and Camaros pass in front of me. One of the Chevys—a loaded-up, jacked-up coupe—stopped just in front of my lane. That's all the cue I needed. Rapping the engine in acknowledgment, I turned right to join the line of cars, the aroma of hydrocarbons and the thudding tones of glass-pac mufflers filling the air around me. The procession tamely made the turn on the road around the back of the school, and then, as if there was an invisible pace car that turned off into the pits, the cars picked up the tempo, the V8s winding up and the speeds stepping up as we swept along the road lined with eucalyptus trees and oaks. I was in second gear most of the way but shifted into third as we picked up speed, hearing the engine reach deeper. We turned left to the road that led up the mountain, effortlessly outgunning gravity as we wheeled our way in close formation up the narrowing road.

I forgot for a moment that I was in a twelve-year-old makeshift hot-rod Chevy. I was just one more link in the steel and cast-iron chain wrapping its way around Fire Mountain.

The next day, Saturday, Mark pulled up to my house, beeped the horn, and jumped into the passenger seat of my '57 parked in the driveway.

"We're going for a ride."

"Mark, I've got chores, and I have the shift at the drugstore." I sighed. "Where are we going?"

"Just down the street …" Sure enough, Mark directed me to pull over to the curb in front of Dotson's garage. There, hooded by the half-open, pivoting garage door, Dotson could be seen leaning over the shell of his

Speedster. He looked up as my Bel-Air lumbered to a halt and just stood there warily as we approached.

Mark strolled up to the Porsche, surveying the primer gray slopes of the Speedster's body. "Nice …"

"It's getting there," Dotson replied to Mark, avoiding casting a glance my way. "So what brings you by?"

"We're just looking," Mark said mischievously. I followed behind Mark and traced my gaze across the rounded shell. It was stripped of its interior, and the doors were attached by their hinges, but there were no windows or handles. The front sloped down to the ground with a thin chrome pipe of a bumper strewn across its face, and the bug-eyed headlights were popped out like the face of a dry skull. The lines of the car flowed—I would grant it that; there were no wasted humps or contrived arches or creases. This was a car that projected an air that it did not have to try too hard to affirm its stature; in its own effete way, it was saying it was all business. On that level, it did command some measure of my respect. Yet it is one thing to shun nonessentials in the design but quite another to have never thought of them at all. In that way, the Speedster's leanness was austere to an extreme. It was so lacking in anything ornamental or interesting, it seemed lifeless.

"So." Dotson had braced both hands on the doorsill, his head lowered as if inspecting something in the interior. He looked up at me underneath his eyebrows. "First time you've seen a real Porsche, I'll bet."

I glanced at the shell from front to back as if to remind myself that's what it was. "Yeah, actually, this close, yeah."

Dotson paused, surprised by my tone of respect. "And what do you think?"

I almost responded instinctively—something casual, even polite, like, "Looks great. It's coming along, just like you said." Gallantry would have dictated that—after all, I had won the bet; I had smoked the tires in front of him on the front lawn. I had emerged victorious; he was vanquished. I was in a position to take the high ground, say something that left him with some dignity and showed my strength of character, something that perhaps even began to forge some mutual regard. I looked at the Speedster—its bare wheel wells, the missing headlights, the drab, gray body, sitting there on blocks—and it came to me.

"I think it looks like a dead turtle."

I'm not sure that I really thought about saying that; it just seemed to come out because, well, it did look like a turtle—a turtle that somehow managed to shuffle out across some desert road and just died from the exhaustion and heat, and over time its innards just shriveled up and its legs fell out of the sleeves of its shell and its eyes shrank back into its skull. That kind of dead turtle.

Mark screeched in glee at the comment and then looked at me in half admiration and half alarm. I had just stood in the mighty Dotson's garage—the Porsche Palace, treading on holy ground of all things German-engineered—and pronounced a 356 Speedster as nothing more than a dehydrated reptile. That part was good. The part that was bad emerged nary two seconds later when we realized that we were standing in the garage of a guy who was six inches taller and forty pounds heavier than us, and he had blunt-force tools in his hands and we were defenseless. It would have been nice to think that Dotson really didn't care what some jerky guy with a faded blue '57 Chevy with a dumpy interior and shag carpet really thought about his vintage 356, but Dotson glowered at us and moved around the side of the car in our direction.

Mark and I just took off, running slightly harder than we were laughing. We jumped into the '57. I turned the key, and the trusty 348 seemed to sense the urgency of the moment and roared to life. Mark clattered his palms on the metal dash all the way back to my house.

# # #

Chapter Ten

What do these people do—lick their car clean?

My wife Carol and I stroll through the tightly cropped lawn of the park, taking in the view. Bugattis, Packards, MGs, Aston-Martins, Shelbys, Austin-Healeys, Jaguars, Triumphs, Porsches … the array is staggering. A chorus line of chrome, rolled fenders, and spoked wheels. Flexible exhaust pipes streaming out of 1920s-era roadsters with headlights as large as Mr. Magoo's eyeglasses. They are grouped by era: prewar (the First World War, that is), postwar, European classic, modern classics, American performance, racing …

The Cincinnati Concourse D'Elegance, a pretty respectable sidekick to the marquee Monterey Concourse D'Elegance classic car show, has another category that gets less attention and a lot less drool on the fenders from passersby—American classics. I know that section will be a letdown after seeing dozens of hand-crafted road machines from an era when building an automobile was a sensual absorption as much as a mechanical process. Face it—you look at most of those roadsters from back in the 1920s through the early 1940s, whether U.S. or European, and you are looking at a female form. Well, I am, anyway.

My phone vibrates in my pocket, and I glance at the number.

"It's Mark," I tell Carol, my finger poised over the answer button.

"If you answer that and tell him where we are, he'll be jealous …" she cautions.

"No," I respond. "He'll be depressed." I slide the phone back into my pocket.

We wind our way through the crowds to the American classic section of the lawn. There aren't too many feminine curves in sight, at least not on the cars. After experiencing such nuance and refinement in the European and early twentieth-century American cars, the classic car section is a blunt force assault on subtlety. It is the rowdy, unshaven cousin with the jeans and Grateful Dead shirt who shows up at your wine party hollering for a Bud Light. The cars are arranged on the lawn in a loose chevron pattern, slung low over the grass. I had forgotten how big they were. The Dodge Charger and GTO parked close to each other look like a pair of doublewides at a trailer park.

Carol and I drift down the hill to the concession stand and spot a car off by itself, tucked under a broad oak tree. I can tell right away it is a '57 Bel-Air. That part was easy.

The problem with this car is its color. It's *turquoise*. I'm half expecting Ozzie and Harriett to come bounding out of their Cape Cod house and cheerily invite us to pile in and go out for ice cream. This car is spotless, but in a prissy way. Innocent. Tame. *Nice.*

They must lick these cars clean. This car needs to get roughed up a bit, take off its high-heeled shoes and dance barefoot with some guy with a Ducks shirt on and a smirk on his face. Don't just sit there, man, and pamper it. Drive this thing.

We wander around the lawns of cars for another hour but then drive home. As we park the car and go in the house, Carol turns to me, puzzled.

"Is that what they really look like?"

"What does what look like?"

"The car," she says. "The '57 Chevy. The one you always talk about. I didn't know that's what they looked like in real life."

They don't, I say to myself. *At least not mine.* Carol hangs the car keys on the hook by the laundry room and sits down at the kitchen table to sort through the mail, but I head downstairs to the basement, to the cabinet where we have all the photo albums. The one I'm looking for is not hard to find—it's the oldest, a cracked vinyl tan binder with "Old Paul stuff" scribbled on the binding in Magic Marker. I flip to one of the first sheets in the book, gingerly sliding out the black-and-white photo, snap the album closed, and take the basement steps two at a time to the main floor. Carol is still at the kitchen table flipping through a magazine. I push the mail to one side and slide the snapshot in front of her.

"There," I say, tapping the photo with my finger. "That's what they look like."

Carol puts down the magazine and passes her fingers carefully over the glossy image of the Beast shouldered against the curb in front of my parent's country-club house. She gently picks at a few spots as if they are not real—the jutting exhaust pipes, the chrome moon hubcaps on the front wheels, the jacked-up suspension, the mag wheels with the thick tires in back—and then looks up at me like I am some kind of stranger.

"I never would have gone out with you if you had shown up in this car."

To: paul
From: mark
Subject: keeping up

---

burnside added headers to his roadrunner ; he was worried he could drop 1 spot to the mythical 57 beast brat added carbs and lowered his corvair. he said paul cant win the curves sorry my typing is bad, right arm does not work anymore

"I'm in loooove!"

Mark was never one for understatement, and today was no different. He and I were in the stockroom of the drugstore on a school-day afternoon unloading the weekly short orders of pharmaceuticals, toothpastes, deodorants, hair sprays, bandages, and dozens of other items. The weekly shipment from the supplier only had two or three of each product since Mac was old-fashioned and thought it was wasteful and stupid to have too much inventory around in back, even if that meant he failed to qualify for volume discounts.

Having convinced Mac from the start that we were better as a team, we designed a nifty synchronization routine to sort the goods so we could put them on the shelves more efficiently. We had the store memorized by now and even cajoled Mac into letting us rearrange some of the shelves so products had what you might today call some "affinity"—shaving creams for men and women should not all go together, we told him. Men's shaving cream should be by the men's deodorant; women's shaving cream should be close to their skin lotions or shampoos. Our thought was that guys shaved standing at the sink, where they brushed their teeth and rolled on some deodorant, so their products ought to be together because guys don't like to think real hard when shopping. Women shave in the shower, so their shaving cream ought to be close to the shampoo or hair color. Mac eyed us suspiciously but warmed up to the idea pretty quickly after befuddled customers no longer peeked over the high drugstore counter to ask him where to find the shaving cream.

So with the store now grouped by affinity product set, I would arrange four or five baskets—labeled for men's stuff, women's stuff, baby stuff, injury stuff, and so on. Mark would sit on a low stool a few feet away at the larger bins of unsorted products we just received from the supplier. He would then reach in randomly, grab a bottle or jar, and toss it my way with instructions in mid-flight; I would catch it and toss it into the assigned basket, which we would later take to its respective part of the store and unload it more efficiently.

Mac was, at first, bewildered with the scat-talk in the stockroom, but then would give us one of his avuncular smiles when he saw how quickly we could unload the weekly shipment ("Men's deodorant!"—*clunk* "Bandages!"—*smack* "Acne!"—*clunk* "Diapers!"—*thump).*

This particular day, Mark was off-stride. "Women's shampoo"—*thump.* "Speaking of which, I'm in loooove, I'm telling you!"

"Mark, pay attention!"

"Toothpaste"—*smack.*

"Mark, that's not toothpaste; it's Neosporin."

"Whatever. I'm in looooove ..."

"With whom?"

"Jolene. She's awesome; she's beautiful. She's a varsity cheerleader. You've seen her; she hangs around Denise."

"I guess," I said, just to amuse Mark with the conversation. I sure knew who Denise was, but when she was around, I had eyes for nobody else. "Okay, but keep tossing, buddy."

"Clearasil!"—*smack.*

"Wait—men's or women's?"

"Doesn't matter. I sat next to her on the lawn today and we started talking and she is just so cool. Very friendly. Mouthwash!"—*clunk.*

For the next half hour, Mark extolled the virtues of Jolene. I got the full report: her hair, her eyes, her smile, her humor—and yep, her estimated proportions, but done with a dignity not always seen from Mark when he described girls. The only unknown was whether he had a shot at getting a date with her.

Mark ventured that maybe, just maybe, he could leverage up a date with Jolene to have the four of us—him Jolene, me, and the goddess

Denise—on a double date. Oh yeah, right. Denise wouldn't give me the time of day. She probably hates my car. She goes out with guys with new cars. Mark chuckled one of his laughs that meant he knew something you didn't know, which was fairly often.

"I'll tell you what she said to Tony when he asked her out in his new Cougar Eliminator." Mark fell quiet to see if I would take the bait.

"I'm listening …"

"Tony asked Denise out and was bragging on his car and Denise tells him she wasn't impressed, that Paul at least built his by himself." I doubted that was exactly what was said, but it made me feel better to leave it unchallenged. It was pretty hard to imagine that my determination to rebuild the Chevy from a junker had drawn the attention—and certainly not the affection—of the cutest cheerleader in the school.

While Jolene would be Mark's brass ring out of reach, I was back in the open waters of dating now that my Chevy was out of dry dock. After a couple of dates when the girls asked guardedly if the odor in my car was a flatulent skunk or when they seemed repulsed that their shoes were sticking to the shag carpet, it became apparent to me that my car was not exactly a chick's car—well, some girls liked it a lot, but I was not always sure I liked them. When you work on an engine for that long, especially jumping in and out of the driver's seat cranking the ignition, the car acquires a certain aroma and glaze that can only be associated with petroleum-based residue. One of the junior varsity cheerleaders felt sorry for me and volunteered to do an assessment of my car's interior from the standpoint of a potential date. A proxy with pigtails.

The audit was exhaustive, careful, and unrelenting. She opened the passenger door and flinched at the creaking sound. The seats were hard and soft in all the wrong places. The steering wheel was very *stock*, meaning very large and very retro *Ozzie & Harriett*. She twirled the knobs on the AM radio as if it was some kind of quaint novelty. She whisked her hand across the headliner fabric and then squinted her eyes and coughed as dust drifted over her face and she wiped her hands on my shirt. Her real dismay was reserved to the end for the carpet—it was green shag, probably installed a few years ago by whoever swapped in the 348, but after weeks of engine rebuilding, its strands were caked, matted, and stained with dried gunk.

She stepped back and surveyed the car with one long lingering gaze before issuing her report.

"This is really disgusting."

We spent the next half hour making a list of what needed to get done for my Chevy to be a date magnet—new steering wheel (small, chrome with a padded foam rim), a new headliner (cream), a serious scrubbing of the seats (Formula 409 and a brush), new carpet (we went with a dark blue loop), an eight-track (sigh; Mark clips me for another twenty-five dollars for a used Craig), and window cranks that worked. It was a tough laundry list, but when you've come this far in the dating game, you don't want to punt on the third down. I dutifully recorded her instructions but then proudly suggested one of my own.

"How about new interior trim on the doors?"

"Oh, I didn't know you could replace that," she said, scratching her fingernails across the blue vinyl armrests and two-tone panels.

"Sure." Actually I had no idea if you could replace the panels, but ignorance hadn't stopped me yet. I volunteered for some extra hours at the drugstore and plowed the money into the new interior appointments. I saved the best for last, clutching my last twenty dollars and breezing into a fabric store.

"I need some vinyl," I told the clerk, who motioned to a rack of rolled material against the wall. There were plenty of good choices—black, dark blue, white, and nice cream. Left on my own without an advisor, I don't know what came over me, but I landed on something that I thought was nothing I had ever seen in a car before—gold Naugahyde embossed with black swirls. I'm not even sure if I had even seen such a fabric on the worst Barcalounger ever made. Over the weekend, I pulled off the interior door panels and set about cutting out the templates to glue the Naugahyde into place. My family, one by one, stopped by the garage to offer their encouragement:

My younger sister: "You're obsessed."

My younger brother: "Interesting."

My youngest brother: "Cool."

My father: "What was wrong with black?"

My mother: "Oh, Paul, I would have gone with you to pick something out …"

By the end of the weekend, I had mastered the art of replacing interior door panels and replaced the green shag carpet with dark blue pile. So now I had the only steel-blue '57 Chevy Bel-Air in the town—well, perhaps in the nation—that had dark blue pile carpet and gold Naugahyde interior. The chicks would dig it.

Cristy was a cute blonde who attended the school in the town three exits down the freeway from our school. She attended the church where I was the resident rock star, playing my pseudo-spiritualized versions of songs by the Doors and the Yardbirds. She sang back-up vocals in our little church musical group and would cast a knowing smile at me when I would slip a Rolling Stones' Keith Richards guitar lick into some song I was doing for communion. Early stage cognoscenti. I had talked with her several times but never really considered dating her since I was hopelessly smitten with some other girl at the time. The latter potential pairing cooled off—or more accurately, never had chance of heating up. Meantime, Cristy joined a large group of us who went on a ski trip to Tahoe. On her first run down the intermediate slopes, she broke her leg and was condemned to spend the rest of the three-day trip at the lodge in a cast. Shortly before the trip, I had been picked to play the lead in our school musical *Li'l Abner* and was not supposed to be skiing at all. So while I secretly hoped to score points for chivalry by appearing to sit out for her sake and keep her company, I was due to mark time in the lodge as well. Cristy and I would just lounge on the open porch and whisper secret commentaries on all the people passing by, a bit like Paul Simon and "Kathy" on the bus in "America" *("She said the man in the gabardine suit was a spy; I said be careful, his bowtie is really a camera ...").*

We talked for hours and developed a friendship that certainly had its romantic twinges, but expressing any serious affection for each other seemed an awkward imposition on a friendship that we both enjoyed too much to ruin. We found that we simply liked to be with each other, especially at times when it seemed too hard to be with anyone else. We both dated other people during the time we knew each other closely, but there was no jealousy or resentment that I recall. The expression "Let's just be friends" was the kiss of death to any guy in high school, but for Cristy and me, we seemed to know that and accept that—and we rather enjoyed the freedom it offered.

Cristy was actually one of those rare girls who actually knew, and appreciated, something about cars. I could tell her that I just picked up some "Hookers" and she wouldn't slap me but knew those were the hot brand of exhaust headers. Some girls, even after my interior makeover, would sit in my Chevy tentatively, as if they thought it might explode. Cristy loved the sounds and sensations of power from that car; she was not afraid of it. She understood its capabilities could actually tell when the engine was running a little rich or the spark was a little too far advanced or retarded, and would have had no hesitation slipping into a baggy pair of jeans and crawling under the Beast to help line up the linkage on the transmission or pumping the brakes while I bled the brake lines.

She also liked music, almost all kinds, but especially Motown and the Memphis soul sounds of Stax. We had the kind of relationship where if either one of us went to a dance separately, we could dance together more than once during the night even if everyone else was still pacing around the perimeter of the gym. We could dance fast and not feel embarrassed if we did not have all the moves; we could dance slow and not feel like the closeness took on any great intimacy.

While I tried to keep my car as something of a rolling palace after the interior makeover, it still had a truck-like role—hauling equipment for our new soul/funk band Bedlam Showboat. We practiced on Saturday afternoons at a junior high school gym, an arrangement Mark somehow had set up through someone he knew at the school, hoping that the gigs would follow. Everyone was responsible for hauling their own gear, but Mark went with me on the first trip so we could pick up the bass guitar and bass amp he had arranged for me to borrow. We lugged the massive amp and the guitar case to the Chevy's trunk and unloaded them a few minutes later at the school's gym. Mark was mouthing rhythms, humming, and drumming his fingers on just about any nearby surface. He was so thrilled with the prospects of being in a band.

We waited until each band member arrived—we had never really met each other before, and some awkward introductions and nervous chatter marked each arrival—feeling out each other on our musical tastes and background. However, when Hampton, our black singer, showed up, we all fell back a bit and really sized up the person who would be the most critical member of the band. He was of average height and build, so we were not dealing with some over-pumped Isaac Hayes, and he carried himself with a grace that allowed him to seemingly glide across the room toward us. He was, by any measure, a pretty handsome guy, which Mark whispered to me would be a good attribute in case he couldn't sing. Roger Daltrey of the Who had already shown the music industry that you don't have to be able to sing to be good, and he wasn't alone. David Clayton-Thomas of Blood, Sweat & Tears and the drug-rusted Jim Morrison of the Doors also were not great singers, but chicks still swooned with their stage presence. As Hampton came toward us, though, we noticed another figure coming right up behind him—it was Dawn, older sister of our high school goddess cheerleader Denise and apparently Hampton's main squeeze.

"Hey," I elbowed Mark, "I thought we agreed 'no girlfriends' at practice. We have work to do."

Mark's eyes were glazed on Dawn, who was every bit as gorgeous as her younger sister and, being nineteen years old, showcased the added refinements and blossoming of adulthood.

"Hey, Mark …" I nudged him again.

"*S-h-u-t u-p!*" He hissed as he stared transfixed at her. "It'll be fine." Then almost to himself, "*Real fine!*"

When I opened up the borrowed bass guitar for the first time on the school's creaky wooden stage, I was swept with remorse. Rather than a Fender Precision or even a Jazzmaster—much more the norm for a funk or rock band—it was a Hofner bass. The Hofner bass was a somewhat obscure brand that had been adopted early on by Paul McCartney back when he didn't know how to play bass either (or buy one, for that matter). The Hofner bass had become a trademark for Paul McCartney. For me, it felt really creepy to be playing a violin-shaped, semi-hollow body bass in a band that was aspiring to play James Brown, Sly and the Family Stone, and Wilson Pickett. In my imagination, I saw people out on the dance floor at a high school prom looking up at us and saying, "Weird—the bass player is playing Paul McCartney's bass." But it, and the amp that came with it, were free. With every dollar I earned at the drugstore going into car parts, I was content enough to be the only funk bass player in the area—if not the nation—who played a Hofner bass.

It didn't sound so bad anyway, considering it was in the mix of a band that didn't sound all that good at first either. It was one thing to sing Otis Redding in the shower or rap out the rhythm to Marvin Gaye's "I Heard it Through the Grapevine" but quite another to pull it off with a half-dozen high school guys in a borrowed junior high school gym, but we got our act together pretty quickly. Mark appointed himself the authority on what songs we ought to be playing, seeing himself as the most astute about what songs were hot or represented some new vanguard of soul/funk music. Our guitar player, Grant, was masterful in knowing complex chords and moving from one to the next with some nice licks, but after I showed him how to play them with more of the "chicken scratch" style of James Brown or Tower of Power, I was appointed the music arranger, calling out the parts and determining whether the song was to be done as soul, funk, or rock. Davis, our sax player, was in charge of background vocals and working out brass section parts with Mark. Hampton's job was, first, to look good; second, to look like he owned the stage, as he did; third, to get the lyrics right, since just about everyone in the crowd would know these hits by hearts; and fourth, to sing on key. He nailed the first three.

At the end of our first practice, I was packing up and heading toward the twin metal doors that led to the parking lot when I realized that Mark had vanished. I leaned into the restroom and hollered for him but got no response. I went back toward the stage and pulled back a heavy, musty curtain covering a stairwell and found Mark curled over on the steps, his hands pressing against the sides of his head.

"What, had enough of our racket for the day?" I joked, poking him on the shoulder. He said nothing but shook his head, which was still cupped in his hands. "Hey, you all right?" I dropped down to the lower step to look up at him. He dropped his hands and looked out with a glazed stare.

"Man, I feel like my head's cracking in half."

"Got a headache?"

"Noo, man, it's when I play trumpet. It's like I get shin splints in my skull." Mark was a runner in track, so the best way he had to explain his agony was the feeling of runners who suffer nearly hairline fractures in their legs from running too long on a hard surface.

"You look like you're really hurting," I said. "Maybe this trumpet thing is not good for you." Mark's glazed stare boiled into a fiery glare.

"*I'm playing trumpet!*" he said through gritted teeth. "I got this band going, and I'm not about to bail because of a simple headache."

I stood there in stunned silence for a few seconds, and then Mark bounded up and grabbed his trumpet case. "I'll be all right," he assured me as well as himself and then headed out the door.

# # #

Chapter Eleven

"You sound tired." I'm calling Carol at a break in a client meeting in DC. Normally she's busy around the house by now or running errands. This morning, she's just running on empty.

"I was up late, or rather early," she sighs. "Mark called."

"Mark? When?"

"Two o'clock."

"In the morning?!"

"He was calling you, but I told him you were out of town. He wanted to talk."

"So you talked with him ..."

Yes, she says. For an hour. He probably just got confused about the difference in time zones, she says. Nothing was up. He was feeling okay, maybe a little down. Mostly just seemed to want to talk.

"He doesn't need to be calling you at two o'clock."

"Okay," Carol says. "Then be home the next time he calls and I'll hand the phone to you."

Mark calls again the next week. He is all wrapped around the axle about forgiveness—does God really forgive everything? Mark, I remind him, we covered that early on. Yes, I told you, yes. You need to accept and move on. Still, he persisted, beating on himself over it, like he either was desperate to be sure or just couldn't believe it.

Oddly, he never told me what it was he was afraid of. I'm pretty sure he has told Carol, because she just has that way of listening that lets people talk, but she never told me what it was if she knew.

It didn't matter. If I believed in forgiveness, it couldn't matter.

Mark is in a wrestling match of his own making over the next few weeks. The more he learns about God, the more he seems to get morose over his life and the mistakes he has made. The calls pick up in frequency and duration, and they come at all hours. One time he calls again in the middle of the night, when I am out of town on a consulting project. Again, Carol talks—*listens*—for an hour and then tells Mark that most problems don't feel as big after a good night's sleep, so go back to sleep.

"I'm not okay with this," I say testily as Carol tells me again of Mark's nocturnal call. "I'm going to talk with him."

"Don't." There was a firmness in Carol's voice. "If you do that, he might think we don't want to talk with him at all and he might stop calling."

Get him a clock for his birthday, I think to myself. One that is already set to Eastern Standard Time. I mean, I'm thrilled that I tracked down Mark. We shared a lot of good stories. He had a great week at the track, at the museum, sitting around the kitchen table; it's been great to catch up, and I love how he is so supportive of Lesley. I'm thrilled that he has accepted Jesus. Maybe I'm feeling a little absolved at this point for having knitted up all the loose ends. I'm even a little worried about the guy, with his moods and all. But the middle-of-the-night calls? I didn't buy into that. Mark should understand that. Most people would understand that.

I'm home this time when the phone rings in the predawn darkness of our bedroom. I reach for the phone to tell him off. Carol presses my arm back on the bed until she feels my muscles settle.

Then she answers the phone. I go back to sleep.

That weekend, I can hear my cell phone ringing, but I cannot find it—I am curled and cramped under the dashboard of my BMW, my arms buried deep into the wiring underneath and my pants pockets jammed up against the seat. Carol was going to call me when she finished driving to Louisville to visit some friends. I'd better get this. By the third ring I have pried myself loose enough to slip one hand into my pocket and pull out the phone. Without looking at the screen, I just punch "Answer" and press the phone to my ear.

"Paul, this is Mark."

"Oh, hey." Mark wasn't calling at two o'clock anymore, but just about all other hours were open season. He normally calls when he had something on his mind—even his impulses had a sense of mission. But mostly I am learning from Carol to listen. This day my listening matters. I hear it in his voice before he ever finishes with the words.

It's too much, he says. Too much time lost, too hard to make other friends who would put up with him, too hard to figure it out all. He wants to end it. He says he just wants to be with his Father-God where he can be safe.

"Mark, let's think this through." I know I can't just talk him out of it. He is too stubborn for that. I pull myself out from under the dash and stand against the car so I can concentrate. "If you really want to do this, at lot of us are going to miss you pretty badly. But you also need to be logical about this."

"I am," he counters.

"No, you're not. Have you made a will? Do you have someone lined up to take your dog? Have you arranged to have your magazine and newspaper subscriptions cancelled? Have you even catalogued your baseball card collection? You have a lot to do first." I keep going until I run out of tasks, hoping the obsessive part of him will click in.

"Okay," Mark says quietly. "I hadn't thought of all that."

After carefully going through the list, I remember something else.

"Mark, you said you always wanted to learn to play guitar. When's that going to happen?"

There's quiet on the line for a few seconds. "There's not enough time for that, Paul."

"Mark, there is as much time as you make for it." I promise him I will give him lessons over the phone. He buys it. By the time we finish the conversation, he is already talking about forming a blues band.

The whole thing is so surreal that it doesn't really hit me. I stuff the phone back in my pocket and crawl back under the dashboard. I snake the wires of a palm-sized engine diagnostics reading device up into darkness near the fuse box, plug them into a module, and look back at the blue-white screen of my PDA, peering at the screen and scrolling through the list of fault codes. You can just stop by an auto parts store and have them tell you what the benign and mindless "check engine" light means, but there is something to be said for self-sufficiency. Maybe I'm just cheap.

My neighbor Ray thinks I'm pretty amazingly smart to use all this technology. I don't. I feel dependent—enslaved to engine-management systems, on-board diagnostics, three-dimensional stability-control systems, and more built-in electronics and computer capacity than Jim Lovell had in front of him when he limped Apollo 13 back home after crewmate Jack Swigert accidentally blew up the oxygen tanks.

It is hard to argue with the quest for safety, but it has come at a cost to authenticity. Today's cars are antiseptic, distant, and so in control that they no longer invite or allow you to lose control. My current car's traction-control light blips on before I even hear the tires slipping. The engine-management light flashes me before I even feel the engine stumble, if it does at all. Everything is monitored and cross-checked in megabits of data per second against a database of performance parameters—anything out of whack and you get scolded with an amber "check engine" light, even if it is something as simple as being a few weeks away from needing to replace an oxygen sensor.

When I rebuilt the Beast, it spoke to me in a language that we makeshift mechanics understood. It was tactile, sensory, and instinctive—we could feel the heartbeat of the engine through the gas pedal and sense any out-of-place murmur as well as the best cardiologist reading the blips on an EKG. Before power steering took over, we knew what it was like to feel the road and could tell you with impressive precision whether the left or right front tire was scuffing from a slight misalignment or was just lacking a couple of pounds of air. When you grabbed the Hurst shifter just right, you could sense the spin of the synchros in your fingertips and just knew the exact split second to slam that transmission into the next gear, without a microchip somewhere adjusting the engine speed to match the gear. You knew the difference in whine between a failing wheel bearing and a differential pinion gear.

When you build your own engine, when you install your own clutch, when you tear down and piece back together your own transmission and differential, you know—you just *feel*—how things work together, and you can see them in your mind as they do. It is hard to argue against safety systems; they save lives and often rescue less-experienced drivers from their ignorance or reckless drivers from their stupidity. But there are times when modern systems are relieving us of our most basic responsibility to manage our lives. On my current car, I have to pull the door latch twice from the inside because some safety-crazed designer wants to make sure I don't just open the door accidentally for no good reason and fall out. If you ever saw James Dean playing chicken with Buzz in *Rebel Without a Cause* seconds before they reached that ocean cliff, you know darn well why you sometimes want to get out of a fast-moving car quickly—on the first pull of the door handle, thank you. These systems today would not have saved James Dean; they would have killed him. Then again, if he had airbags in that Porsche Speedster, maybe he would have been up on that Oscar stage doing dueling push-ups with Jack Palance back in 1992.

To: paul
From: mark
Subject: the beast lives

---

that one guy couldnt beat you so we beefed up his stereo instead, said his sound would bury you. ha ha we had good time hope you dont get frustrated with my speed; my vision still blures at times

I wasn't tired of Mark; I just needed a break sometimes. I had worked so hard on the Chevy that I felt a little burned out. You can get so caught up in the fury and the noise; you become trapped in it. I needed to get my bearings, settle into the routine I had missed so badly during most of my junior year. I was drawn to the notion of feeling settled a bit. Mark never settled.

I was also watching time in a way that Mark never could appreciate. While I had some friends among the juniors, many of my other friends at this point were seniors. I'm not sure how that happened, as dorky as I felt coming into the school, but it just did. As the spring headed toward summer, the second semester nearing its end, I became much more aware that part of my tenuous social network was about to unravel, and I wanted to spend as much time with them as I could.

Bones's gravel driveway continued to be the gathering place for that on most Sunday afternoons—me and Frankie, and Dirk even came by sometimes with his rusted, dented Bug. I was a little ticked at Frankie. There was a girl I had been chasing for a date for a few weeks, and Frankie thought it would work if we double-dated with his girlfriend. He never told me where we were going, and he offered to drive in his '57 convertible. We pulled up to a house on a quiet street where it looked like a party was ready to go into full swing, with cars lined up on both sides of the street and the front door ajar. We went in and just strolled around a bit, being polite to everyone but not seeing anyone else we knew. Then, almost on cue, everyone started drifting to the living room and sitting cross-legged on the floor in a circle. Somebody pulled out a guitar and everyone started singing; then one guy older than the rest flipped open a Bible and started reading from it.

I was livid but kept it inside as I turned to my date and asked her to join me in the hallway.

"I'm sorry," I said. "I did not know this was going to be some Jesus freak meeting." We couldn't leave since Frankie drove, but I asked her if she just wanted to sit outside until it was over.

"No," she said gently. "I'm actually okay with it. I'd like to stay."

I rejoined the circle but stayed on the outside edge, counting the minutes until the study and singing ended. I met Frankie at the front door.

"Thanks," I spit out. "I finally get a date with this girl and you pull this over on me."

Frankie apologized, but in a way that seemed to suggest regret on the approach but not the intent. "I thought you might like it," he said with his hand on my shoulder. "Sorry, really, but I hope you might want to come back someday."

We never talked about it again, even on the next few weekends when we were hanging out in the black-lighted out-building or crawling around on the gravel of Bones's driveway working on the cars. For the Chevy owners, Bones's driveway was a mini-junkyard of its own. Behind a shed next to the house was a lean-to, normally reserved for lawn mowers and tools, but we had evacuated its more urbane contents and stuffed it with a cornucopia of Chevy parts—manifolds, carburetors, linkages, shocks, even a crankshaft with rusted journals. It was somehow comforting to work on your car amid such flotsam—it was not so much that any of it was usable, but it created an ambiance that seemed to authenticate us as real backyard mechanics.

Every culture set, though, has its subcultures, and ours was just around the corner and a half mile down the road at the home of Napper, one of Bones's buddies. The homes on his street were decidedly more modest; some were just really a mess—paint peeling from garage door panels, driveways scarred with cracks and holes, weeds lying lazily on what were once lawns. Napper's house was like that—it was a small ranch home that had not had a coat of paint since Eisenhower last played eighteen holes at Congressional. The front door was faded and hidden behind a screen door that had long ago lost its place in the doorjamb opening, and it suffered gaping holes like a pair of torn fishnet stockings.

Napper himself displayed some raggedness and road wear for a guy his age. Swarthy and thin, with a plaster of black hair greased and combed back in not so much as a style as to keep it out of the way. He was a senior at our high school, but I rarely saw him there. Most times when I saw Napper he was lying on the crackled asphalt of his driveway taking apart or putting together a motorcycle.

The first time I met him, Bones had driven me over on a Sunday afternoon when we got tired of fiddling with our respective Chevys. When we pulled into Napper's driveway, I saw him stretched out on the driveway, his round-toed boots sticking up from the end of a stained pair of jeans. He wore a white T-shirt; actually he *always* wore a white T-shirt—or at least one that used to be white. The sleeves were usually either rolled up or cut off. From the garage, a makeshift stereo blared Creedence Clearwater Revival. The speakers were small and hung from the rafters of the garage with coat hangers. The turntable was perched on a wooden shelf, covered by a scratched plastic dust cover.

Sadly, I did not know much about motorcycles. My only reference point was fragile and comical, having grown up to the Hondells' "Little Honda" *("First gear, it's all right ... third gear, hang on tight ...").* I knew that there were more formidable machines out there, but I somehow had never encountered one in close quarters, except for my hitches on Rocky's Harley. Napper's bike was unlike anything I had ever seen. There was nothing elegant or refined about it. It was pure utility and raw machinery, stripped down to the frame, with a balloon-like gas tank draped over the top bar and heavy gears and an engine that was caked with grime. Throttle cables hung from the handlebars; the rubber grips were shiny from wear.

As Bones introduced me, Napper rolled out from under the bike and punched a thumbs-up and a toothy grin. I kept looking at the bike trying to spot a logo or some other evidence of its make. I gave up.

"It's a Beezer," Bones noted helpfully.

I was too embarrassed to ask what a Beezer was, so I just nodded knowingly.

"I have an Indian in the garage if you want to see it," Napper called out from under the bike. I shuffled over to the garage and looked inside its dark interior, half expecting to see some antique wooden Indian figurine like you might find standing guard at a general store or tobacco shop somewhere in New Mexico back in the '50s. With the stereo blasting "Green River" *("Yeahhhh ... c'mon home to Green River ...")* I glanced over to the wooden workbench. It was nothing more than an old, thick pine door, scarred with knife marks, hammer blows, and deep fissures, laid across two saw horses. Spread all over its surface were parts—pistons, piston rings, valves, valve springs, piston cylinder sleeves, gear housings, single-throat carburetors, throttle cables, headlights—enough parts to put together a whole extra Beezer, I had to assume, if you knew how to put together a Beezer. In the back, half-covered by a musty canvas tarp, was another motorcycle, this one also in a state of repair or disrepair. I took that to be the Indian but did not ask.

All that hardware spread throughout the garage was like an entire box of Legos or Lincoln logs strewn across a carpeted living-room floor on Christmas afternoon—everything you needed was there, but it took some fierce imagination and even more time to assemble it into anything workable or recognizable. I wouldn't have known where to start, but Napper did. By this time, I was pretty comfortable taking apart a Chevy engine, but motorcycles seemed different. There seemed to be some level of improvisation, especially when you were swapping engines, changing gear ratios, and chopping and extending the front forks. It was a vocational art form to get all that geometry right and get everything to fit without finding yourself frying your pant leg on an exhaust pipe that stuck out too far or spitting flames up your crotch from a too-rich carburetor coughing back an intake backfire.

Sunday afternoons at Napper's were all about bikes—and Creedence Clearwater. There is only so much of "Suzie Q" and "Willy and the Poor Boys" you can stand. One day when CCR was grating on my nerves like a four-inch grinder cutting through a driveshaft, I found a few dog-eared album jackets in his garage—Jimi Hendrix's *Are You Experienced,* Led Zeppelin II (with its signature opening track "Whole Lotta Love"*)* and Marvin Gaye's *What's Going On.* I tried to slip the latter on top of the turntable when Napper rolled out from under the Beezer and tossed an open-end wrench my way.

"Hey, leave it," he scolded. "I like CCR." Napper's old turntable had an arm for holding up a stack of records; if you just lifted it up and away from the center spindle, the tone arm would think the album was a new one and would just go back to the beginning and play it over and over. To this day, I think I can remember the order of all the songs on the A-side of the *Green River* album.

One particularly bright Sunday afternoon, a machine-gun blast of four-stroke exhaust notes slapped the air behind us, and the driveway crunched under the tires of a motorcycle pulling into Napper's place. We turned around to see a monstrous machine of light blue lacquer and chrome, thick tires, and the grinning face of Rocky, his meaty hands wrapped around the grips, twisting the throttle as the engine barked out through the twin exhaust. Napper spun out from under the Beezer and practically leaped in the air.

"Whoa—you got a Trump!"

Now I was really lost—first a Beezer, then an Indian, and now a Trump.

"Triumph," Bones nudged me. "That's a kick-ass bike."

(whump—whump) "It's (whump-whump) a (whump-whump) 650!" Rocky bellowed above the thump of the engine and then cranked the throttle as if to validate the statement. (whap-whap-whaaapp) The ground shook, and waves of pressure from each pulse of the engine enveloped me.

"My last blast before The Marines get me and stick me in a helicopter," Rocky said as much to himself as anyone as he shut down the engine.

So now Napper's driveway each Saturday and Sunday afternoon, and often Friday evenings, was a biker haven of sorts—Napper, the skinny, quiet mechanic, and Rocky the bawdy, beefy counterpoint—all drenched in the sloppy and mindless guitar leads of Fogerty and CCR. It actually surprised me that Napper was so devoted to the shallow and carping sound of CCR; he was actually quite bright. That was never more apparent to me than when my parents were getting rid of an old console stereo and I managed to strip out the old tube amplifier that was buried in the cobwebs and dust in the base cabinet. Unknown to me, the amp was to drive the bass speakers only, so when I tried to hook it up in my garage to serve as a more permanent stereo than Mark's Impala with its windows open, the sound was muddy and booming. I nestled it in the trunk of my '57 and took it over to Napper's, hoping he might know something or be willing to trade it.

When I explained the problem, Napper carried the amp to his grimy wooden workbench, blowing off the dust on the tubes and digging his wiry fingers into the mass of wires and components.

"This is easy," he said to himself. "There are too many capacitors running to the ground in the middle power circuit. Kills the high end every time." Without hesitation or permission, he sorted through the tools on the bench, gripped a pair of needle-nose wire cutters, and quickly reached into the jungle of wires. I winced at each snip—snip as he clipped the capacitors and they skittered to the floor.

"Here," he handed the amp back to me. "That should do it."

It did. I never saw Napper in an electronics class; there were no Popular Science or Modern Electronics or Stereo Review magazines anywhere in that garage. Yet when it came to simply knowing what needed to be done with just about any kind of equipment, Napper had a knack. Over the next few weeks, I watched him at work on his motorcycle. To the annoying bleating of John Fogerty, Napper took apart that whole Beezer and put it back together—tuned, aligned, and tight as the drum kick in Chicago's "25 or 6 to 4." But what really amazed me was that when he first started it up—a crucial and defining moment for anyone rebuilding an engine of any size or purpose—he shut it down within seconds.

"It's not right," he declared. "It's running lean, and the timing's a bit early." No scopes, no gauges, no fancy sensors, not even a manual or tune-up guide. Napper eschewed them all; instead he just listened to the engine, held his fingers lightly against the cooling fins, or held his palm against the exhaust, sniffing the invisible residue like it was a fine wine. Then he just went to work and fixed it. First time, every time. Watching Napper, I learned to set aside the more clinical tools you might use to analyze or tune up an engine and went with the sensors built into my fingertips, nose, eyes, and ears.

If you listen carefully, you can tell when the mixture is too lean—the engine literally *sounds* thin and anemic. Same with too rich of a mixture— it sounds thick, heavy, the way your voice gets just moments before you need to cough up some phlegm. Ignition timing is the same way: retard the spark too much and the engine lags and almost sputters when it tries to accelerate; advance it too much and the engine feels rushed and strained. It is hardly some Zen-like deal to be "of one" with a cast-iron machine that has no soul, no ties to the earth, no regard for natural rhythms. Yet there was something to be said for knowing the idiosyncrasies and nearly subconscious nuances between you and your car and its engine.

I learned a lot from Napper. We all did. Rocky got his Trump running for the dirt. I learned how to set ignition timing without a scope. Bones learned how to adjust the bands on his Powerglide transmission. No books. Just Napper.

I also learned that, as capable as someone is on any given day, it does not always mean they feel they have control. Napper's stereo was cranking out Fogerty's "Run Through the Jungle" when Napper just stood up from his crouch near the bike and sat back on the leather seat.

"You know what that's about?" he asked.

"No, I don't pay attention to Creedence."

"It's about 'Nam, man." Napper shrugged, like we were all supposed to know. "Run through the jungle, two million guns, devil's on the loose." He got quiet.

"You worried about 'Nam?" I asked, curious about a side of Napper I had not seen.

"I try not to worry about things I can't change by worrying about them, man." His voice had a resigned, weary sound to it. "Everybody else is going to get off by going to college, maybe Canada if they're chicken. Me? Heck, I don't know. I'll probably end up there. That's how it works."

The rest of the day seemed quieter. Up to that point, I was a junior who was, in every other way, treated as and considered a senior. But at that moment, I realized there was a world of time and place between being seventeen and eighteen.

Early on the Fourth of July weekend, a bunch of us planned a party on Fire Mountain. It was to be a good crowd—Greek, Mark, Burnside, Sconze with his new set of headers and side exhausts on his Nova SS, Brat with his newly lowered Corvair, Boomer with his latest wheels on his Vega, and a matching number of girls, mostly from the varsity cheerleading squad. The gathering, though not openly expressed, had an ominous undertow—it was the day the Vietnam draft lottery numbers would be announced. The Vietnam War seemed far away during most of the school year. Strangely, as much as the culture of our experimental high school invited and fomented fierce political debate and social consciousness, the horror of the Kent State shooting barely earned a passing comment on the front lawn at lunch the next day from the junior class. Maybe it was too far away, that small college in Ohio, or maybe the whole concept of America being rent in half over a war a half world away was too surreal.

On this day, though, the war knocked on our front door and dragged us all out of bed to the front lawn, naked, waiting to get our number. The draft lottery numbers were to be drawn by birthday. Get lucky and get picked in the top third and you were going to 'Nam, baby, unless you snagged a deferment. The easiest although not always the most reliable path was to simply get a pass to go to college, the odd rationale being that a mind was a terrible thing to waste on a riverbed in the Mekong Delta. The other deferment was physical—you had to have some chronic malady or incapacitation that made you unfit for the rigors of a swift boat or jungle patrol. I was 4F—hopelessly nearsighted and amblyopic in one eye, so I was in the clear. The myths and methods that built up around 4F were legendary, the best being Mark's advice that if you swallowed aluminum foil scraps the day before your x-ray, they would show up as stomach ulcers. It could easily have been, after swallowing all that aluminum foil, that those blobs on the x-ray *were* stomach ulcers.

The most unsettling deferment was CO—conscientious objector. Despite the clearly liberal slant of our faculty and the growing presence and voice of the antiwar crowd at our school, there was still something *unmanly* about saying you just couldn't muster the emotional fortitude to serve in the military. For a lot of us Ducks and the jocks, the view at the time was to take your odds, but if your number came up, you get over it and do your job. If you survive, come back and vote out the bastards who sent you over there, but you don't get to pick when to be a citizen and when not. There were a couple of COs in our class, and somehow everything was different between them and their classmates the rest of the year, once they declared what to some was courage, to others cowardice.

On this date in early July, not everyone knew his deferment status. The odd thing about the lottery was that you had the game plan ahead of time. You would know your number, and then you could scramble around to get a deferment if you wanted to avoid getting called. It is debatable whether the draft was needed or the right thing to do in such a scalding, divisive conflict like Vietnam, but it sure did wonders for convincing high school guys to go to college and get good grades.

Normally, when we drove up the winding road to Fire Mountain, Mark was exuberant, looking every bit the part of a dog sticking its head out of the window as he leaned out to relish the sound of the Chevy's exhaust echoing off the rock walls. Today, he was moody and sullen. I rarely noticed Mark's mood swings before, other than what we all knew to be his propensity for taking his emotions to whatever precipice was nearby, but they seemed to be appearing more frequently, sometimes at the slightest provocation. They were not just fleeting bad moods. They were full-lock power slides into a dark funk. When he was in one, I could not talk him out; I just had to wait it out.

"I'm screwed," he muttered, staring out the window but clearly not really taking in the view. "I'm going to 'Nam. I can just feel it."

He did not cheer up much when we arrived at the mountain's peak, where other students were unloading their caches of burgers, soft drinks, and the occasional contraband six-pack. One car was declared Music

Central—it had a powerful enough stereo and a decent collection of eight-track tapes where it would serve as our boom box. But as the party wore on, another set of radios began to compete. They were tuned to KFRC in San Francisco, which was going to interrupt their Top-40 playlist with a bulletin announcing what dates had been drawn for the lottery draft.

The mood thickened as the hour approached. Mark and I retreated a bit from the crowd and sat on my '57 as the music stinger sounded on KFRC, signaling a news bulletin. Everyone fell silent as the announcer made some introductory remarks that were totally unnecessary for this crowd; we knew what this was, why it mattered, for crying out loud. Just get on with the numbers.

It did not take long. The first date picked—the number-one slot that assured someone born on that day would be getting their draft notice during their senior year—was July 9. You could hear an "Oh, crap!" in the crowd around the radio, and then everyone spun around to see who it was. Danny, a popular guy in our class, a varsity wrestler, one of the Ducks, was standing there as if someone had slapped him. Courtesy dictated we wait until at least a few more dates were called; none elicited the shock of Danny's date getting picked. Being number twenty was not good; neither was twenty-eight or thirty-three. But to be number one in the Vietnam War lottery draft was a real punch in the gut. It felt like they had singled you out.

# # #

Chapter Twelve

Mark hasn't brought up suicide again since I gave him the list. Neither have I. Why bring it up—let him work off the list and come back for more. Our conversations have shifted to guitars, blues music, some politics, a lot more about God, and back to music. I'm more patient now, maybe just because I see how patient Lesley and Carol can be with him. Sometimes, frankly, I'm a little envious. I'm working every day, traveling most, trying to keep up with things, never mind have a decent conversation with Carol over the phone from some hotel or on a Saturday morning when I have a clock full of chores ahead just to catch up. We're tight—that part's good—but we're busy. Mark gets to talk whenever he wants to, as long as he wants to. As long as Carol will listen.

So maybe it's good that Carol and I have switched roles in managing this relationship with Mark. At first, I was the one ready to put off some daily tasks to track him down, make those first calls, get him out here to visit, even take him around town for a week, while Carol just watched politely from a distance but kept everything else in the household moving.

Now I'm finding it hard to talk very long on the phone, even though Mark seems to need to talk more and longer than ever. His conversations sometimes are deep but also meandering, vulnerable. His view of the future is through a short-focus lens; he can look forward to something the next day but seems to lack the hope or confidence to see beyond that. He also, oddly enough, does not dwell on memories. It is as if his past and his future are both too far away from today.

So I'm really okay with Carol talking with him; it's my proxy for feeling like I can still be there for him when, really, I am not. But even she's getting disciplined about it. She cradles the phone on her shoulder and goes about the house doing the things she normally does—cleaning up the kitchen, doing my business accounting work on her computer, making lunch, picking up our dog's poops in the backyard when I'm away traveling—all the while seeming to give Mark all the time and attention in the world.

Sometimes when she hangs up I can see her quietly smiling. Other times she has been quietly crying.

It's a gift; I'm telling you.

It's been a few months now since I talked to Mark about getting a guitar, and a few weeks since our last lesson on the phone ("Mark, the pentatonic scale is easy. It's the opening guitar line to the Temptations' 'My Girl' … "). We've missed his call today, being out at dinner, but see the message light blinking when we come home that evening. We punch the code for voice mail and hear a rustling before Mark's voice comes on.

"Check this out!" There is more rattling as we can hear that he has propped the phone up on a counter, and then the sound of his guitar. The riff is unmistakable: the opening George Harrison guitar part to "Here Comes the Sun."

Mark had mastered it.

To: paul
From: mark
Subject: the beast the best

Funny when you blew you engine ha the Beast is dead but you never gave up my hand is real tired … sorry

My younger brother Mike started taking an interest in the car now that it was running and really taking shape, often finding excuses to have me drop him off somewhere so he could goad me into lighting it up at a stoplight. He often would be riding his bike down the street with Cindy, our Weimaraner dog, on a leash galloping behind him and would pretend to race me when I drove past. One Saturday, I was working under the Chevy trying to adjust part of the suspension and I could hear Mark and Mike whispering and scurrying back and forth around the back of the car. I finished up and slid myself on the cardboard mat out from under the car and stood up to see the two of them waiting for me.

"Hey, big brother," Mike said with a practiced air of casualness, "ever wonder how fast Cindy can run?"

"Not really." I said. "Fast enough, I guess. Why?"

"Nothin'." He shot a smirk over at Mark. "Just wondering."

Mark and I had to go to the auto parts store, so I backed the Chevy out of the garage. Mark jumped in at shotgun, Mike got in back, and Cindy stayed behind obediently in the garage. Just as I started to accelerate up the hill, Mark and Mike both leaned out of the window and shouted in unison "C'mon, Cindy, fetch." The dog leaped from a dead stop, put her head down and locked in her olive eyes on my rear bumper and came at us like a gunmetal gray missile.

"Go! Go!" my brother yelled over to me. "She's catching up." I shifted into second and fed the engine with about a half throttle as the 348 responded with a growl. I watched her fall back in my rearview mirror, but then she kicked into another gear and quickly closed the gap.

I was coming up to a right-hand turn near the thirteenth hole of our golf course, the same turn I had made the first day I got the car running. I made the turn and looked in the rearview mirror—no dog. My brother was yelling out the side window, "Yeah, Cindy, c'mon girl." Rather than continuing to trail behind my Chevy, Cindy had cut across the thirteenth green, her paws churning up some of the manicured bent grass green, trying to cut us off at the pass. A group of golfers approaching the green stared in horror and fury. That was it—I braked the Chevy to a halt. There was a thump from the rear as the Weimaraner leaped against the back of the car. I heard growling as I jumped out of the car and ran around to the rear. On the rear bumper, tied with twine, was a mangled package of ground beef.

By now Mark and Mike had jumped out of the other side, high-fiving each other and patting the panting Cindy on her head for her role in the escapade.

My brother called her over and opened up the door.

"What are you *doing?*" I reached to close the door.

"We need to take her back home. She's exhausted."

"We are *not* taking a dog back anywhere in my car," I was not about to have dog hair and slobber on my nice new interior. I knew enough to know that having your date pick gray dog hair off her pants or blouse was not conducive to the prospects of a second date. So my brother Mike and Cindy trudged home as Mark and I went on to the auto parts store in silence before Mark finally spoke.

"That was *awesome,* wasn't it?"

With the Chevy now falling into place as a date machine and band bus, I was enjoying it fully for the first time. It was a point of pride, and equal reassurance, to walk out to the car in the early morning of a summer day, wipe the dew from the outside mirror and window with my shirtsleeve, and turn the key knowing that the 348 was just waiting to get on with its work for the day.

I should have just let well enough alone, but a few days after I scored a new carburetor—a Holley 650 dual pumper—from a guy who was "parting out" his car (slowly dismembering a car that may be worth more in pieces than whole), I was at Bones's place bolting it on and reattaching the linkage that connects the rod from the gas pedal to the throttle of the carburetor.

"Sure that'll fit?" asked Bones.

"Yea, it's a straight bolt-on," I assured him and myself.

Later that day, I had brought my younger brother Ed to town to pick up something and while driving back must have made a big brother boast about having installed a new, larger carburetor.

"Punch it, then," he coaxed.

I guess there's something about younger brothers that makes you do stupid things to show how smart you are, so I floored it. We were on an open stretch of the main road, at least a half mile away from the freeway overpass where we might have to watch for traffic, so I was fine just grabbing a little rubber in a couple of gears before I would have to back it off. When I shifted into second gear, I kept my foot on the gas to smoke the tires a bit but was pleasantly surprised with how the car seemed to surge forward as if the engine was really enjoying taking in the air/fuel mixture in such large gulps. I shifted into third for just a second to prove I could burn the tires a bit but then quickly let off the gas to start slowing down before the overpass.

The gas pedal did not come up. The car, rather than slowing down, was streaking ahead. With a chill racing through me like an ice shower, I looked down at the tach to see it climbing steadily. In a split second, I realized that I had a stuck throttle. My brother was still whooping it up in the passenger seat, but I swept into action, cramming the toe of my shoe under the gas pedal to pry it up. This should not be a problem. Throttles can just stick sometimes. I lifted my toe back hard to pop the gas pedal back.

The gas pedal did not budge.

By now, the tach was sweeping toward a redline of sixty-five hundred rpm, the 348 was screaming for its life, and my brother suddenly fell silent. With sounds that I never want to hear again—popping, shrieking, thumping, grinding, and a searing howl—the engine blew.

My brother pulled his white-knuckled hands off the metal dash and stared out the window. "Wow!" he breathed. "Did you mean to do that?"

I sat there for a few seconds, taking deep cleansing breaths, squeezing and releasing my hands on the steering wheel. Then I reached for the door handle, stepped to the front of the car, and gingerly released the hood latch to survey the carnage.

It was as if someone had died of a heart attack but still had their last expression frozen on their face. The engine appeared normal, despite some ominous hissing and groaning. I poked around and found the culprit—the carburetor had a massive linkage plate on the side that had caught on the intake manifold when I floored the pedal, and it had jammed in a wide-open position.

I slid back into the front seat and turned the key. The only noise was a rasping clatter from the starter motor, metal against metal. The engine ignoring the prodding, silent in death. It was "locked up" in the parlance of gear heads. I felt like I had died with it.

I called Bones, and he came down in his Chevy with an armful of thick rope. Back then, we did not have the luxury of rigid tow bars, so we just looped the rope around his back bumper and my front bumper, trying to leave a respectable amount of slack between them so I had a chance to stop if Bones did. Bones towed me and my brother all the way home, with me riding the brake nervously, keeping my speed the same as his lead car. No reason to have me get a reputation for taking out two '57 Chevys in one day.

We rolled the Beast into the driveway, unhooked the ropes, and stood there for a moment, letting the magnitude of the event sink in.

"Sorry, man," Bones finally spoke. "You worked on that thing." He coiled the rope around his long arm, tossed it in his trunk, and drove away respectfully.

The next morning I went outside in denial, as if the event had been a bad dream overnight. I turned the key with as much confidence as a paramedic uses shock paddles on a guy dragged from a muddy river and was met again with the telltale grinding of the starter motor against the flywheel.

So months of work—no, toil—and it was wasted. I was no longer some cool guy who had rebuilt a junker into a respectable muscle car. I was just a fool with a junker again. I broke the news to Mark that night on the phone. He was, as always, reassuring and optimistic, but I knew that this was not something that got fixed easily, or affordably. I called Cristy and she, characteristically, asked if she could help. No, I told her, not this time. This was serious stuff. Which also meant that I had no idea where to start.

Frankie came to my rescue in a most unsuspecting and even sacrificial way. By now, Frankie had all but despaired of getting his '57 convertible running well, with its balky and esoteric fuel-injected engine. Also, as a graduated senior, Frankie was pondering his options as the Vietnam draft loomed and the more frivolous distractions of high school were beginning to pale. Frankie made a proposition: he would trade his 283 straight across for my locked-up 348. He's nuts, I thought. His engine works; mine doesn't.

"Nah," he shrugged. "I'm just not into it any more. I'm going after a college deferment or something, so I have to start landing a college placement and stop messing around with cars. Your car is just getting going. Mine is shot. I'm going to junk it, but it ought to have an engine in it, even if the engine doesn't work."

Frankie said the whole deal was fine, as long as I did the work. He had no idea how to swap engines. Neither did I. The only guy I knew who either knew everything there was to know about jerry-rigging cars or made it up when he didn't was Woofer, my persona non grata guitar buddy from church. First, anyone who can keep a real early '50s Jeep Willys rolling under its own power is way ahead on points right there. He also had served on the pit crew for a well-known off-road racing team at the Baja 500—maybe it was a Baja 1000; I don't remember, but it sounded impressive—and seemed to have a nonchalant confidence about what it took to keep a four-wheeling truck rolling across the desert as parts fell off of it. Sure enough, when I broached the project with him, his response was typical Woofer: "Sure, sounds fun. When and where do we do it?"

The answer came with my next call to Bones. We needed to pick a time when his father was out of town flying; otherwise there was no way we would ever get away with using his garage. Bones said his dad was flying Friday night, returning late Saturday night, so we would have a clean twenty-four-hour window to pull it off. Should be easy.

Mark did not know Bones very well and had never met Woofer, but I called him anyway because he had been such a part of everything to this point, and I was sure there was no way he was going to miss this.

"Oh, man," he groaned over the phone. "I'm working all morning at the drugstore."

"Okay, that's fine," I said. "You can just stop by Friday night for the first part."

There were a few moments of silence on the other end. Then he practically giggled. "I can't make it, man. I mean I *can't* make it!"

"That's fine, but what's up?"

"I'm in looooove ..."

So you got the date with Jolene that night. Good for you, buddy.

At eight o'clock sharp, with Bones's dad on the road out of town, we knotted a thick rope between my Chevy and Woofer's Jeep and dragged the carcass of my '57 to the gravel staging area—the driveway at Bones's house.

Woofer was the pit boss and, we discovered, a pretty respectable equipment and supplies manager. He unloaded a giant dark green metal toolbox, an extra hydraulic jack, three bags of potato chips, and two six-packs of beer.

"So," he said, inspecting the garage bay. "Where's the engine hoist?"

Bones and I blinked blankly at each other, and Woofer blanched. "You don't have an engine hoist? How are we supposed to pull an engine without an engine hoist?"

Bones improvised on the spot, untying the drag rope from my car and looping it over the center roof beam in the garage. With one person guiding the engine and transmission out of its resting place, and the other two—okay, maybe we would have to call Napper to help—hauling on it for all their weight would allow, we should be able to lift out the whole mess with a few testosterone- and adrenaline-fueled pulls. Woofer and Bones spent the first hour psyching up for the procedure by drinking beer while I nervously paced around my and Frankie's cars trying to size up the situation. By nine o'clock, with the sun fully retreated for the night and with only a couple of bare bulbs in the garage to shed any light on our situation, we began.

Pulling Frankie's engine took a while—until well past midnight— simply because we kept forgetting to disconnect something and would have to lower the engine each time to do it. Woofer also needed to fashion a rig with some chain and bolts to secure the rope to the intake manifold.

With Frankie's engine lying on the garage floor, we wheeled his convertible out of the garage onto the gravel drive and then rolled my moribund Chevy into the operating room. I draped the front seat with a towel. "I don't want you guys sitting on my nice clean seats with your greasy pants," I explained. "And keep your grimy elbows and mitts off the door panels. They're brand new."

By now, we were fairly adept at the pre-op protocols and had my engine lying beside Frankie's within a couple of hours. All three of us had had enough beers and done enough work that night. When we saw the old plastic clock on the garage wall showing 3:00 am, it was all we needed to convince ourselves to crash for a few hours and renew the project by the early light of dawn.

By morning, fortified with sugar-frosted donuts and orange juice, we set about the second part of the project—getting my engine into Frankie's car and his into mine. For some reason—perhaps it was the beer or the lack of sleep—we started on Frankie's car. It really made no sense, since the engine didn't run, and destined as it was for the junkyard, we could have put the engine in the trunk for all we or anyone else cared. Nonetheless, we were now into the late morning shoehorning the 348 into Frankie's car, with me underneath trying to line up the engine mounts and Woofer and Bones hauling on the rope.

"Down a bit. No, too much. Up a bit. Wait …"

"We can't hold it! *Hurry up!*"

"Okay, I got it." *Clang* "Wait"—I dropped the bolt. "Okay, up again, just a little …"

"Dammit, Heagen—can't you put a bolt in a hole?"

And so it went for what seemed like hours. We rolled my Chevy back into the garage for what was now our fourth and final engine procedure. As before, we lashed the rope to the Woofer rig on the intake manifold and hauled the 283 to where it was dangling above the engine compartment, creaking slowly on the rope as I slid underneath to line up the engine mounts. We had this down cold.

On cue, Woofer and Bones lowered the 283 and it nestled into place, a ship coming home to a familiar dock. We were lining up the mounting flanges when suddenly a *c-c-c-rack* echoed through the rafters. We froze. Bones looked up to where the rope was tensed like a piano wire over the center beam of the garage. At first, you could only hear it, not see it—another *c-c-crack*—and then Bones saw the crack come into view in all of its inevitable clarity. The beam bowed, and the crack fissured its way across the grain of wood.

"*She's gonna go!!!*" We all stood paralyzed again for that same half second as our brains ran the calculus—will the beam hold out long enough to get the two engine mount bolts in, or do we save the beam and end up with an engine on the floor, with no way to get it in the car, and with Bones's dad now just a few hours away from returning home?

Bones made the call.

"*Go! Go!! Go!!! Go!!!!*"

I spun around under the car and slammed the first engine mount bolt home with the heel of my hand, reached behind me without looking, grabbed the next bolt while rolling on the floor like Warren Well in double coverage snatching an over-the-shoulder bomb from Ken Stabler in the end-zone, and slammed that one home as well.

"*Got it!*"

Bones and Woofer released the rope, and the beam wheezed once more and then fell quiet.

"I'm screwed," Bones declared, looking into the darkness of the rafters. It was now three o'clock, only three hours before the Angel of Death appeared back at the garage. Woofer, the ebullient and resilient innovator, came up with the notion of cranking the beam back into place with a makeshift jig—stacking everything we could find to make a tower in the middle of the garage and then using a car jack to crank the beam back into place. Bones rummaged around the shed in back and emerged with a couple of two-by-six boards, which we then nailed into place on both sides of the crippled beam. With barely an hour to spare now, we buttoned up the remaining two mounting bolts on the Frankie engine now in my Chevy and rolled it back to the driveway, scurrying back to the garage to put all the tools back on their felt-marked places on the pegboard, throw away the beer cans and potato chip bags, and polish away any oil residue on the floor.

We were back out in the driveway reattaching linkages, drive shafts, fuel lines, and wiring when we heard the gravel crunching as Bones's dad pulled into the driveway.

"Hey, Dad, how was the flight?" Bones called out with poker-faced innocence.

"Fine," he replied as he spied my legs sticking out from under the Chevy. "You boys keep those cars out in the driveway."

That was the last time I ever saw Bones. As we headed into late summer, Bones, Napper, Woofer, and Rocky were crossing over into that opaque new world called "early adulthood." Rocky went into boot camp, coming back for a two-week leave looking and sounding like nobody we knew. Frankie was thinking of working at a drug and alcohol rehab center. Woofer went to Reno, got his degree, and slipped into a small town to be a firefighter. I lost track of Bones and Napper.

Everyone's lives were now being absorbed with college, pondering their options with the Vietnam War draft, paying for apartments, having a parting hug or a parting argument with a parent, breaking up with a high school girlfriend, knowing that their lives would forever change. The last thing on their minds after that Saturday was whether a Holley 850 fit on a stock 348 manifold (it did not) whether you could replace the worthless fuel-injection system on a 283 with a regular manifold (you can) and what a junked-out '57 Chevy convertible with a blown 348 engine would get at salvage (who cares).

For those twenty-four hours or so, we were just friends helping friends; a bunch of guys doing the impossible and having an impossibly good time. Life would inevitably be harder for all of us in many ways after that day—scoring deferment-qualified grades, getting jobs, getting on with what life throws at you to manage—but for a day we had done the hardest thing we knew how to do at that point, and it wasn't so tough after all.

#

Chapter Thirteen

Carol and I are on the phone now with Mark several times a week. Carol has this way of encouraging him when he is down and admonishing him when he becomes too self-absorbed in his views. It's those questions she always asks after she listens. *So, Mark, what do you have to be grateful about?* I find myself most often just listening and offering some advice where it seems to fit or is welcomed. Mark is fierce about his faith—it is more than a lifeline; it is a steel cable that somehow keeps him tethered to something bigger than just daily realities. One thing about giving a Bible to a person with obsessive/compulsive disorder—they'll read it. Mark read the Bible four times through in the space of a year. In many ways, he is obsessive and compulsive about his relationship with Jesus; I am not always sure if it is a consuming passion or just consumption. When he talks about God, he seems calmer, more settled, and more centered.

Yet at other times he seems fretful, desperate, needing to talk with someone. We often do—for hours at a time, and at all hours of the day or night. We know something is wrong, but we do not know what. Lesley keeps up her notes despite the pressures of law school. Carol answers the phone amid the demands of a grandson under her care during the day. I call back when I can, even though it is often on a cell phone at a distant airport.

"Heard back yet from Mark?" Carol greets me at the door after another week on the road.

No, I had not. I had called three times that week after we didn't' get our normal flurry of calls from him. Usually he gets back in a day or two, but not this time. Carol calls that night and leaves her own message. It's not a big deal, I convince myself. Maybe he drove down to Fresno again to visit his aging grandmother. Then again, Mark is not driving as much these days, with his bad eyes and all. We wait two more days, with another message in there somewhere, and finally call another number, one that had never left my memory, even though it had been at least thirty years since I last called it.

"Paul, oh my. How are you doing? How is your family?" Mark's mother's voice seems timeless to me. She may have been terrified of the Beast back then, but she treated me like a second son and never complained about the racket when the Beast pulled into her driveway on those summer days between my junior and senior year.

"Betty, sorry to bother you, but I've been trying to reach Mark. He always calls me back, but I haven't heard from him."

"Oh, you know what he did, Paul?" Betty sounds amused by it, but still with that unmistakable tone of a mother caught between scolding and concern. "He slipped in the shower last week and hit his head. He's still a little dizzy, but he'll be fine, I guess. He just needs some rest."

I finally get through to Mark three days later but then make another call to Betty. I'm startled by how Mark sounds so unfocused, his speech sluggish. He had fallen again, twice, she says. They will be taking him to the doctor. He may have pinched a nerve.

Something like that.

---

baby moon covers; 409 w duals w glass packs and rear air shocks because of wide meats and small racing steering wheel and ah that craig 8 track good memories friend.

Frankie's 283 engine was simply not like my old 348. It lacked the punch and grunt of the 348. Mark heard about a guy in the next town who was selling a 409 short block—basically just the lower part of the engine with the pistons, crank, and flywheel but no heads, valves, or intake manifold—for a whopping one hundred dollars. The 409, the center of lyrical attention in the Beach Boys' 1968 hit "409," was a beast in its own right. It easily generated 400 horsepower and equal numbers of torque and, with only a modest amount of coaxing, could push 425 horsepower or more. To buy one for a hundred bucks, if it was in any shape at all, was a steal—and it would be all I needed to convince myself that my temporary

283 had to go. I bought the engine the next week with eighty dollars cash and a promise to make up the rest in a month.

The only problem was that I had no place to do the work. My dad was ready to scatter nails on the garage floor to keep me out of the third bay now that I had the car running, and Bones's garage was clearly off-limits.

Cristy and I were driving around on a Friday night, trolling for parties, when she came up with the answer.

"We have an auto shop class at my school."

"How do you *know* these things?" I looked over at her with awe. She just smiled back with that same knowing smile she used to give me at church.

It was an exchange program between our two schools—kids from one school could take weekend classes or workshops at the other. It would be tough to fit it in between homework and the drugstore job, but I was desperate. That Monday I signed up. I told my mother that I would be working after class at the drugstore, something that my dad expected me to do anyway, but that I thought it would be good to take an extra class at the other school—something mechanical to give me an appreciation for basic shop skills. I did not say much about my plans to swap the engine, since there was no reason to diminish her pride that I was taking my education so seriously. I convinced a friend of mine to haul the 409 engine to the shop building the next week in his pickup truck. I was in business.

When I first entered the shop floor, it was as if I was standing under a cool waterfall on a hot day. Instead of Napper's scarred, greasy workbench, there was a gleaming counter of stainless steel that ran along one wall. Instead of Bones's spider-infested rafters and bare bulbs, the ceiling was criss-crossed with white-painted steel girders and ribbons of fluorescent bulbs across the whole room. Instead of my stained garage floor at home, the floor at the school shop was finished with polyurethane that gave it almost a marbled look. Tools of all sorts were in their places, even if their locations were not prescribed by felt marker outlines. A solvent tank—rather than the makeshift laundry bucket I used at home—held cascading waves of cleaner.

But what really caught my eye was the painted red device sitting right in front of the work area: an engine hoist.

To get credit for the course, I had to endure several weekends of classroom instruction. It was pretty agonizing after the last year of transplanting two engines, suspensions, drive shafts, and four generations of carburetors to sit at a cramped wooden desk in an adjoining classroom and endure lecture after lecture about compression ratios, combustion technology, fuel/air mixtures, piston design, and the lubrication characteristics of oil. Sure, look at the nice line drawings about how to rebuild a carburetor, but go ahead and show me how you can slap one together and get the float angles right just by eyeing them, especially after spilling the whole kit all over the garage floor and chasing little springs and rubber grommets all over the place. There were some things you just could not learn in a textbook.

After the textbook section, we were unleashed into the shop, which for a group of teenage boys was like unleashing a herd of Rottweilers into a rabbit pen. Those of us who had a project already in mind and could prove its relevance to the course and our reasonable competence at carrying it out were allowed to do what essentially was independent study—work on our own as long as we followed safety practices, did not steal tools or parts, and did not wait too long to ask for help if we got stuck.

The shop teacher was wired into the local car scene and did help me trade my entire 283 for a nearly new set of 409 heads with the larger valves—I was already in 425 horsepower territory and had not even put the engine together yet. I was to find out the hard way that it was not a straight drop-in proposition—more than once I had to get the shop teacher over to my bay to help figure out how to move the radiator and modify the engine mounts to shoehorn the 409 into place. I got a great deal on a Holley carburetor from a guy in the class who needed someone to help him rebuild his brakes and another carburetor he was using on his Chevelle SS. All those nights learning how to do brakes and chasing little springs and washers around on the garage floor during a carb rebuild paid off handsomely.

As much as that school auto shop was a palace, I remember very little about the work I did in it. The whole scene was sterile, mechanical, rote, and lifeless. Every tool I needed was in that shop. I did not need Woofer's improvised rig to attach the rope to the engine to pull it; the shop had one that fit all. I did not need Bones's wrist-thick three-strand rope slung over a rafter; the engine hoist came fitted with a shiny chrome chain. I did not even need Bones and Woofer hauling on the rope, laughing and drinking beer as I fought to pound in the engine mount bolts; the engine hoist at the shop had a hydraulic piston that did all the work, without complaint. I didn't need Napper to help me discern the source of a mysterious tapping near the valves; the instructor would come by and measure the rocker arms with his feeler gauges and tell me. The only sounds in the shop were those that were generated by the work itself—hammering, drilling, engines being turned over; there was no radio on the workbench pumping out Wilson Pickett or James Brown or Junior Walker or, God forbid, Creedence Clearwater.

More than anything, there might as well not have been anyone there. Everyone kept to themselves. This was a class, not a culture. We were here to make grades and finish projects, not to make friends and finish well-known punch lines. The only person we saw was the instructor, who would stop by and inspect our work and offer some suggestions, but he never picked up a dead blow hammer like Rocky could and pound out a suspension bushing with one swing, or hook up all those hidden radiator hoses like Bones could, or crank a head bolt to just the right tightness without a torque gauge like Napper could, or set the points on a dual distributor, or adjust the fuel mixture screw like Woofer could. Most importantly, I did not have Mark there bothering me with his latest lost-and-found love life, or the betting line on me versus Dotson, or whether we needed a new keyboard player for Bedlam Showboat; nor was he there getting in the way handing me tools rather than letting me find them myself.

I got that 409 running in two weeks, compared with something close to three months with the 348, yet I lacked any of the satisfaction that would come with that. Here all along I thought the whole deal was the car, that owning a muscle car was the goal, the source of the pride and the satisfaction. I could walk around that car and touch every part of it and know it was not just steel and rubber and iron. That crease in the front fender was the time I forgot just to reattach the hood latch and the hood flew up and over the side of the car as I raced down the street. That scratch in the blue paint on the dash is where Mark let his screwdriver slip when helping me install the second Craig eight-track. That dimple on the side of the trunk lid is where I slammed the trunk down too hard and fast after a Bedlam Showboat gig without realizing there was not enough room for the microphone stand that Grant tossed in there. That slightly rusted scar on the back bumper was where I hit Dirk's VW.

So if Mark was right that the goddess of our school thought it was at least worth points, if not a date, that I built this car myself rather than bought it, I would have taken those points. But I'd have to pass them around to a few people. You don't rebuild a '57 Chevy on your own.

At least not one that means anything.

It was on a clear Saturday afternoon when I turned the key and the 409 rumbled to life. A few of the student-mechanics looked up from under the hoods of their cars to spot the source of the steady growl and acknowledged my achievement with a knowing nod of their head and then turned back to their own toils. The instructor put me down for full credit for the class since I finished the project successfully. Mark had just returned from a day trip at his grandmother's in Fresno, so I picked him up at his house and we tooled around town the rest of the day, honking at people we knew, racing the engine at stoplights, and every once in a while laying down a little rubber like a Doberman pees on a tree. It was a good day; we had the windows open, Mark was in love again with Jolene, the eight-track was blasting out Booker T., and we had the rest of the afternoon—and the rest of our lives—ahead of us.

Surprisingly to me, after working so hard to transplant the 409 into my '57, I did not make much of a show of my car during the rest of my first semester as a senior. It was Thanksgiving now and in the thick of football season, so I took the Beast to home games on Friday nights, but I felt strangely unmotivated to be part of the normal parade lap of muscle cars that line up near the gate, racing their engines in front of the students streaming into the stadium.

Since I had installed the engine at the auto shop at a different school, not everyone knew I was running a different, and much more formidable, power plant under the hood. Despite my more reserved mood, Mark had coaxed me into taking the Chevy on a lap around the circular drive at the front lawn of the school. At first we did not draw any particular attention, since my car was a familiar fixture at the school at that point. When I gunned the engine, though, and the 409 cleared its throat through the headers, a few guys who knew the tenor of a 409 compared with a 348 turned their heads toward the noise. I revved it to the requisite three thousand rpm and popped the eleven-inch performance clutch I had installed with the 409. With the 4.11 differential, I was almost unprepared for the explosion of torque that poured through the drive train. The 348 was a respectable power plant, but the 409 was a beast of a different order. My Chevy seemed to stand still for a second as the engine, clutch, driveshaft, and differential all wailed away as if friction did not exist.

The whole experience was sensory overload; the howling engine, the deep hiss of the intakes sucking air through the pizza-pan-sized air cleaner, the tight quiver of the Hurst shifter, and the smell of fuel all added to the sense of unbridled power and speed. At first my senses were filled with the engine and the drive train, but they soon were replaced by the high-pitched wail of the tires against the pavement. We started to edge forward and then gained speed as the warm rubber bit into the pavement. Respecting and maybe even a bit wary of what the 409 could do in close quarters, I backed off the accelerator, the car nosed forward, and we were enveloped by a milky cloud of hard-boiled rubber. Two other drivers near us rolled up their windows as the cloud passed over them. Mark and I were again met with the mixed clatter of applause, catcalls, and yelling as we now more slowly drove the car down the backside of the driveway and down to the parking lot.

For Mark's sake, it was worth it. It was fun, but for me it suddenly felt a little silly. Maybe I was just getting more serious.

It may have been the conversation at our house before Christmas that finally did it. My father had called everyone to sit down in the living room, and as soon as we did, you just knew something was wrong. My father was in his high-back chair, but he was far from relaxed. My mother stood behind him, kneading his shoulders with her hands. My father stuttered into his talk, and I forget most of what he said other than the part about him getting fired. The company had decided to move out of San Francisco and go private, knocking out most of the executive team. My father was game about it—he always was—but even then I could see in his eyes that he had no idea what do to next.

My younger sister, two younger brothers, and I looked at each other as if seeking signals on what to do or say. Then we all lined up in front of my father and, one by one, gave him a nervous hug and said something like, "It'll be okay, Dad." He was embarrassed, and we were bewildered, so there was no reason to make theater of the whole thing.

I can't say that I felt there was much I could do, but I did sense that I needed to back off a bit on the car. Drive it, enjoy it, sure; but maybe stop doing stuff to it. It was not just the money—it was this feeling that my dad did not need any more problems to deal with, including from me.

Blackhawk Canyon was an arroyo that swept around the far side of Fire Mountain and eased into the flat meadows south of town. It was not much of a canyon—a shallow, wandering swale of land punctuated by a two-lane blacktop road with a few farmhouses here and there. A wooden fence hugged the side of the road in most places, its brown, lopsided posts and rails long beaten and broken by the years, looking like a bad set of teeth.

The road was straight enough in most places—straight enough where somebody at some point figured out that you could go for a good quarter mile with your gas pedal flat-ironed to the floorboards before you would need to ease up as the road rose up over a small hill.

Friday nights, the cars would come one by one, cruising down the road, prowling. It was never anything formal or even declared, but once four or five cars had pulled off on the side of the road with their engines throbbing in the twilight, someone would pull the traffic cones from their trunk and square them up to create the imaginary starting line. Then the same car would drive down the road, slowing down to a crawl just as its odometer showed that a quarter mile had passed, and the cones would come out again, tracing the finish line. On a nice night, if there were no basketball games or a dance to compete, other cars would show up and park well ahead of the start line or well after the finish line, and the teenage passengers would pile out and sit on the hoods or trunks for a better view.

The start of the races was like a street fight breaking out. One minute everyone was standing around; then, as if provoked, two cars would grind their way off the gravel shoulder and square off at the starting line. The guy who placed the cones served as starter, holding aloft a white T-shirt, which he twirled in the night air as if teasing a dog with a bone. Then the shirt whipped down and the air exploded with the howl of engines and the scream of tires as the two cars leaped from their standstill and wormed down the road, their taillights jogging a bit as the drivers switched gears and jammed the gas pedals again to the floor. It was over in a few seconds, and it was a miracle that we never repeated the scene in *American Graffiti* when the cars sideswipe each other and tumble in a ditch.

It was fun, but it was serious.

I went there with Mark several times, sitting on the hood of his Impala, usually just off the finish line, where Mark felt all the real action was. The *whoosh* of the cars passing by us after their run fluttered our shirts as we raised our arms to cheer on our favorite contenders.

Mark wanted me to bring the Beast down for a run, but I never did. I'm not sure why, other than the whole scene struck me as vaguely felonious and perhaps dangerous. I would not have won all the races by any means, but I would not have lost more than my share either. Maybe it was more that I did not want to skewer my driver's license or frayed relationship with my dad any further by being just stupid. I also did not want to peg my chances for being seen as a winner or loser based on whether my car won or lost.

It was another Friday night when, instead of blending into the crowd at Blackhawk, I drove alone east of town and turned left on the two-lane road that trailed alongside Interstate 680. The road was quiet, with just a few homes tucked back in the shadows behind groves of oak trees. I slowed the Chevy and lined it up close to the faded white on the left and glanced to my right to measure the distance to the gravel shoulder. The windows were rolled down, and a slight breeze rustled through the openings as thick clouds ahead darkened what was left of the sunset.

I must have idled there for a couple of minutes, not so much thinking about anything as *feeling and hearing*—feeling the seat beneath me gently rock with the torque of the engine, pushing the clutch to the floors and flicking the shifter in and out of first gear to sense that satisfying *click* as the gears meshed, and listening to the hiss as the engine sucked air through the filter and down the throat of the carburetor.

It had been a while since the Beast and I just hung out together by ourselves, without Mark or the Ducks or anyone else around. I drifted for a bit, remembering the early days when I imagined how the engine worked, seeing the parts pumping and rotating in unison in the *Motors Manual* and in my mind, and now here it was on a lonely stretch of road east of town and it was real. The space between the memories and the present compressed; the work and toil between then and now seemed to vanish. Time flies when you're having fun, they say. Or maybe time just flies.

I was nudged from my thoughts by the *splat* of raindrops on the windshield—not enough to turn on the wipers but enough to know it was time to get going. The clouds ahead were rearing and tumbling, with bursts of lightning streaking to the ground in the distance.

I checked the rear-view mirror and flicked on the high beams to scan the road ahead and then jacked the shifter into first and left it there. I pawed the accelerator a few times to wake the engine out of its lazy idle and then pressed the pedal more purposefully until the tachometer strapped to the steering column fluttered at three thousand. I popped the clutch as I jammed the accelerator to the floor, gripping the steering wheel tighter. The hood lifted a bit as the car hurled forward and the back tires seared on the pavement. I just jammed into each gear as the needle passed six thousand, feeling the wheel shiver in my grip. I was in fourth gear before I snapped my eyes off the tachometer and looked down at the speedometer. It waved past 90 ... 95 ... 100 and was quivering toward 110 when I just quit, lifting my foot from the gas and feeling the engine sigh. I downshifted the next few hundred feet and only used the brakes at the very end to slow the car to a halt.

We sat there for a couple of minutes; the engine nodded back to its lazy, rolling idle as the raindrops got heavier, splattering and hissing on the hood and stirring up little wisps of steam over the hot metal. I would have stayed there longer, just listening to the rain and the engine, but the floodlights came on at the house just behind me on the left, so I quickly shifted into gear and drove away, the smell of burning rubber and water-drenched soil filling the passenger compartment.

In many ways, Mark and I were a twisted helix—always connected in some way but always switching positions. Call it yin-yang—opposing forces that somehow complement each other and balance things out in the end. Most of the time this mutual dependency, this reciprocal nature of our whole, moved forward. But as winter started to give way to spring, the strands of this creation began to stretch and fray. Up to that point, the Beast had been our common root on the surface, although the taproot deep beneath the soil was something different. I needed a muse, a guide, someone who "had it all together," while Mark needed somebody who could serve as a vicarious channel for his optimism and perhaps his need to be needed and useful. It was the human condition—the urge to have a raison d'être, to belong, to feel needed, and to need—played out between us in ways as teenagers we never understood.

It all came close to being uprooted one day in the library. There never seemed to be a question in our minds that we were going to go to college together. Only we had never had the conversation about where to go. Mark was at one of the tables in the study section of the library, fiddling with a folded triangle of paper, flicking it around on the tabletop playing his game of "football" while I had college registration and orientation books stacked in front of me. I had taken an English Lit class that semester where we had to write something—anything—every day, and the teacher said he thought I should consider a career in journalism. So I was crosschecking the lists for schools that were ranked for journalism but also wondering where Mark wanted to put his check marks.

"Mark, what about Sacramento State?"

"Too boring," he said as he spun the paper wedge to an imaginary goal line. "I thought you wanted to go to Stanford anyway."

"I did, but I don't have the grades, and," I said more quietly, "my dad doesn't have the money." I went through several names—Humboldt State, San Diego State, San Jose State—but Mark would just mumble, "I don't know; maybe ..." to each one. I slapped the books shut and pushed it at him.

"Mark, c'mon, man. We have to decide this. Where do you want to go, and what the heck do you want as a major?"

Mark didn't answer for a while. I was stewing; we were already late for early acceptance, and any more delays were going to limit our options and raise my dues.

"Fresno State," Mark said finally. I had to look it up. It was about two-and-a-half hours away. It had a journalism school—a good one, I was to find out with later research, so that was fine. "Why Fresno, Mark?"

"My grandmother lives nearby. I can visit her on weekends."

I always considered Mark the smarter guy, the one who knew where he wanted to go, what he wanted to do, but that day I was both frustrated and alarmed. Gee, Mark, this is the ball game—picking college, deciding what to do with ourselves. Get in the game, Mark.

As the last semester of our senior year hit midpoint, many of us in the senior class evidenced an odd juxtaposition of sober determination and reckless frivolity—at times being quite focused and purposeful as we faced college entrance exams or Vietnam while at other times falling easy prey to the last-minute distractions and delinquencies of vanishing youth. Mark and I reflected the disparities in our final gigs with Bedlam Showboat. For my part, I had learned bass lines in my spare time by cranking up my stereo in my bedroom and sticking my fingers in my ears, blocking out all sound but the bass lines until I got them right. And of course, Hampton did what only Hampton could—he owned the stage with a cool that comes from somewhere deep. He got better about singing on key, and when he did miss a few notes, he more than made up for it with a silky, slick sound to his voice that made you think you and Otis were sittin' on the dock of the bay dipping apple slices into caramel. Hampton discovered, though, that he did not do well with the occasional guttural screams that came with some soul music back then. He didn't mind James Brown, but there was something about Wilson Pickett's scream that left Hampton worrying that he would lose his voice the rest of the night. So when it came time for "Mustang Sally" or "Midnight Hour," I picked up lead vocal duties. Mark would say for decades later that I was the best at it. All I know is that we were the only funk-soul band in the area that had a black lead singer and a white bass player who sang the Wilson Pickett songs.

Most members of the band took our playing seriously; you did not get the next gig if the word got around that your last one was sloppy. Some members of the band were content to play out the songs we knew; both Mark and I were a bit more restless, pushing the group to try something new each time. By late May, though, the pressures on everyone in the band to move on made it obvious that one high school dance we were doing on the last Friday night of the month would be our last. Mark was simultaneously ecstatic and moody, playing his heart out but also edgy and tense, knowing that each song brought us closer to the last song by the band he had created.

When the gig was over, Mark was desperately agitated, still brimming with nervous energy—enough to salve his persistent headache from the trumpet. Our routine was to wolf down a massive fifteen-inch pizza at Round Table after each Bedlam Showboat gig, usually critiquing ourselves and mapping out some improvements for the next gig. But tonight there was no next gig. Mark and I stuffed down a fifteen-inch pizza each—an impressive performance in itself since I weighed in at 135 pounds and Mark was a few pounds lighter than that. Even after a pair of huge-sized sodas and the pizza we did not want the night to end, so we decided to cruise the Creek in my '57. In a way, Mark and I probably both knew that this might also be the last Main Street strut by the Beast, and Mark made the most of it. He cranked the eight-track as if he were warring in a decibel derby with the other cars and rode for several blocks sitting on the door sill, whistling at passing girls, taunting guys in other cars, and generally letting the Creek know that Mark was there and may not be there again.

At one stoplight, in an unsettling repeat of the bumper bumping between Greek's GTO and that Impala in my first journey down the Creek, a lowered Ford Galaxy tapped us and revved its engine. As we sat there in neutral, Mark reached over, honked the horn on my Chevy, and then jammed his foot over mine to punch the accelerator. The 409 roared, and Mark turned around in his seat to make some faces at the car behind. At the next light, the Ford pulled to our right and the driver rolled down his window and started arguing with Mark, who was taking great delight in letting things escalate. I had been to the Creek enough times by now to pick up some folklore—the driver was Lonnie, a street thug of sorts who apparently was going nowhere with his life and wanted to make sure you didn't get ahead of him.

Lonnie and Mark exchanged some feigning blows—although if they were closer, they may have landed—and I decided it was enough of a show. We used the next few blocks to dodge and weave our way through traffic to ditch Lonnie. As much as it would have been hard to admit, we both were a little afraid that we had kicked a junkyard dog and needed to back off from this fight. As we turned down a side street, I was privately breathing a sigh of relief. We had steered through some back streets and come out on the far end of Main Street, awaiting the light so we could turn and head back home, when suddenly the Ford drove by. Mark screeched, "Hey, there he is!" and reached over again to lean on my horn and offer another gesture out the window. The Ford slid to a halt right in the middle of Main Street, and Lonnie came running our way, cursing and waving his fists. I leaned over and rolled Mark's window up just as Lonnie reached it.

We now had a window-full of enraged maniac on the other side of the glass, pounding on the window and pushing against the Chevy. In one of the most definitive displays of insanity I ever saw from Mark, he reached for the window crank.

"Well," he said, "let's see what he wants." I tried to slap Mark's hand away but was too late. By now, the window was down and Lonnie was pummeling Mark on his head, as Mark was both laughing and screaming. It was becoming apparent that Mark was losing the battle, so I did the only thing a good friend would do under the circumstances: I reached under the flying fists and rolled the window back up, right on Lonnie's churning arms. Now our would-be assailant was wailing and thrashing against the side of the car, his venomous threats of only a moment ago reduced to panicked protests.

I put the Chevy into gear and slowly started to drive away—made sense to me at the time. Our once-protagonist was now in full-flight terror, clawing at Mark inside the car with his trapped hands. Just then, two police cars skidded to a halt in front of us, their red lights streaking across my windshield. They came up to Mark's side, put Lonnie in a headlock, and ordered Mark to roll down the window.

"Tell him to stop beating on me!" Mark barked in an impressive show of hubris.

"Stop beating on him!" the cops ordered. Mark rolled down the window, euphoric in victory. As one cop handcuffed Lonnie, the other cop came to my side of the car. I was ready to step outside and get thrown against the car and handcuffed myself when he surprised me.

"You guys okay?"

I looked over at Mark, who had a bloody nose but was grinning from ear to ear. Mark started to say something to the cop, and I mouthed, "*Shut up!*"

"Yeah, we're fine," I replied as calmly as I could.

"You guys ought to quit while you're ahead," he said. "We're taking Lonnie in. He's nothing but a troublemaker." As they muscled Lonnie into the squad car, I looked over at Mark—bloody nose, still making faces at Lonnie through the windshield. "Yeah," Mark scoffed. "A real troublemaker."

The next morning, I spotchecked the Chevy interior for any remaining blood spatters or spilled sodas from the encounter and then drove down to the drugstore for my early Saturday shift, mostly checking inventories, taking out the trash, and helping Mac file some prescriptions and notes from the day before. I punched out in early afternoon and headed home. My dad had a late tee time, and my mom and brothers and sister were all out somewhere for the day, so it would be nice to have the place to myself, maybe do a little work on the car and catch up on some studying for finals. As I crested the hill to our street and neared the house, Cindy, our Weimaraner, came around the side of the house as always to greet me, her mouth stretched with the familiar bulge of the tennis ball she always carried around. This time, though, I noticed she was lethargic and unsteady.

"Hey, Cindy, c'mere girl," I called to her as I walked around the side of the house to her dog run. She wobbled up toward me but then stopped as if disoriented. Reaching down to take the tennis ball from her, I realized that there was none there, yet her cheek was billowed out as always. Now concerned, I scanned her head and eyes to see if I could figure out what was wrong; then I spotted the telltale twin puncture marks on her lower lip—*rattlesnake.*

Cindy seemed to collapse in my grasp, her legs trembling, her olive eyes glazed. I ran into the house and raced through the cards and notes plastered to the refrigerator and found the one for the veterinarian in Cedar Creek. The card said the clinic was open until 1:00 pm on Saturdays; it was already 2:00 pm. I dialed the number, and someone finally answered after several rings.

"My dog got bit by a rattlesnake," I blurted out. "What do I do?"

"Get her down here—*now*," he instructed. "I'll wait for you."

I rushed outside, unhooked Cindy from her leash, and carried her to my Chevy. Afraid that she might panic if left her in the back, I put her up in the front seat, folding her legs underneath her. The 409 started on the first turn of the key, and within seconds I had the Chevy racing up the street.

I went too fast around the turn at the thirteenth green, drawing a few scolding looks from a foursome lining up their putts, but I barely noticed and cared even less. I went as fast as I dared through the familiar streets to the main gate and punched it as I turned out to the main road out of town. Cindy was quivering on the seat, barely able to lift her head. Drool trailed out of the wounded side of her mouth, and as I turned onto the freeway, she gagged and vomited on the door panel and carpet.

"That's okay, girl." I reached out and patted her head. "We're almost there."

I never felt the Chevy run so well as it did that day. Inanimate objects do not share the human quality of urgency and purpose, but if they did, my '57 seemed to know what it had to do that day. Within minutes, I had screeched the Bel-Air into the parking lot and gathered my near-lifeless dog into my arms and kicked at the locked door with my foot. I kicked again, and within a few seconds a hand peeled away the drape and flipped the lock on the door. We ran to a table in back, and I gently stretched Cindy on the cold stainless-steel surface. The vet inspected the bite, measuring the distance between the two bloody dots. I paced nervously as the vet pulled some bottles and syringes from a white porcelain cabinet. Cindy, who at first was panicked and trying to climb down from the hard steel table, now was becoming quieter, maybe too quiet. The vet went about his work calmly but purposely, especially at one point when Cindy appeared to have stopped breathing. After some injections, including apparently some adrenaline injected directly into her heart to help restart it, Cindy's breathing seemed to settle into a more natural rhythm, less forced and desperate.

"That was close, but I think she'll be all right now." The vet held Cindy's jaw in his hands and swept the small flashlight across her pupils. I don't even remember how I paid for it all—maybe I gave him my parent's phone number and address to send a bill; maybe he did it all as an act of mercy. I carried Cindy to the Chevy and laid her down in the back seat and drove home. By now, the rest of my family was filtering in from their Saturday pursuits, wondering why I, the Chevy, and Cindy had been gone. After recounting to them the near-fatal episode, I led Cindy into the house to rest and I went back out to the driveway to clean my Chevy.

The front seat looked like the back porch of a fraternity house after an all-night party—vomit, drool, and matted dog hair were everywhere. Mark came by later that afternoon to borrow an eight-track and saw me scouring the seats and shampooing the carpets.

"Never can be too clean, can it?" he affirmed as he scanned the interior, unaware of the events of earlier that afternoon. I didn't have the heart to tell him I had a vomiting, drooling dog in the front seat just three hours earlier. When I was done cleaning the Bel-Air, we took another hour and cleaned out his Impala. Mark was fastidious about his interior, so it was quick work to bring it to a sheen. As I polished the dash, there seemed to be more torn matchbook covers than ever bristling from nooks where panels met or where the radio or gauges were fitted into the metal, like a post-pubescent boy has little scraps of tissue stuck to his face after his first attempt at shaving. I wriggled the cardboard silencers loose to clean the area and considered tossing them into the trash but instead carefully slid them back into place.

There were now just two weeks left of school, and the sense that we were about to leave an important era in our lives was palpable. The playwright Arthur Miller once said that an era can be said to be over when you no longer hold any illusions about it. With only days remaining, we all understood that our time was nearing an end, and any illusions we had—for grandeur, coveted dates with some cheerleader, being named class president, or even getting an A in biology class—were over as well. The yearbook had been published, and at lunchtime you could see people passing them around to write little notes that would mean something at the time, much less in a few years, and sometimes more than ever decades later. The muscle cars were in full display, rumbling along the circular drive—one last lap in front of the grandstand.

It was later that week when Denise came toward me. I didn't presume that she was headed my way; I had never attracted much of her attention. As I lay on the grass eating my lunch, she stopped in front of me and knelt down.

"Can you sign my yearbook?" She smiled at me. It was such a common request at that point in the semester that there was no reason to consider it anything special; yet it still felt nice. As I wrote something typical, one of those hurried "I've enjoyed knowing you. Have a great summer and let's stay in touch …" kind of memorials, she then startled me.

"Jolene is coming over tomorrow night to go swimming at my house," she said, almost shyly. "Maybe you and Mark would like to stop over." It was an invitation posed as a question, and it took a moment to sink in before I stammered an answer.

"Sure, cool."

So just like that—after nearly two years wondering what it took to get a date with Denise—Mark and I had our own personal invitation to come over to her house to go swimming. It was a shot that some guys would have traded a Hemi to get. I wondered if this qualified as a date. Not really, I ruminated, since we really weren't going anywhere like Round Table Pizza and, at least by the standards of that day, the guy initiated most dates, not the girl. Still, after months of Mark imagining the prospects of a double date with Jolene and Denise and perhaps all of his scheming over how to pull it off, it landed at our doorstep, a feather from heaven.

I called Mark.

"I *told* you!" he blurted out. "I told you, I told you, I told you …"

That Friday night Mark and I rumbled up to Denise's house in The Beast, turned off the engine, took a deep breath, and walked up to the backyard gate. Denise and Jolene were both in the pool and waved us in. We brought swimsuits but really just planned to wear the cutoff jeans we had on, which was fairly typical then and fine with Denise. So there we were in out cutoffs gazing at the two cutest girls in our school in the pool in their swimsuits. We were in awe.

There was no time for ogling, though. Mark let out a whoop and did a perfect belly flop off the side of the pool, and I followed with a decent cannonball. We played Marco Polo and hoisted the girls on our shoulders and tried to tip each other over in jousting matches; Mark did more cannonballs off the diving board. We must have been there for two hours, and the time flew. Oddly enough, one image that did stick with me was seeing Denise—yes, every bit as stunning with wet hair plastered to her face—as she broke the surface of the water, laughing and sputtering after a dive and no longer having to live up to anyone else's view of her as the prom queen. She was just simply being a high school girl who was enjoying being herself, being silly, being who she was in ways that others sometimes would not let her be. For those two hours that night, she was not some unapproachable goddess and I was not the overanxious guy who sometimes tried too hard at everything. We knew that after that night, a lot would change, and despite whatever you wrote in a yearbook, we probably would never see each other again. For those two hours we were just two people who might have been friends under different situations, but were at least friends tonight, holding off the future for just a few more hours.

The larger memory, the more enduring memory, though, was of Mark and Jolene. She seemed more relaxed around Mark, more at ease in being with him and letting him be his frenetic, crazy self. And as I watched Mark that night—whooping and laughing and splashing around with the woman of his dreams—I also realized that I had never seen him happier.

The week before we graduated was a blur—final exams, hurried yearbook signings, cleaning out our lockers, and asking for, and for once listening to, some last-minute advice from trusted teachers. Caps and gowns for graduation arrived at the school office, and the seniors were streaming in at lunch to pick up their packages. Mark tracked me down on the front lawn that day.

"Let's get our caps and gowns." He tugged on my arm. "I was thinking, too, that we could take your '57 to graduation and do some final burnouts in the parking lot afterwards in front of all the parents. Wouldn't that be cool?"

"I'm not going," I said quietly, suddenly struck that I had not told him until now.

"What do you mean you're not going?" A puzzled, fretful look flickered across his face. "You're not going to your own *graduation?*"

"I promised Cristy a few weeks ago that I would take her to the Motown Battle of the Bands that night. I didn't realize it was graduation day ..." I shrugged.

"Wow." Mark processed the whole struggle in a range of facial expressions. "That's the pits, man, even if it is Cristy." He darted away, strutting across the grass, dipping into clusters of students as he went, chatting it up, laughing, cackling at his own jokes, and stoked by every chance to broadcast his goofy smile at anyone who looked his way.

The Saturday of our graduation, I gave the Chevy's interior a quick once-over with Pine-Sol, washed the outside, Armor-All'd the tires, and went inside to shower and change. I snatched my keys from the kitchen counter and headed for the front door. My father was sitting in the living room, reading the newspaper in the high-back chair in the corner by the fireplace. He lowered the paper to his lap and looked up over his reading glasses.

"Heading out?" His voice sounded tired and almost meek.

"Yeah, remember? I'm going to the concert ..."

My father folded the paper onto the side table and stood up. My parents had accepted several weeks ago that I was not going to graduation; it may not have been indifference so much as their growing anxieties and preoccupation with what to do next with my father out of work. Still, for some reason I thought I was about to get a lecture: *I hope you know you are missing an important event in your life. I hope you know your mother and I are disappointed with this. All you care about is music and your car.*

Instead, he reached into his back pocket and drew out his wallet, peeling open the leather folds, and pinched out two dollar bills.

"You work pretty hard on that car." He spoke as if he had thought about what to say. "You need to relax and just go out and have a good time for a change." He straightened the bills and handed them to me. I was taken aback with the gesture and then took the two dollars from him, mumbled a "thanks," and stuffed them into the front pocket of my jeans. By today's measures, two dollars is not much. I knew on that day, at that moment, that it was a lot to him. To me, it was also a half tank of gas, more than enough to get to and back from Oakland with room to spare for a few laps cruising the Creek.

Rather than sitting back down, my dad looked outside the window at my Bel-Air parked at the curb and pointed his thumb toward it. "Car's running pretty good?" Talking about my car was not something that came easily to him, but I could tell he wanted it to be that now.

"Yeah, pretty good." I wasn't sure how much he really wanted to hear, but it felt good to tell him at least that.

"Drive carefully." He reached out to shake my hand, something he did with all of us kids. "Don't be out too late."

I turned to the foyer and closed the front door behind me a little more quietly than normal and then took the stone steps two at a time to the curb. I started the Chevy, but rather than rapping the engine, I just let it idle gently before giving it just enough throttle to work up the hill. A few minutes later I was thundering up the steep road to Cristy's house with a Temptations cartridge in the eight-track just to gear us up for the concert. We drove the main freeway to Oakland, trading opinions on what songs would be performed that night and which ones were best. For anyone who loved Motown—and Cristy really did more than me—the concert was an immersion. As hackneyed a sound as Motown can be, and as moon/June/swoon in structure were some of the lyrics, Detroit knew how to crank out songs that you could sing in the shower, even thirty to forty years later. They spoke to, and of, the experiences that were central to our world—the girl we loved, the girl we always hoped to love, the girl whose love we lost. The imagery of a Smokey Robinson and his Miracles was pressed into the memories of a generation, the painted face of a clown hiding the track of his tears. We all could imagine Gladys taking her midnight train to Georgia; David Ruffin of the Temptations basking under the sunshine he'd got on a cloudy day. It would be almost two decades before that Rod Stewart song would be the one to best capture the essence of the era with one of the most evocative lyrics ever in the history of rock 'n' roll: *"Bring over some of your old Motown records, put the speakers in the window and we'll go on the roof and listen to the Miracles echo through the alley down below ..."*

On the long drive home that night as we approached town, I wheeled the Chevy up a narrow lane off the main road right outside of Cedar Creek. The road hugged the side of a hill and was pockmarked by potholes and cracks. At the crest, I swung the Chevy into a U-turn and coasted to the side on a shoulder of gravel that overlooked the town below. Setting the parking brake a little more firmly and notching the Hurst shifter into first, I turned off the Chevy and rolled down the windows. We sat quietly together for a few minutes, the 409 and its radiator hissing and popping quietly under the hood as they cooled down in the late spring air.

Cristy nuzzled her head into my shoulder, and we just watched the lights of the town—the headlights of all the Chevys, Dodges, Chryslers, and Fords coursing their way back and forth between the Creek and our town on a Saturday night. We talked about our summer. I was going to put in as many hours as I could at the drugstore to save money for college. She was going to stay at her older sister's and get a summer job. I was going to Fresno State in three months to try my hand at journalism—not yet any real passion of mine but just something that my English teacher told me to consider. Cristy said she wasn't looking forward to her senior year; there was something about her that hinted at a restlessness, an urge to get away from *something*, or maybe she simply wanted to get away from what she might have thought would be *nothing* in our town. She thought she might want to go to Southern California and maybe study oceanography. Maybe, but maybe was a year away, and for her that seemed like a long time.

We stayed there for a while longer, just listening to the horns honking in the distance from kids driving around at post-graduation parties. We would giggle from time to time as we tried to mix the harmonies of a Temptations or a Gladys Knight song from earlier that night; other times we just allowed ourselves to be absorbed by the growing quiet.

Then, as if we both understood that our time was up, I snapped on the headlights, softly released the parking brake, and pushed in the clutch, turning the hood-mounted gun sights of the '57 back toward the paved road, the gravel crunching outside our windows. I rested my foot lightly on the brake as we coasted onto the pavement, taking the first turn or two in silence, the tires humming gently on the road. Then I slipped the shifter into second, turned the ignition key one notch, lifted my foot off the clutch, and compression-started the 409. The engine surged to life, took over, and reined the car at an easy pace as I gently steered around the familiar turns, neither one of us saying anything. We rumbled our way down the rest of the hill and out onto the flow of traffic on the main road.

# # #

Chapter Fourteen

They could have picked a better time of the year, you know. If you want people to stroll around outside for hours, ogling and cooing over the rows of immaculate artwork, why do it in August? It's a swamp out here—microscopic bugs licking the sweat off your neck, prickly needles of heat stabbing your forehead, your shirt darkened with wedges of perspiration, the sky white-washed with humidity, the stewing asphalt sucking at the soles of your shoes.

Yet we come in waves and endure the caldron. Thousands and thousands of overheated people weaving through the rows of antique hot rods and roadsters, hundreds of the machines lined up in formation for as far as you can see in the sprawling parking lots around the Louisville Fairgrounds in Kentucky. I don't have the geometry in my head, but I'm looking at dozens of acres of pimped-out street rods—millions of dollars worth of steel, chrome, and leather, all competing for attention. It's quite a show.

For a while, anyway, you don't notice the heat. Your nostrils are immersed in the aroma of oiled leather, high-octane gasoline, and carnauba wax; your eyes glazed with the reflection of blazing chrome and custom paint jobs; your ears gathering in the cacophony of racing engines.

This is the first time I have been to this car show—the largest collection of "street rods" in the country—and for a while I am fascinated, mesmerized. Where did they get all these cars? How do they put all this effort into them, to stand there *in this heat* and show off a car to people they don't know and may never see again? Are they nuts? Maybe they're just crazy.

It's amazing, captivating—but after a while the heat just overwhelms you and your mind wanders away and the cars all start to melt into a gooey haze. My shirt is plastered to my chest like cellophane on mayonnaise, sweat dripping off my eyebrows onto my glasses like rainwater from a rusty gutter leaking down a windowpane. It's just too hot to stand here anymore. Obsession has its limits, especially as my body sags from the swelter. I worm and knife my way through the throngs, finding the doors to the air-conditioned exhibit hall. Maybe there are some cars inside; maybe not. Maybe I don't care right now. I just need to clear the fog of condensed humidity on my eyeglasses for a bit; then I can get my bearings.

The air conditioning recharges me, and I renew my wanderings. Inside, the palatial hall bristles with booths hawking T-shirts, spoilers, wheels, upholstery, sound systems, chrome valve covers, and just about every device you can imagine to spit-polish your baby. There are no cars here from what I can see, just people retreating from the heat and wandering through the rows of booths, debating the merits of different brands of radar detectors, gazing forlornly at aftermarket wheels or hood scoops, rocking steadily in the sonic wake of massive trunk-mounted sound systems, and curiously reading the labels on the bottles of nanotechnology polymer car finishes. This is not a car show inside; it is a carnival, a flea market, crass money-changers in a temple built for car worship.

I am about to leave with my half-chewed hotdog and monster-sized soda when I catch a glance of the gleaming, jet-black '57 Bel-Air coupe off by itself, lounging under a bluish flood of mercury-vapor spotlights. It is as if it were lording over the hall on a throne. This car is fabulous, flawless. A masterpiece. Every bolt, every trim piece, every knob on the dash seems brand new, brimming with color and shine. The ebony paint is deep and wet, shimmering under the lights. The chrome sparkles with a crystalline brilliance and clarity. Every surface is completely without blemish—no fingerprints, no haze or swirls. The interior is understated perfection. The seats emulate the stock bench seats of the original but are re-created in supple leather. The nap of the carpet is full and alert. The windows are so clean they disappear, especially the trademark wraparound windshield.

The hood is open, so I lean over into the cavernous engine compartment, breathing in the view. The clatter and chaos of the exhibit hall fades to a dull buzz as I find myself studying every part, tracing every line of the engine with my eyes, reassembling it piece by piece. I am in awe, not only of the perfection of the car, but that it had been restored to such majesty, as if it had earned its place in that hall.

I close my eyes and mentally touch every part from habit on the Chevy. It's not hard to do when the car is part of who you are. On one side is the battery, where you would already know which one of the terminals is negative or positive for all the times you disconnected it to make sure the engine did not kick over by itself. In back is the distributor, held down with a single bolt and clamp. You know that since you had to loosen it with a box wrench to turn the distributor just a few degrees left or right as you pointed a strobe light into the depths of the front pulleys to align the timing marks at four degrees before top dead center, more if you were running a hotter camshaft. You can trace every hose and wire, especially if you recall doing exactly that when you replaced them more than once, pulling an engine to rebuild it.

If the owner had let you, there would be enough room to stand in the well in front of the radiator or in the spaces on either side of the engine to work on it, because you could, certainly, back when you were a teenager. Without checking, you would know that a nine-sixteenth-inch socket fits over the bolt on the intake manifold and that you would have to move up to a five-eighth-inch socket for the head bolts.

You would also know, without having to ask, which side of the head gasket faces the engine block; especially when, for a lot of reasons, you don't want to forget.

I gaze at the car for a while longer, taking it all in, letting my eyes wander one more time over its classic lines and bold form. The din of the exhibit hall seeps back into my swoon; I now hear some people behind me chattering in admiration of the car, peering around me for a better view. I move out of their way but turn back toward them for a moment, suppressing a smile and announcing to no one in particular:

"I had one of these."

When I get home, I check the phone for messages. Nothing. The calls have taken on a bit of urgency since Carol made her comment about his e-mails. Something wrong? At first I thought that was silly. Now I'm not sure. This is nuts. Betty told us last month that the doctors didn't find anything. Now he's on different medication. Maybe it was a concussion he got when he fell. He doesn't answer any calls any more, not even from Lesley or Carol. You call now and you get one of those standard greetings that say that this customer's voice mailbox is full, and please call back another time.

Our routine of talking with Mark by phone is replaced by talking with Betty. Each week it is something different—he keeps falling, his arms are weak, he has stopped playing guitar, his hands and feet are cramping. Some crank of a chiropractor said it was a pinched nerve in his neck; I told Betty it had to be more than that. By now, we hear from Bruce, our old friend in high school, that Mark is having trouble eating, and when he falls out of bed he cannot get back up. We call Betty and can hear Mark moaning in the background. He has moved back in with her and his father; a neighbor comes by each day to help Mark in and out of bed to take a shower or use the bathroom—it's that bad. Carol and I are in a panic. We can't see what's happening. We are left to only listen carefully to everything we hear, searching for clues. More doctors. I offer to come out and take him to a specialist, but Betty says not to come out yet. Give him a chance to rest up, get back on his feet. She has put a computer in his room; he has never used one, but he looks at it and tries to type things. She gave him the password to her e-mail account, and he has been writing notes to someone, she says. It keeps him awake, she says, but it keeps him going.

Merely days later, the talks with Betty now are shorter; I can feel the anxiety and fatigue in her voice. Mark does not want to come to the phone, even though we plead. Betty and Wayne say he is embarrassed with his slurred speech. The last time I talk with Betty on the phone, she is crying.

It is later that week, in the midnight quiet of my office, that I get all the e-mails.

Then they stop.

---

good memories friend. can think of more but really tired now need to go to bed and try to get sleep talk later

The classified ad in the paper was simple enough: "1957 Chevy, Bel-Air, two-door, 409 w/4-speed manual, light blue, gold interior, good tires. $900 or best offer."

There is only so much you can say in a classified ad without paying more for the extra lines. I could have added something about the eleven-inch clutch or the 4.11 rear end or the Hurst shifter or the Holley 850, but that would have cost me a few more bucks, and by then, especially with my dad out of work, I needed to save every penny I had for college.

Either way, I could only afford one car, and I had already bought our sax player Davis's '59 Opel Kadett. He had rolled it a few months before after a party up on Fire Mountain but just took it to Earl Scheib's and told them to paint right over the dents since it wasn't worth doing all that Bondo work on a '59 Opel with a four-banger and three-on-the-tree. He told them to paint it turquoise; Davis was like that. I paid sixty-five dollars for the whole thing, including the half tank of gas still in it.

Brat decided to join Mark and me at Fresno State. Mark was going to keep his Impala since he didn't owe anything on it and it ran great; he would need wheels anyway since I was selling my '57 and the Opel couldn't take the packed boxes of two people going to college. Brat wouldn't part with his Corvair. He was hoping it would turn out to be a classic and he might be able to sell it for more in a few years and maybe use the money to put down the security deposit on his own apartment or buy equipment he might need if he went into geological-survey work like he wanted to do.

The Opel barely ran. I fixed a few obvious things, but all I wanted to do was make sure it got me to Fresno State and perhaps back a few times if needed. The manual transmission shifter was mounted on the steering stalk but had a worn-out spring on the gate; to go from second gear to third, you couldn't just throw it down like normal. You had to tease it out of second with the clutch down all the way, settle it in the middle between gears, jiggle it back and forth a few times until the synchros slowed down and the spring would jam, and then slap it into third before the linkage locked up on you. Davis showed me how to do it. I could have fixed it, I suppose, but I never tried. It was okay the way it was.

The Opel was wobbly enough that we agreed, for the trip down to Fresno in early September, that Brat would be the lead car, I would be in the middle, and Mark would take up the rear in his Impala. It would be weird to have Mark behind me instead of beside me—nobody riding shotgun, motoring on about his love life with Jolene, nobody punching the channel button on my eight-track, nobody trying to tag road signs with a crushed soda can as we raced by.

So we knew how we were going to get to college together after all; right now I just needed to sell the '57.

One of the first calls I got from the ad was on Saturday from a guy in the Navy on Treasure Island near Oakland. I gave him directions, and he called me twice along the way when his buddy driving him got lost. About noon, they slowly rolled down toward my cul-de-sac and then pulled up to the curb when they saw the '57 parked in the driveway.

"This is a nice car," he said, just a bit nervously but excitedly.

"Yeah, thanks," I said, swept with some regret. I should have been proud but almost found myself annoyed as he passed his fingers over the tail fins and crouched down to admire the dual exhaust and the five-spoke mag wheels. We popped the hood, and he and his friend let out a whistle.

"That's a machine," he whistled out.

"It's a 409," I said, not sure if that meant anything to him. "Cranks out about 425. Holley carburetor. Dual distributor. Solid lifters …"

I suddenly realized that I was talking to myself, as he was listening but not really understanding what I was saying and was not even looking at the right things as I called them out. I asked him to move out of the way as I pushed the hood closed.

By now, he had opened the driver door and was glancing all around inside.

"Who did the door panels?" he asked as I tensed up.

"I did."

"Nice work," he said as he brushed his palm across the armrest. "Mind if I start it up?" It was an odd sensation. For a moment, I was not Paul; I was Rocky. The kid sliding into the front seat was not some overanxious Navy kid; it was me. Of course you can start it up. You're supposed to start it up. You don't just go buy a car like this and not make sure it runs right. I wondered then, as I never wondered before, if Rocky just gave up on that car, gave up on his dreams for it, or was it really just because he was going into The Marines and couldn't take it with him. I wanted to believe that the car meant something to Rocky too and that he didn't just dump it. I wasn't going to just dump it.

The kid turned the key and flinched when the 409 sprang to life. The car nodded to one side from the torque as he punched the accelerator a few times; then he shut it down, like he was getting off a horse that was too wild for him to ride.

"Do you know how to own a car like this?" I said more than asked. It was a rude question, but I was strangely drained of courtesy as I struggled with the indignity I felt.

"Yeah, I think so," he said back, missing the subtle insult. "I can learn with this baby, that's for sure."

Sure enough, he never asked to take it around the block. We settled on $850, and I counted out as he peeled the bills into my hand. With the hood as a table, I smoothed out the pink slip and scribbled my signature on it.

I stood in the driveway as he backed out. He ground the gears as he put it in first—stupid kid—and lurched forward when he released the clutch too soon and the 409 started to throw its weight around. Then, as deep and smooth as thunder on a summer night, the car rumbled up the street and disappeared over the hill. I stood there for a minute, kneading the bills in my fist, and then walked into the garage and closed the door behind me.

After fifty years, there are only two real destinations for a '57 Chevy.

One is what was once called a junkyard. Now they are rebranded as auto reclamation and salvage facilities. Despite their airs of feigned sophistication, these outfits do one thing—wring serviceable parts out of old wrecks and then crush and shred what's left to make washing machines in Mexico or China.

The industry's equivalent of organ donation is blunt-force surgery. Cars are first strip-searched; anything easily accessible and removable goes first. In the case of most cars, that means the wheels, taillight trim, mirrors, shift knobs, and just about anything that will yield easily to a firm grip or a twist of a screwdriver or pliers.

In the case of potentially classic cars, the operation takes on more precision and more determination. Emblems, hood ornaments, and distinctive trim pieces are all carefully extracted. A good reclaimer knows what to look for, like the chrome racing horse on the front grille of a '65–'66 Mustang. Any kind of engine designation are prime picks: 283, 302, 327, 350, 383, 396, 398, 427, 440—they are the badges of badness that define a car's heart and soul to a performance-oriented classic car restorer. The back window slats of a Mustang 2+2, a wing-like rear spoiler from a Road Runner—anything that was a signature design element is golden.

For the '57 Chevy, the prime pickings are the faux air vents on the side of the front fenders, the raised aluminum panels that drape down the side of the tail fins, and, of course, the massive front bumper. Even the distinctive "V" on the front of the hood can command upward of fifty dollars in the aftermarket. This part of the extraction is done with great care—any needless damage can diminish or destroy its value.

The other dismemberments are less delicate. A trained junkyard mechanic armed with dead-blow hammers, a pneumatic socket wrench, and pry bars can pull apart what's left within a few hours. Gears are unbolted and yanked from their attachments, quickly inspected for wear, and either stockpiled for inventory or hurled into a scrap metal dumpster. The "bones" of the suspension are spared—leaf and coil springs, tie rods—but shocks and bushings, the soft cartilage of the car, are not.

The whole process is accompanied by painful noises: the shriek of scraping metal, the staccato whine of a reciprocating saw, the clang of parts falling lifelessly to the concrete floor, the crack of rusted bolts yielding to a breaker bar or the echoing blows of a mallet, the groans of the rubber mounts as engines and transmissions are pulled from under the hood and chassis.

By now, the car lies lifelessly on jack stands or concrete blocks. Stripped of its headlights, bumpers, and grille, its face has lost its personality and is just a bony frame. It looks like it could never move again, as it cannot. The last step is for a tow rig or fork lift to hoist or drag the carcass of the car to a crusher—a leviathan of hydraulic cylinders, support beams, a massive crushing deck, gears, and a diesel engine—that bears down on the skeletal body of the car with a force of as much as 150 tons, flattening it to mere inches in height. Another unit, descriptively enough called a baler, then closes in on the pancaked wreck and compresses it into a mangled but compact rectangle not much larger than a small file cabinet. A magnetic crane picks up the bale and drops it into another bin, where it will later be sold for scrap and melted down or shredded.

If the crushed car had held any attachment to anyone, the whole process would be gruesome, clinical—and conclusive.

Some Chevys died of neglect. On the Internet you can find a photo of hundreds of '57 Chevys and other classic cars of the era wasting away in a shipping port storage area. They supposedly had been manufactured in Tarrytown, New York, and shipped to Rio de Janeiro but languished in a parking lot at the port when the customs authority in Brazil slapped such a high import tariff on the cars that the registered or prospective owners simply could not afford to buy them and abandoned them to rot and rust. A picture from that era shows the cars neatly lined up at the port with doors so rusted at their hinges that they fell off and just rested hopelessly against the cars, like shingles or clapboard siding falling off an abandoned farmhouse in Oklahoma after the Dust Bowl.

By contrast, once a year, in the parking lots of the casinos, grocery stores, and hotels of Reno, Nevada, you can find dozens of '57 Chevys along with their older siblings, '55 and '56 models, preening in front of crowds of admirers. Reno's Hot August Nights is an annual love fest of the American muscle car and street rod, attracting more than fifty-five hundred street machines from the West Coast for an orgy of chrome, cast iron, and leather. In a staggering display of nostalgic indulgence, these cars fill up display areas that amount to more than fourteen football fields, with another nine football-field-sized areas stuffed booth-to-booth with vendors selling everything from carb-rebuild kits to T-shirts silk-screened with pictures of hot rods or hot chicks.

More than nine hundred cars change hands during the week at auctions, either on the spot as the buyer inspects the prize under the hot sun of the day or the mercury vapor gleam of night or in quiet sales next to a beer booth. Maybe the owner was done with his dream, maybe other physical or financial burdens weighed in, or maybe he just wanted to recoup the hundreds of hours in the garage and out on the driveway to start all over again with another one needing some time and attention.

There are a few "stockers" in the crowd—cars that have been meticulously restored to their factory specifications—but most of these machines are tucked and rolled, tanned and tattooed, jacked or racked into rolling showcases of ingenuity and indulgence. The organizers like to cap out the field at 1972—anything newer than that just doesn't qualify as a classic or a bona fide member of the muscle car era. The rule is enforced, but it doesn't need to be—anyone showing up in a car from the late '70s or '80s would feel very out of place, and their best prancing would be met with stony silence or muttered derision from this crowd.

For the free-for-all that is Hot August Nights, it is all about cruising down Virginia Avenue with rock 'n' roll blasting from all directions. You don't have to stand there long as the cruisers rumble past to spot a "cherry" Tri-Five. Some of them are immaculately restored—the classic turquoise-and-white '55 or its beefier brother, the '56. But the '57s turn heads every time. Their massive bumper is a jutted jaw, the hooded headlights are James Dean in a slouch cap, the dual nacelles on the hood are Chuck Yeager's gun sights over the Pyrenees, and the notched hump that starts the tail fins are Rocky Marciano's deltoids.

Just say "a '57" to most anyone more than fifty years old and chances are that somewhere in their brain two cell clusters are firing synapses to each other and completing the phrase "a '57 *Chevy.*" Drive down the road and pass one and see if you don't cast a glance its way, no matter what your age. See one in a parking lot—usually parked off by itself—and see the crowd that gathers around it.

The car deserves much of the credit. It was a one-of-a-kind, a "get outta my way" retort to the *Ozzie & Harriett*, grey-flannel suit decade before it. Some of its legendary status was reinforced in our popular culture. A movie back in 1975—*Return to Macon County*—was perfect casting. Nick Nolte (Bo) and a pre-*Miami Vice* Don Johnson (Harley) set out on their dream cross-country drive to enter their heavily modified '57 Chevy in drag races in California but are diverted when they take on and take in a small-town pistol-wielding waitress with dreams of Hollywood and attract a convey of state police in pursuit. It's not much of a movie by today's standards—nobody gets killed, there are no special effects, and no aliens or axe murderers leap out of the trees—but it makes the point that a '57 Chevy is cool enough to attract some trouble but is fast enough to get you out of it too.

But you did not have to own a '57 Chevy to appreciate what the car and the muscle-car movement meant to a nation. We were a strong, visceral, and visionary country with ambitions for our future. Staring at the cold war, the space race, and racial tensions, we had our insecurities; but we covered them nicely in hubris as needed.

We as a nation made that '57 Chevy and the dozens of muscle cars that followed it. We were too young in high school to plumb the depths of our motivations and psyche, but on reflection I wonder if our obsession with cars and their role in our identities was bigger than just getting a date on Friday night. Maybe it was Vietnam—hey, dump the clutch and go for it, because who knows what tomorrow will bring. Maybe it was that last fling before we confronted what we knew would be a very different world. Maybe we knew the good times couldn't last forever.

There is a reason why we keep the '57 Chevy, and cars like it, alive.

It keeps us alive.

After a half century, there is only one thing that determines whether a '57 Chevy ends up discarded and sprawled within a scrap heap or rolled out to bask under the lights of a classic car show: It's who owned it when it came to the end of its natural life.

# # #

Chapter Fifteen

I was out of town a few days later at a client's office when I saw the call come in on my cell phone. The area code told me it could only be one person: Bruce.

"It doesn't look good, Paul," Bruce said quietly. "You might want to find a way to get out here by this weekend. I'm heading to the hospital now."

All the pieces of the last few weeks suddenly tumbled together. Falling in the shower, not being able to raise his arms, unable to eat, the slurred speech.

"It's ALS, isn't it?"

"Yeah." Bruce's words were choked. "It's moving fast, too."

"ALS" makes the whole thing sound so simple; just three letters that roll off your tongue and stick in your mind. This monster's full name is far more intimidating and as puzzling and confusing as the condition's cause: Amyotrophic Lateral Sclerosis. When you translate that into something you don't want to know, it means that the nerve cells in the voluntary nervous system just wither, just give up their only job: translating the impulses, dreams, and drives in our head into signals to the muscles to swing a baseball bat, dance, make love, play a guitar, write, sing, laugh, and eventually, breathe.

They call ALS a condition because it's hard to call it anything else. It's not something you can see through a microscope. It doesn't show up as black or white blobs on an x-ray. It's not anything by itself. It's not obviously some outside agent gone wild in your system. It's a *condition*. It's all yours.

No one really knows how long ALS has been lurking in the shadows. It first came into the spotlight of the public consciousness when Lou Gehrig stood gently trembling and bowed before a packed Yankees Stadium and declared himself the luckiest man on the planet earth. It is a strange legacy to have a fatal disease named after you.

It does take luck of a sort to get ALS. Medical researchers sifting amid the ruins of the disease have come up short in trying to uncover the black box that would indicate its cause. Is it hereditary? Not really; it rarely strikes more than one child in a sibling unit. Is it environmental? No; there are no clear patterns of location or lifestyle that leave their telltale fingerprints. Is it viral or triggered by some esoteric organism? Not that anyone has found. Until we know more, the only answer is luck.

Bad luck.

ALS is a biological termite gnawing silently into the timbers and wiring of your body. One day a wall falls through or the basement lights flicker off, and then it is too late anyway. Over months, and often after three to five years, the body slowly shorts out.

It often starts with some involuntary twitching deep under the skin like a low-grade, subterranean earthquake warning of havoc to come. Most people, and some doctors, ignore it—oh, it's just stress, or cut down on salts, or drink less coffee. Then you're walking down the hall and the carpet just heaves into a lump, snags your toe, and trips you. That's the only explanation. You've walked down that hall a hundred times and never stumbled there before. Or you find yourself fumbling for the soap in the shower—it just won't seem to stand still in your hands. Maybe it's just muscle strain or stress that can be relieved with some aspirin, if only you could open the bottle that you remember opening without pause just a month ago.

If you're a guitar player, like Mark was later in life, it's puzzling and discouraging that you can't hit that blues riff on the fly like you did just last week. Your fingers, rather than gliding across the strings by instinct, now tangle into each other like too many logs floating down a stream. Before you realize that you are losing your motor function, you lose your confidence. Every step is more tentative, every stance more tested, especially in the shower or bathtub where you fall down three times in one month. Scrubbing the floor and putting down rubber mats doesn't seem to make you feel any safer or more stable.

By now, you know that it is something more than fatigue. That knob on the back door that always used to be just a little balky now seems more stubborn than ever. You find yourself, for the first time since being a child, reminding yourself how to hold a fork or tie your shoes, and then you realize that it is not your memory that has failed you.

ALS is insidious and deceptive. It's not like it shows up on a panel in a blood test, in a petri dish in the lab, or as a speck on an x-ray or MRI. It is furtive and mysterious. It arrives from nowhere, and the only evidence that it has visited another part of your body is the rubble it leaves behind. ALS somehow attacks motor neurons and shreds the circuitry. With ALS, what begins as a simple tremor or numbness advances to muscle weakness and then full atrophy. No longer asked to stay alert and active, muscles wither and waste away. Hands, feet, legs, and arms fall prey first, but ALS seeps into other areas of daily existence—our swallowing reflex being the most perilous. I worked on-site with a client for about a year and watched one of the senior executives decline each day from ALS. After a while, the mere act of sipping water became a life-threatening exercise.

It is perhaps a testament to the imperative of living life consciously, if not purposefully, that the diaphragm—the massive membrane that acts as a bellows to draw air into our lungs and expel it again so routinely—is a voluntary muscle. But its status as a muscle we manage, even if below our daily awareness, is among the eventual and ultimate targets of ALS. The disease does not ravage the body like a virus or bacterium; it simply shuts the body down, limb by limb, organ by organ.

Cruelly, while ALS ravages the body and its muscles, it leaves the brain unmolested. While there is some evidence that the brain begins to slip into dementia with some victims, most others are agonizingly alert. The expression "a mind trapped inside a body" is never truer than in ALS.

What would be oddly merciful is if ALS would wreak its havoc quietly and painlessly, but it shows no such mercy. Victims have no ability to move their limbs or even their torso, yet they can still feel, even to the point of being hypersensitive to touch. Defining what is tortuous to someone suffering with ALS is an endless and ironic task, but to lie in bed and not be able to do something so simple as scratch an itch takes on its own disproportionate form of torture. Like sitting in a car too long on a road trip, muscles that remain in position for too long begin to cramp. ALS patients, unless attended to by a physical therapist, can suffer agonizing cramps without relief and can be, depending upon the state of the disease, unable to cry out.

Bottom line: You don't "get" ALS.

It gets you.

Right after Bruce called, I called my wife. "You know," she insisted more than suggested, "Lesley and I will want to go with you."

Carol, Lesley, and I pack somberly but purposefully for the flight to the Bay Area. We are in a race against time and in a fight with our emotions, given the suddenness of Bruce's report.

When I make that right turn off the exit at the hospital sign, we fall quiet. I park the rental car in a long-term parking space on the far side of the lot, and we enter the world of hospital smells and sounds.

I hold no illusions about what we will see when we enter the room, but we are taken aback, still, by the ferocity with which the disease has reduced him. ALS takes its time taking you, but it can move swiftly where it faces no opposition. In Mark's case, his near-fatal bout with encephalitis had bruised whatever part of our brain is responsible for mounting counterattacks against the daily assaults our bodies face from bacteria, inflammation, and viruses. His immune system never was able to rally against this latest menace. It had been only five months since he first complained to us about falling down in the bathroom to the point now where he is sprawled, emaciated, on the hospital bed.

"Hey, buddy ..." I call out quietly.

Mark rolls his head to our side and pinches his face as much as he can into a faint smile. We had not rehearsed our protocols for the visit—who would speak first, who would stay, how long we would stay. Lesley steps forward first and holds out her iPod and drapes the headphones over Mark's ears.

"I have something special for you, Uncle Mark. Listen." Lesley stands patiently as the opening guitar riffs of "Here Comes the Sun" crackle through the headphones. "Sounds just like you, doesn't it!"

Mark barely nudges his shoulders into a shrug and smiles wanly but warmly at her; still his dark, shadowed eyes also speak clearly to his embarrassment that she would see him in this condition.

Mark is only able to form wisps of words with a breath that would barely rustle a candle flame. We devise a system where we recite the alphabet and he blinks when we come to the next letter of the word we want to say.

I watch in awe as this man, wracked with cramps, spells out his gift to Lesley.

"I a-m s-o p-r-o-u-d o-f y-o-u," he patiently tells her. "Y-o-u w-i-l-l d-o g-r-e-a-t."

Lesley braces herself against her welling tears so the last thing Mark will see of her is her smile. Mark rolls his head to the other side to gaze at Carol. She spells out the letters patiently, but Mark's responses are jumbled, disjointed.

"I? Okay, next letter. J—K—L—M—N ... no? Back to M? I—M?"

Mark looks at her pleadingly and tries to shape the words with his slack mouth.

"That's okay, Mark. Spelling is better." Carol leans over him and rests her palm on his forehead. "You just tell us whatever you want to say ... is the next letter N? O? P?"

Carol goes over the alphabet several times and tries to lace together the letters. "Okay ... I—M—D—Y ... I can't get the next letter ..." I have already formed the word in my mind by then and am getting ready to say it when Mark sucks in a breath and with every bit of strength he has forces out the slurred words "Dying ... I am ... dying."

I stand at the foot of the bed, forcing my eyes to stare out the window rather than at the horror in front of me. The image of the trees and parking lot outside began to swirl as the tears flow over my eyes. Carol strokes Mark's face tenderly and presses her cheek to his ear and whispers to him.

"It's okay," she murmurs. "Mark, you're going to be with Jesus, and you'll be able to play your guitar for him."

He gasps out quietly in reply, "Don't ... be ... sad."

I push the tears from my face with both hands and turn to Mark, gamely aware that both Carol and Lesley are about to witness the end of a thirty-five-year bond that, in many ways, has defined us both. "Hey, Mark, good to see you."

He mouths something I cannot understand, but his eyes are riveted on mine. We just look at each other for a few quiet seconds—both trying to get a grasp on the whole situation, and then I just start with the first thing that comes to my mind. "I got your e-mails. I kept all of them."

Mark labors a swallow as some tears pool in the corners of his eyes; then he pulls in a breath and pushes the words out of his faltering body.

"Fifty ... seven ... Chevy."

I grin back at him and nod. I spell out the alphabet—ten, twenty, thirty times and never tire of it, always rejoicing when we hit a letter on cue or I am able to anticipate his next word. I don't know how long we talk, but we cover a lot of ground. As I look at him curled on the bed, his head bent painfully to one side, his mouth hung open, I am wrenched by the indignity of it all.

Throughout the day, we take turns sitting by Mark, combing his hair and wiping his face with a cool cloth. The nurses give me some ice chips in a paper cup with a plastic spoon, and every few minutes, I carefully slide some of the chips onto his tongue so they will melt before he tries to swallow them. At times, he wants to talk, and we walk through our alphabet language; other times he just stares out the window, either oblivious that we are there or perhaps comforted that we are. I spell out to Mark that Brat was in Nevada but got my message and wanted to come down the next week. Mark forces a weak smile and spells back: "I-n h-i-s C-o-r-v-a-i-r !" When Mark had first stopped breathing at home and was rushed to the hospital, Bruce had arrived within a few hours from Lake Tahoe after calling me and is now racing back to take care of some things so he can return to the hospital for the duration. I'm hoping he makes it in time.

We spend some of the afternoon in the hospital lunchroom with Betty, Mark's father Wayne, his sister, his brother and his wife, and their three girls. We feel like intruders in a way—to be here not only seeing Mark die but seeing them die a little with him. Carol and Lesley need to take a break from the scene; honestly, so do I. They go to an outside patio to get some fresh air. I am too nervous to sit.

"I'm going to drive around for a while," I tell them.

"Where?" Carol asks tenderly, wondering if she should go with me so I am not alone.

"I don't know. I'll find something."

# # #

Chapter Sixteen

Measured against the brutal realities of the hospital room, the scenes in the town seemed very far away, yet they are a strange comfort. I find myself making turns and driving down roads a bit by instinct or faded memory, even though the town now is peppered with new shops and mini-malls, the nearby hills blanketed with sprawls of cookie-cutter homes. I struggle to find familiar scenes through the windshield—the drugstore on the corner is now a major pharmacy chain store; the Chinese restaurant is still there across the street but now has a blinking sign in the window boasting of their sushi bar; the hamburger stand where I gained and lost my first job has been leveled to make room for a luxury-car dealership.

I turn back under the freeway and follow the two-lane road as its gentle turns and rises seem to welcome me home. A couple of miles later—a shorter distance than I remember—I sweep the car around the familiar curve as the walnut groves yield to the sprawling campus of Stoned Valley High.

Might as well stop by. Can't hurt.

Ouch.

I inspect the dirty scar on my pants leg and ruefully rub the spot to calm down the sharp pain in my thigh muscle. I cuss at no one there, which I find is always the most satisfying time to cuss. I'm not old enough to be walking into things mindlessly, but those steel posts weren't there before.

You can't really tell when the four posts were put in, but the blacktop all around them is pot-holed and cracked. They had been painted, easily three or four times if you pick at the colored flakes with your fingernail and count the layers underneath.

The intent is obvious—the posts were put there to block anyone from driving their car from the lower parking lot at the school to the circular drive that sweeps in front of the main administration building and borders the front lawn.

So whose dumb idea is this? Some overanxious school administrator years past, I guess, who maybe fielded some complaint by a parent that it just wasn't safe to have those big, noisy cars driving up on that circle all day, distracting students from their studies, making all that racket, showing off. As I look around, the evidence of our litigious and controlling paranoia is everywhere—No Parking, Caution, Stay on the Sidewalk, No Loitering, Bicycles Must Stay on Path, No Shouting, Don't Have Fun … whatever.

The school looks different now, even though some vestiges of its experimental past endure. It is almost like visiting the original Disneyland in Anaheim after twenty-five years; the "Magic Kingdom" entrance is the same, there's that famous castle with the "It's a Small World After All" ride, the spinning teacups, and the ubiquitous monorail, like it was the set for the TV cartoon *The Jetsons*. Yet you did not have to go too deep into the park to sense that it is now in a different age—the rides are designed to thrill, not stimulate your imagination. They go fast, but they do not take you anywhere. Whereas the old Disneyland shaped you, the new Disneyland has been shaped by us.

As I walk along the sidewalk bordering the circular drive, the administration building, the original gym, even the odd geodesic "learning pod" buildings are still there, but rising up from behind them, almost consuming them, is a megalith of educational infrastructure—a massive new library, a science lab, a sprawling sports training center. At our old campus, my generation adapted to what we had; here, they are adapting the school to a generation. Whether all these new facilities represent enlightenment or narcissism is worth a good argument.

They are not done expanding the campus. Ricocheting off the roofs and walls of buildings, I hear the *whack-whack* of hammers and the *clacking* of two-by-fours as they are tossed around. The *clacking* falls into a steady rhythm as the workers toss the boards onto the roof one after another. I work my way around the plywood barriers and ropes marking the area under construction and through the debris scattered on the dirt lot. Two cutoff sections of two-by-fours are mixed in with the construction junk. Picking them up, I slap them together to shed their sawdust, hearing the sharp *crack-crack* echo off the walls of the old gym to my right. Pretty loud, actually. If I saw some kid doing that, I would probably have told him to put those blocks down and stop making all that racket.

I turn back toward the circular drive, this time worming my way carefully past the steel posts to the parking lot below. The pavement is clean, pristine, with parking slots painted in perfectly parallel, regimented rows.

These kids must all have rich parents. The average age of the cars cannot be more than two years old. A lot of Rice Rockets (mostly Hondas with deep-dish wheels and oversized exhaust pipes that look like a failed hemorrhoid operation), Subaru WRXs with the garish hood scoops, a few three-series BMWs, two—count 'em—Porsche 911s, and at least four Audi coupes. The European sensibilities that have overtaken the parking lot are a testament to globalization but also a visible snort at Detroit and the slop they have produced over the last twenty years. Okay, thirty years.

Several boys shooting hoops at a Lucite backboard never even glance over as the gray-haired man walks over to and gets into the beige rental car, turns left out of the parking lot, and fades from view through the walnut groves around the curve.

After thirty-five years, the country-club entrance on the right is easy to spot, even though the brick walls are draped with ivy, eucalyptus trees hover over the streets, and there is a polished and pruned feeling about the whole place. It may not have felt like a country club back when I was in high school, but it sure does now. It is quieter than I remember, certainly neater and better groomed. Then again, so am I.

My old house looks the same. Change is not welcomed in this place. It is so damn hard to even get approval to paint your house a different color from the control freaks that are most architectural committees of homeowners' associations. Don't ever think money always buys you freedom.

I pull up to the curb—this is really weird; I'm parking in the same tentative spot as my first day with the Chevy—and step around to the driveway. These days, if you just walk up someone's driveway without a really good reason and decent identification, you could be inviting a feeding frenzy by a pair of Rottweilers with no appreciation for nostalgia or stupidity. I do not see any animals clawing at the window, so I walk slowly up the driveway to the third garage door.

I almost step right over it without noticing, but there at the toe of my right shoe is an oil stain—the *only* oil stain on the driveway, and I suspect the only oil stain in the whole prissy and prim country club. It has to have been mine. It is like sticking your hands or writing your initials in wet concrete on a city sidewalk—a mark in time for destiny. The adult in me is feeling a little bad about it—I abhor oil stains on my driveway today—but another part of me is smug about it. Well, sure, maybe it was somebody else's oil stain, but today I'm claiming it.

I had been here.

For the next hour, I drive around a bit aimlessly—I'm not on a quest to revisit any particular scenes-of-the-crimes, but it's not hard to come across them. Dotson's house is still there on the corner near the other entrance to the country club; the garage door is closed as dictated by the neighborhood association, and two massive SUVs command the driveway. Turning right out of the club, I wait for Bones's ranch house and garage to come into view. Gee … must have driven right by it. I turn around and cruise by the familiar cut in the curb but cannot make out the shape of the house or the garage through the overgrown trees. The gravel driveway is now paved, with sculpted granite borders, leading to a massive three-story estate home under construction. From the looks of things, I'd say I just missed seeing Bones's house before that bulldozer showed that ceiling beam what a real crack looked like.

It is an easy instinct to drive from there to Napper's house, but as I see one modern home after another that have overtaken the street, I never imagine that Napper's ragged, stucco house would have survived the assault of affluence. Yet there it is, stubborn and out of place. I pull to the side of the road and peer through the trees to an embalmed scene—the house is still hunkered there, most of the paint long peeled away from the trim, the driveway scarred with potholes and fissures; even the torn screen door clings to the door frame. I think about going up and knocking— "Hey, remember me? We used to watch you build motorcycles and listen to Creedence ..." But as I survey the condition of the house, I press the impulse back where it belongs. Some memories are better left unstirred.

It's time to go back—to check on Mark, to maybe just sit with Carol and Lesley on the patio, to meet with Mark's family—but I impulsively turn the car around and speed down the two-lane road, around the curve past the walnut trees, wheeling the rental car up the circular driveway, past the posts, to the crown of the front lawn. One more look.

The lawn today feels different. Back then our school's janitor just mowed whatever grass was there with a rotary Sears mower. The grass was matted, worn, and trampled in certain spots, evidence that it served a purpose. It was our common ground, our community, where we gathered as teenagers out of the classroom to have the conversations that edged us toward, or harbored us from, adulthood.

Now it is manicured, mowed both ways like a golf-course fairway. Rather than the stubby and coarse St. Augustine grass of my day, the carpet is now a fine-bladed hybrid. It's *perfect*. Perfect for what, though, is the question. I spot the back of a sign over to the side and lean around to read it: Keep off the Grass.

The last time I was on this lawn was when I told Mark I was taking Cristy to the concert instead of double-dating with him to our graduation and smoking the tires of the Chevy in front of the whole crowd of parents. As I stand on the grass, the *clacking* of the construction work nearby fades to a muffle and is replaced with the sound of Mark's raucous laughter. I can still see him bounding from one person to another; the clarity of his exuberance, his determination, even his recklessness are coming from someplace deeper than the scenes I imagine in front of me.

A corporate general counsel I know spent a month studying in Dublin. I asked him if he thought Ireland was quaint. He pondered that for a moment and answered with the same annoying precision that characterized any question posed to him: things are really only perceived as quaint when they are juxtaposed with things that are not quaint. Thus, since everything in Ireland looked about the same to him, he never thought about them being quaint.

Some people are so intrinsic in their being or self-absorbed in their minds that they know who they are and their uniqueness without some kind of outside reference point. Most of us, whether we realize it or not, use some other measure beyond ourselves to gauge how we are, where we are, even who we are. We model ourselves after those we admire; we are repulsed by those we detest. Our measure of growth, then, is calculated by how far we move ahead of those constructs.

As I stand on this lawn and perhaps too long in the bright sun, I keep thinking that who I am—or at least my self-view—could have been very different had my years in high school not been rooted in my time with Mark and with that Bel-Air.

When I look back on it, I realize that I could not have done it without him.

Maybe more important, I *would* not have done it without him.

I wonder sometimes whether if I had never bought that car, if Mark had never leaned against the window to check it out or stop by that Saturday to first help, I would have acquired as much self-clarity. Our air-brushed images of who we were at that stage in our lives are often convenient and retroactive ("Oh, I always knew I would be a writer/doctor/pilot/teacher" is largely nonsense). What I do understand, standing on this lawn, is that all that wrenching, banging, twisting, and bending I did on that Chevy was shaping me in ways I never imagined. True, too, is that Mark served as my reference point and counterpoint—he was so vivid, his margins and edges so crisply drawn, his identity so pervasive in his actions, that it was easier and faster to carve or at least see those defining lines in myself. Who I was to become was defined by how Mark and I were similar and how we were different.

To Mark, being in the center of things was natural; being a friend to everyone was normal; assuming that everyone was his friend and enjoyed his company, without being arrogantly presumptive, was uniquely Mark. Conversely, that relaxed sense of interacting with people was a practiced skill for me. I was comfortable, even centered, on ideas and challenges. Mark accepted things and made the most of them; I wanted to change them, change my circumstances. There were times when I wished I could be as at ease as Mark, but I was also wary of his bent toward distraction, impulses that I often judged as a lack of purposefulness. Yet Mark had changed me—perhaps intentionally, but more likely simply by irrepressible osmosis. I was confident—not born of hubris but from a deeper resolve that someone had to change things, so it might as well be me—restless, and bold, not because I attached any particular nobility to those qualities, but because to live life any other way seemed so listless and wasteful. Yet Mark slowed me down, made me laugh more often than I might have outside of his influence, and stirred an impish humor that served as a refreshing counterweight to the times when I was inclined to bear down too hard on myself and others.

I, too, without intending it, changed Mark. I settled him, focused him, and occasionally quelled his reckless impulsiveness before it lost its charm. I don't think I ever diminished his energy, but I directed it to more consequential pursuits.

As I replay in my mind that scene of Mark scampering from one friend to another on that front lawn, it takes on a tint that I probably never really saw at the time. In many ways, Mark and I were alike—determined to explore, challenge, and push ourselves, unencumbered by caution or, at times, wisdom. However, in my case I approached life with my head down, fending off distraction, a little more introverted than some might know, immersed in the task, even at the cost of being too stoic. If I faced an obstacle, I would generally head-butt it out of my path.

Mark, on the other hand, lived with his head up—high, leading with his chin into the world, accepting that he might take a hit, but having confidence in his irrepressible spirit to plaster over whatever damage might be done. He smirked his way through every encounter, dodging and weaving—not always with a sense of where he was going so much as a dogged resolve to keep moving. For me, to move, I needed to know where I was going. To Mark, merely moving was going somewhere.

Mark may not have been voted the most likely to succeed in our class, but he would have been hands-down victor for the most likely to have a great time trying.

# # #

Chapter Seventeen

Carol, Lesley, and I walk quietly up the hallway to the now-familiar room on the second floor. We wait as we always did to make sure we were not walking into a quiet family time. There are two people in the room, but from their silhouettes in front of the window, we can tell that it is not Mark's mom and dad. The woman stands at the foot of the bed, massaging Mark's lifeless feet, while the shadow of a man towers above her, looking out to us in the hallway.

"C'mon in; it's okay." The deep voice resonates from the room. "It's me, Greek."

I have to look up at him to meet his eyes as I always did; I firm up my grip to shake his hand like I always had to. His wife is a hospice nurse and is working with Mark in ways we never could. It is touching and humbling to see her talk with him and seem to just sense when he needs his head turned in just such a way or to have a cramp worked out of his neck or to be shifted just so in the bed so he can better see visitors.

When I introduce Lesley to Greek, she looks up at him for a few seconds as if to size up the reality with the legend. Then, with a wry smile, she says, "I have a couple of things I want to confirm with you."

Greek looks down at her, both puzzled and amused. "Shoot."

"I hear you are pretty good at kicking in headlights." Just for a moment, the pall and the weight in that room lifts and Greek laughs just like I remembered him doing in high school. "Yeah, that would be true, back then anyway."

"And," Lesley continues, like a prosecutor cross-examining a witness, "I understand that you were also part of this *thing*"—she slathers the word with mock scorn for dramatic effect—"the Ducks, I believe they were called?"

Greek winks over at me. "So you know about the Ducks too, huh?"

Early that afternoon, after everyone has left to find lunch, I go back up to the room by myself. Mark does not see me enter, so I just stand off to one side, out of range of his weary eyes, and struggle to fit my image of Mark—my high school shotgun-riding, Bedlam Showboating, double-dating buddy—into the image before me. The only sound in the room is the gentle *blip–blip* of the monitor marking his heartbeat, his blood pressure, his breathing. The numbers are all too low, as if the life they represent is now just a trace, a whisper of what it once was. I step around the back rail of the bed to come into Mark's view.

"Hey, buddy …"

Mark's eyes plead with me, his mouth forming the word "water"—over and over, no matter what I say back to him. I anxiously scan the room and the supply cabinet out in the hallway looking for the cups of ice chips, but they are nowhere to be found.

"He can't have them," the nurse at the station says clinically when I tell her what I need. "His swallowing reflex is very weak, and he might choke."

"Okay, but what about water?"

"No, he might aspirate it and develop pneumonia." For a moment, though I stay reserved in front of her, I am furious. The argument rages in my mind, even if not on my lips. How insulting, how insane. My friend is pleading for water. How dare you decide how he is to die? He can do little more now than blink one eye and move his jaw and you are worried about pneumonia? Pneumonia would be merciful.

"My friend needs water," I beseech her. "He is asking me for water. I'm his friend. Please …" The nurse looks up at me for a moment, perhaps understanding the real request, and then gets up and walks furtively to a refrigerator behind a door.

"Here," she explains, handing me a cup of water and a fistful of plastic-wrapped sponges on paper sticks. "Dip the sponge in the water and roll it around on the inside of his mouth. He won't feel so thirsty. Not too much water, now …" She is cautious but seems actually a little relieved to be in on the conspiracy. I pause only long enough to make sure that she knows my "thank you" is not casual and then scamper to Mark's room. After I outline for him the warning the nurse has given me, Mark blinks his eyes that he understands, and then, for the next hour, I feed him water on a sponge. At first I am in control of how much to give him. Yet the way he sucks so hard on that sponge speaks to his stubborn independence. This is a dying man, and I am just riding shotgun, along for the ride. Just like he would hand me those wrenches that I asked for while lying on my garage floor, Mark mouths "more" to me and I dutifully dip the sponge into the water and put it in his mouth. He knows what he needs. And I know what I need to do. We do not speak; in the near silence of the room and of the moment, I just watch his eyes and mouth for the next signal that he is ready for the next Popsicle stick sponge of water—as the heart monitor keeps its cadence.

(blip)

The afternoon sun dips below the windowsill as Carol and Lesley come back up from the cafeteria. It is time. One by one we say good-bye. When it's my turn, I sit down next to him. Most of his body lies lifelessly on the bed, his arms and legs unaware of their awkwardness, cramped and bent in the last position they took before the ALS finally sucked the life from them. The sound of his monitor is the only evidence of time passing.

(blip)

Mark's head has rolled to one side, his neck no longer having the strength to right it. His mouth is half open—unable to move or speak, too weary to close. His eyelids are heavier than the day before, like someone fighting off the urge to sleep, but his dark eyes are intent and intense, the remaining thread to the world around him and the fragile voice for whatever is still inside of him. Like tunnel vision, I shut out all but his eyes in front of me and speak slowly.

"Mark, this will be over soon and you will be in the arms of your Father-God." A peace seems to settle in on both of us. I lean over and hold the side of my face to his.

"I'll miss you, buddy. We'll all miss you."

———————

It is early afternoon the next day—as Carol, Lesley, and I sit quietly on an airplane heading east over Kansas—that taking just one more breath becomes something that Mark is not able to do anymore.

# # #

Chapter Eighteen

Bruce is sitting on the chipped concrete slab at the base of the stairs leading to the second-floor apartment when the woman in heels and a tailored dress walks tentatively up the walkway from the street. When she sees Bruce, her pace stutters for a moment and she stiffens, but then she gathers herself and strides toward him. The years compress as she comes closer, and Bruce stands and takes in a breath.

"Jolene?"

Her poise and reserve dissolve, and she cries. She cannot stop the tears even if she tries. It has been thirty years, and yet the tears flow.

Bruce stands quietly, leaving Jolene to her world for a moment, as she fights for words.

"When you called ... I didn't know ... I wish I had known ..."

Bruce knows it is as much a question as a plea. It happened so fast, he says. We didn't know where you were. He tries to say more, but it doesn't matter anyway. It has been years—decades—since there was really anything there between Mark and Jolene, yet this whole thing is so abrupt, so violent; it's like she had been running down a dark street and slammed into a wall that she never knew could be there. She and Mark had flirted with a serious relationship at times when he woke up after his college coma, but the two of them were like magnets reversing poles at every whim—at times powerfully drawn together by an energy that neither wanted to question; at other times powerfully pushed apart by forces they did not always understand. After a while, it just became too much—maybe not for Mark, but certainly for Jolene. It never settled into a comfort zone that starts to narrow and define the borders in a relationship. Then there were Mark's drugs. And his impulses. It just got too hard.

Still, you never forget.

She and Bruce talk more and she weeps more, but then there is nothing more to say, nothing more to keep crying about—at least not here, not now.

"Do you want to come up and look around?" he asks as he steps aside to make room for her on the stairs.

Her gaze does not follow Bruce's eyes to the view above of the dented door and the darkened windows; instead she glances off to each side, down—anywhere but toward the steps in front of her.

"No," she says quietly. "You do it. I can't. I have to go."

"I'm sorry. I'm glad you could at least come by …" It sounds oddly out of place when he says it, but both are true. He hugs her gently and stands back respectfully as she turns, brushes her hair back from her face, and walks back down the path.

Bruce waits until he hears her car drive off; then he climbs the steps, the rusted cast-iron handrail wobbling in his grip. He jiggles the key in the cheap lock and pushes open the door to the apartment. He is there to clean it out, but as he flips on the light, it's hard to imagine where to begin. The aftermath of Mark's consuming compulsions is packed to the ceiling everywhere. Not just a wrapped package of paper towels or toilet paper, but cartons of them. Not just a bar or two of soap in the closet, but a case of them. Not just a few collectible baseballs cards on a desktop, but boxes and boxes of them, all stacked neatly in rows by year.

The chaos that overruled Mark's amazing mind and imagination in those final years now had left its detritus behind in the three cramped rooms of his abandoned apartment. Anyone looking at the confusion and excess would have been within their rights to call it a wasteland.

Somberly, Bruce begins to sort through the pillars of boxes.

"What are you doing here?"

The doorway is filled with the tall frame of a man, well into his seventies. He says he's the building manager for the apartment. He's supposed to keep an eye on the place. "What are you doing in Mark's apartment?"

"Mark died last week," Bruce says carefully. "I'm just cleaning the place out for his mother."

The man crumples against the door jamb, tears welling in his eyes; then he straightens. "You don't know me," he says haltingly. "I've been a janitor for a lot of years." Bruce wonders if he is there to oversee the process of cleaning the apartment, perhaps inspect the place before refunding the security deposit, but something tells him not to talk but just to listen as the man fights through his tears.

"I met Mark several years ago, when I was just a janitor. He called me his friend." The man pauses. "Wait, I'll be back."

A few minutes later, the man returns, carrying a large framed picture under his arm. "I used to ride a unicycle, and my troupe was on *The Ed Sullivan Show* when the Beatles were on. Look …"

He turns the large frame toward Bruce. It is George and Ringo and Paul and John—all balancing on or standing around the unicycle. "When Mark saw the picture, he took it down to a local photo shop and had it enlarged and framed."

"Mark called me his hero," he said, "but before he even knew I had that picture, he called me his friend."

The man pauses and then hands the picture back to Bruce.

"For most of my life, I've been a janitor, and most people treated me like I was just a janitor. Except Mark."

# # #

Epilogue

It is a clear, warm June day in Southern California as the three elderly women climb out of their car and stroll across the parking lot to the community center. As they reach the last lane of cars, the woman with the peach dress and white shoes slows her pace as she catches a glimpse of the dark green coupe parked carefully by itself across two spaces at the end of the row. Her puzzled gaze lifts as her eyes follow the muscular roll of the hood and the glistening chrome front bumper to the lean lines of the tail fins.

As her two friends look on curiously, she walks toward the car, tentatively at first and then more briskly as its profile fills her view. She reaches out tenderly and whisks her palm over the sleek ridge that crowns the front fender and the chrome trim of the headlights and then trails her wrinkled hand down the side of the car as she walks past, finally tracing her fingertips over the gold "Bel-Air" on the rear side panel.

She looks back at her friends with a wistful, quiet smile.

"My son had one of these."

# # #